ABOUT THE AUTHOR

Jule Wilkinson began her years of association with the foodservice industry in 1946 when she became Food Editor of *Institutions* Magazine. Her enthusiasm about the industry has never lessened and this book constitutes a special salute from her to the industry and its leaders. She remained food editor of *Institutions* but in the '50s was made supervisory editor of the magazine. In that position, she expanded her interest to all areas of foodservice operation, but food—its preparation, presentation, and merchandising remained a continuing interest. Since 1968, she has been education and book editor of *Institutions/VF* Magazine, having edited more than 50 books on foodservice/lodging subjects under the aegis of Cahners Publishing Co., Inc., publishers of foodservice/lodging books and magazines. She is also the author of *The Complete Book of Cooking Equipment* and *Special Atmosphere Themes for Foodservice* as well as numerous articles that have appeared in the magazine.

Selected Recipes
from
IVY Award Winners

Selected Recipes from IVY Award Winners

JULE WILKINSON

CAHNERS BOOKS, INC.
221 Columbus Ave., Boston, Massachusetts 02116
Publishers of Institutions/VF Magazine

ISBN 0-8436-2069-2

Cover illustration—Tropical Fruit with Breast of Chicken, The Nut Tree; Don Birrell, The Nut Tree design director; Earl Payne, photographer

Printed in the United States of America

Acknowledgements

Publishing this collection of selected recipes of winners of *Institutions/VF Magazine's* IVY Award has been an effort requiring the contributions of many people. It all began on the day when *I/VF Magazine* publisher Chip Wexler told his editors he thought there should be honor paid to the men and women whose performances were uniquely outstanding in foodservice/lodging establishments. This recognition he felt should come from their peers who could fully appreciate the fine points of a foodservice job well done. The senior editors of *I/VF Magazine* refined the idea; named it the IVY Award; devised the method of nominating candidates and polling reader-voters, and launched the effort. In 1971 the first winners were named.

Another major project was to make the awarding of the IVY plaques an outstanding occasion. It has turned out to be an annual challenge, since each year the staff tries to match an evening that was deemed unmatchable the preceding year. The IVY Award dinners have been worthy of the recipients; more could not be said. The *Institutions/VF* staff can be counted on to schedule events that will continue to measure up to these standards.

When the idea of collecting recipes from IVY Award winners for publication in a book was introduced, the first step was consultation with the rest of the editorial staff, who agreed that it would be a book well worth the effort—although none of us quite appreciated the considerable effort it would be for winners, artists, book designers, and the seeming legion of typists, proofreaders, checkers, and cross-checkers that have been involved.

Cooperation from the winners has been more than the author had any right to hope for. The book production staff has exerted every effort in the attempt to keep facts and recipes accurate and, we hope, as nearly perfect as humans can expect. There are too many names to mention individually, but special assistance from Lila Jones should be acknowledged for her work on the recipes; to Carol Ann Ford for her role in collecting facts about the winners, and to Charys Pinney for so ably handling the details that go into cookbook publication.

My gratitude goes to all of those who have been involved at any stage in the development and continuation of the IVY Award program, as well as in publishing *Selected Recipes from IVY Award Winners.*

JULE WILKINSON

Contents

AWARD OF DISTINCTION

TRUE LEADERSHIP STEMS FROM
PROFESSIONALS WHO PRESERVE
TRADITIONS OF EXCELLENCE
EVEN AS THEY ACHIEVE
SUCCESS. BY THEIR EMINENCE
THEY LEND DIRECTION TO
THE WORLD OF SERVICE.
I/VFM SALUTES RESTAURATEURS
OF DISTINCTION, SELECTED FOR
OUR ANNUAL I/V AWARD BY THE
MOST CRITICAL JUDGES, THEIR
COLLEAGUES AND COMPETITORS.

INSTITUTIONS/VFM A CAHNERS PUBLICATION

Homage for IVY Winners

RESTAURANT CRITICISM is not an exclusive profession. Anyone who eats away from home, it seems, considers himself qualified for the job. In addition to the thousands of self-styled critics, there are the professional reviewers: Gael Greene, Craig Claiborne, Jack Shelton, and others. Nearly every sizable newspaper has its restaurant columnist who advises readers on where to eat out. Then, too, bookstores are filled with publications that rate restaurants for the public: *Michelin*, the *Mobil Guide*, *Holiday Magazine*, the automobile associations.

But in every case, these judgments are made by laymen—people who eat in restaurants and are admittedly prejudiced by their own food tastes. As such, they make no attempt to concern themselves with whether or not the operation is professionally managed.

In 1970, the editors of *Institutions/Volume Feeding Magazine* decided the foodservice industry deserved something more. It needed a way to honor its own. While the opinion of a layman is important (and certainly can make or break sales), real recognition comes from other professionals in the same business. Real success lies in the ability to adapt the traditions of excellence to the reality of business.

Thus, the IVY Awards Program was born.

In 1970, a ballot was published in *Institutions Magazine*. The publication's 101,000 readers (all foodservice/lodging professionals) were invited to vote for the people they felt were the most professional foodservice operators they knew.

The ballots were tabulated, and the first IVY Award winners were announced in January, 1971. The only surprise in the results was that there were no surprises. The operators who received the overwhelming majority of votes were the very same men and women who had headed the consumer dining lists for years. Professionalism back of the house, it appears, begets success out front.

Since the first year, the IVY winners from the previous years have been asked to handle the initial nominations of colleagues they believe qualify for the Award. These nominations are published on a ballot in *Institutions* in the autumn of each year. The magazine's 101,000 readers have the opportunity to vote for those they consider the best.

The program is now in its sixth year, and 45 persons possess the coveted IVY Award. Once a person has been selected an IVY winner, the Award is for life.

How do you measure an IVY winner? By the financial success of the operation? By the staff's attitude? By quality of service? Food? Cleanliness? Decor? Creativity? Success is, of course, a combination of all these factors—plus something more. An IVY winner is, in fact, the embodiment of that "something more."

The IVY Award goes not to a place, but to an individual. We believe the place functions as it does because of the attitude, character, philosophy, dedication, and initiative of the person behind it.

The IVY Awards are unique, if for no other reason than that the voters are foodservice executives—colleagues, competitors, and peers of the winners. They are more sharply critical than most patrons of how and when, where and why, things are done within an operation. They look for and vote according to the most stringent standards. After all, if they don't know what is the best, who does?

Over the years, certain modifications have been made in the IVY Program. While the original Awards were limited to restaurateurs, for example, the Program now also includes hotels and non-commercial (school, college, hospital, employee foodservice) operators.

The basic concept of the IVY Program, however, has never changed. It is to bestow honor on those who have won the respect not only of their customers, but also of their competitors. As stated in the plaque presented to each IVY Winner:

"True leadership stems from professionals who preserve the traditions of excellence even as they achieve success. By their eminence, they lend direction to the world of service. *Institutions* salutes restaurateurs of distinction, selected by the most critical judges, their colleagues, and competitors."

JANE YOUNG WALLACE
Editor-in-Chief, Institutions/VF Magazine

Roster of IVY Winners

1971

ANTHONY ATHANAS—Anthony's Pier 4, Boston
BRUNO BERNABO—Mamma Leone's, New York City
VINCENT and ANTHONY BOMMARITO—
  Tony's, St. Louis
EDWIN L. BRASHEARS, JR.—The Drake, Chicago
PETER CANLIS—Canlis' Restaurant, Seattle
RICHARD FRANK—Lawry's Prime Rib,
  Los Angeles
ROLAND and VICTOR GOTTI—Ernie's, San Francisco
ELLA BRENNAN MARTIN, then at Brennan's, now
  at Commander's Palace Restaurant, New Orleans
DON ROTH—The Blackhawk, Chicago
WIN SCHULER—Win Schuler's, Marshall, Mich.

1972

MIKE and LEE COMISAR—La Maisonette, Cincinnati
PETER GOLDMAN—Fairmont Hotel, San Francisco
LOUISE HATCH—Massachusetts General Hospital,
  Boston
SAMUEL HUFF—Washington State University,
  Pullman, Wash.
BOB* and PETER KRIENDLER, JERRY BERNS,
  SHELDON TANNEN—The 21 Club, New York City
DAN McCLASKEY—Century Plaza, Los Angeles
KARL W. MEHLMANN—The Brown Palace Hotel,
  Denver
ED and ROBERT POWER, MRS. ED POWER, SR.,
  MARY HELEN FAIRCHILD, The Nut Tree,
  Nut Tree, Calif.
GERALD RAMSEY—Southern Methodist University,
  Dallas
LOUISE SAUNDERS—Charlie's Cafe Exceptionale,
  Minneapolis
DON SMITH—then at Chateau Louise, Dundee, Ill.
LLOYD and LES STEPHENSON—Stephenson's
  Apple Farm Restaurant, Kansas City

1973

LYSLE and ALBERT ASCHAFFENBURG, BRUCE
  McFARLAND (then also at the hotel)
  Pontchartrain Hotel, New Orleans
JAMES and CHARLES DOULOS—Jimmy's
  Harborside, Boston
FRED GRACZYK—The Vineyards, Southfield, Mich.
FRANK KESSLER—Arizona State University, Tempe
JEAN LAPUYADE—La Bourgogne, San Francisco
MARIE MARINKOVICH—then at Kaiser Foundation
  Hospital, Oakland
JOHN PHILSON—then at Kaiser Foundation Hospital,
  Los Angeles
CHARLES MASSON*—La Grenouille, New York City
JUSTINE and DAYTON SMITH—Justine's, Memphis
LOUIS SZATHMARY—The Bakery, Chicago
LYLE A. THORBURN—Michigan State University,
  East Lansing

1974

ELEANOR ADAIR, Plaza Suite, Buffalo
PAUL KOVI, TOM MARGITTAI—The Four Seasons,
  New York City
JAMES A. NASSIKAS—The Stanford Court Hotel,
  San Francisco
G. WILLIAM PEFFERS—Michael Reese Hospital and
  Medical Center, Chicago
WILLIAM G. QUINN—Hotel St. Francis,
  San Francisco
KARL RATZSCH—Karl Ratzsch's, Milwaukee
HANS WEISHAUPT, CHARLES BELL—
  The Kahala Hilton Hotel, Honolulu

1975

DOMINIQUE BEAUCHARD, JEAN-CLAUDE
  FARDEAU—then at the Ninety-Fifth, Chicago
JEROME BERKMAN—Cedars-Sinai Medical Center,
  Los Angeles
KENNETH HANSEN—Scandia Restaurant,
  Los Angeles
HERMANN G. RUSCH—The Greenbrier,
  White Sulphur Springs, W. Va.
MAVIS and HANS SKALLE—Camelot, Bloomington,
  Minn.

Food and IVY Award Winners

Commercial or noncommercial, an old hand at the game or a newcomer, wherever he/she is located, the IVY Award winner has high and definite standards in the many facets of foodservice.

Care, imagination, and expertise—these are the characteristics that IVY Award winners would agree must go into the creation of uniformly fine food, whatever the operation. Cuisine is considered their most important area of leadership, and seldom are they completely satisfied with their performance.

Always on the lookout for a new way, a better way, a simpler way, theirs is a never-ending search for perfection every time a dish is served— an unattainable goal and one that if pursued, leads to continuing excellence in their operation.

In the following descriptions of the foodservice leaders we have tried to capture the elements that are unique to each. These elements could serve as a guide to others in the foodservice field. Owners, operators, managers, dietitians, foodservice supervisors, or chefs who are interested in making additions to, or changes in, their present menu items, may need to make changes in portion sizes or presentation to meet the needs of a different group of patrons.

The recipe developer's approach to food helps to determine how his or her recipe will fit in a given situation. Knowing what kind of patrons the winner must please helps to clarify the anticipated audience appeal of a dish from that operation.

IVY Award winners also serve well as models in the presentation and merchandising of food. Many of their unique ideas in these areas are described so that they can be adapted for the reader's needs.

Another belief that IVY Award winners share is that *people produce food*. A good recipe and careful supervision are only two sides of a triangle. The third side is motivation plus training. Because these are considered so important, the methods that have helped IVY Award winners motivate and train their foodservice employees have also been described in some detail. The precision with which workers follow recipes and their degree of involvement in the search for perfection are of great importance. Their enthusiastic cooperation can be enlisted. Many tested ways to engage them fully in producing uniformly fine food are suggested on the pages that follow.

Not all the recipes submitted could be fitted into the pages available to us, so an effort was made to balance recipes in the categories chosen for the book. A few winners were unable to meet publication deadlines for recipes and, regrettably, are not represented. For this reason, the complete roster of winners bears the names of persons for whom there are no recipes and descriptive material.

Not all winners submitted recipes in equal numbers; we want to express special gratitude to those who were able to provide us with several of their specialties. We have tried to present the recipes in a style that is easy to read and to follow. Now it is the reader's turn to try the recipes, thus treating patrons to dishes selected from those whose cuisine is considered to be the best there is.

Foodservice at Michael Reese Hospital and Medical Center, Chicago,
holds the record for the number of menu selections among
hospitals in this country operating on a cycle system. Director of food
service Bill Peffers' hotel background and unique organizational
skills are helping him cope with today's soaring costs.

Louise Hatch has been director of the dietary department at Massachusetts General Hospital for 29 years. Here she confers with executive chef Connally. High morale is a hallmark of the department, based on their shared belief that "together we serve."

"People realize that quality costs," said Dominique Beauchard (center), at the time of his IVY Award manager of operations at Chicago's 95th. Belgian-born executive chef Willy Maes and catering director Jean-Claude Fardeau (co-IVY Award winner) were important assets to the 95th team which included 110 employees of 10 different nationalities in mid-1975.

La Grenouille, New York City, serves as a monument to Charles Masson who died in February, 1975. His wife of many years continues to see that there are fresh flowers daily.

Bruce McFarland, 1973 IVY Award winner while at New Orleans' Pontchartrain Hotel, is now general manager at Quail Hollow Inn and Golf Club in Painesville, Ohio.

Jean Laypuyade owns and operates La Bourgogne, San Francisco. There he draws on his French background in building the restaurant's reputation for elegant, haute cuisine.

Hans and Mavis Skalle present an array of colorful continental cuisine in hexagonal dining rooms in a castle designed to re-create the romantic legends of King Arthur. Hans is the host extraordinaire and Mavis, the financial wizard at Camelot in Bloomington, near Minneapolis, Minn.

The four principals of
The 21 Club, New York
gathered here as 1972
IVY Award winners are:
Pete Kriendler, Jerry Berns,
Bob Kriendler (since
deceased) and Sheldon
Tannen. Concern for their
guests' enjoyment heads
their common list of
factors essential to the
operation of "their kind of
fine dining place."

Successful promotion ideas—
an executive women's
club for one, and the kind
of leadership and
training programs that turn
workers into a team are
equally important elements
in Eleanor Adair's successful
operation at the Plaza
Suite in Buffalo, N. Y.

Enthusiasm for Jimmy's Harborside, Boston, registers on the faces of the father and son team who run it together. 1973 IVY Award winners Jimmy and Charles, "Jimmy Jr." Doulos have a staff that is as determined to keep standards high at the Harborside as the owners, despite the demanding pace required by the 2 to 3 times turnover at lunch and dinner.

Lyle Thorburne, manager, dormitories/foodservice, Michigan State University, East Lansing has taken campus foodservice a long way in 30 years. Weighing student demands and keeping abreast of those that are sound is one of his well-developed skills; another is the ability to run a campus dining room that many vote "the best restaurant in the community."

When 1972 IVY Award winner Don Smith was at the Chateau Louise, one of his most popular menu items among the Midwestern patrons was this Baked Stuffed Lobster presented on a sizzling platter with all the traditional accoutrements, and an individual loaf of crusty bread and country crock of butter. A sophisticated selection of wine set a special tone for the feast.

High style food finds followers among Purdue University students and develops tastes that vending machines cannot satisfy. That is one of the formulas that help John C. Smalley, director, keep the university residences and the Memorial Union foodservice contemporary and in the black.

Marie Marinkovich was a foodservice systems consultant for the Northern California Kaiser Foundation Hospital when she became an IVY Award winner in 1973. She gave the lion's share of the credit for the 10 to 12 thousand meals daily that were her assignment to the dietitians in the various hospital units who made the systems "go."

Eleanor Adair

"People say I'm in the wrong business. That I should be a promoter," says Eleanor Adair, general manager of the Plaza Suite restaurant in Buffalo, N. Y. However, Ms. Adair's response is, "I'm in the right business—because I *am* promoting."

While the controversy may continue over whether or not Ms. Adair is in the right business, one thing is certain. She is the person responsible for turning the tide for this luxury restaurant. To do this, she applied every promotional idea she could devise, as well as some intensive training programs.

The restaurant, which is located atop Buffalo's Manufacturers and Traders Trust skyscraper, opened in August, 1967. Almost immediately, it experienced difficulties. It was plagued by one thing after another, ranging from a difficult maitre d' to urban problems which resulted in the exodus of city dwellers to the suburbs.

During this period, Service Systems Corp., operators of the Plaza

PLAZA SUITE, BUFFALO

Delicious

Cherries Jubilee
Luscious Bing Cherries flamed with Brandy over Vanilla Ice Cream.

Crepes Suzettes
Simmered Crepes- flavored in Grand Mariner.

Bananas Calypso
A delightfully different ending to your dinner.

The Red Balloon
Vanilla Ice Cream covered with fresh Strawberries and Champagne.

Atop One M & T Plaza/ Buffalo, N.Y.

Delovely

Coffee Alexander
Brandy and Creme de Cocoa- Hot Coffee- finished with Creamy topping.

Irish Coffee
Strong Coffee- rich cream- a touch of sugar carmalized- and Irish Whiskey as smooth as the wit of the land.

Jamaican Coffee
Tia Maria and Creme de Cocoa blended with Hot Coffee- topped with mounds of fluffy topping and finished to perfection with Bittersweet Chocolate Curls.

Plaza Suite Coffee
Our own special- selected choice liqueurs and Brandy combined with Hot Coffee- finished with oodles of topping.

Atop One M & T Plaza/ Buffalo, N.Y.

Delightful

Chihuahua
Tequila- coffee liqueur and Coffee Ice Cream- Blended.

Sunshine Frosty
Vodka- Orange Juice and Vanilla Ice Cream- Blended.

Velvet Hammer
Cointreau- Creme de Cocoa and soft Ice Cream.

Atop One M & T Plaza/ Buffalo, N.Y.

Suite, tried several managers. Ultimately, they selected Ms. Adair, confident that she could solve their problems.

Service Systems was convinced that Ms. Adair had the right background. After all, she had owned her own restaurant, had managed a small hotel, and, as an employee of Service Systems since 1960, had worked as a troubleshooter in nearly every phase of the organization's numerous operations. But most important, they felt, was the fact that as director of training for the company's foodservice division, she had been responsible for training more than 5,000 of its personnel.

For all of these reasons, Eleanor Adair was selected to become general manager of the problem-plagued Plaza Suite.

Among the new general manager's first tasks was to bring discipline to the Plaza Suite employees. As a first step, she initiated once-a-week staff meetings with department heads.

Explaining her reason for setting up these weekly meetings, Ms. Adair said, "At least, they wouldn't shout at each other during working hours." Her strategy proved to be successful. Gradually the various department heads began to understand each other's problems, and to work together.

Next Ms. Adair instituted training programs for her employees. These further motivated her staff and, very soon, turned a restaurant with a slim chance for survival into a much-talked-about success. However, being a modest person, Ms. Adair insists, "It's the kids behind me that make the Plaza Suite a success."

As soon as the foodservice team was functioning successfully, Ms. Adair turned her attention to other areas, particularly the launching of promotions. She believed that increasing volume was a key to continuing success, and, therefore, she went about the task of developing ways of bringing people into the city and, thus, into the restaurant.

She began by building on the things she knew were popular with area residents. Ms. Adair said, "Hockey is extremely big in Buffalo, and so we started a hockey club."

Explaining how it operates, she stated, "Members get full season tickets, as well as dinner either before or after the game. And we've had lots of repeat business because of this program."

Ms. Adair then developed another plan. This one was a dinner theater, which included shows three times a week. These productions of Broadway musicals, which were put on by talented college students, were extremely well received. In fact, as Ms. Adair reports, "People want more."

Because Plaza Suite has an Executive Men's Club with more than 500 members, and since no women were allowed to lunch in the club dining area, Eleanor Adair started a club for executive women called Grande Dejeuner Les Femmes.

Grande Dejeuner Les Femmes is located in an elegant little room that was formerly a private meeting room, now used to greater advantage as a club solely for women. There need be no discussion over who pays the check, often a problem when women entertain at a public restaurant. No checks are presented; instead, a bill is mailed monthly to each member.

Ms. Adair has turned things around at the Plaza Suite, and she credits fine food, promotion and training for this achievement.

Lysle and Albert Aschaffenburg,
Bruce McFarland (THEN ALSO AT THE HOTEL)

"When I took over this hotel, operating it as a residential hotel, for which it was originally constructed," said Lysle Aschaffenburg, chairman of the board and owner of New Orleans' Pontchartrain Hotel, "it didn't take me long to find out that it was impossible, or nearly impossible, for any hotel to cater to permanent guests and make a profit.

"One evening in the 1930 to 1932 period, I was walking through the coffee shop, and a maiden lady named Ducky Wexler, one of the longtime residents, said, 'Lysle, everybody tells me I'm paying too much rent!'

"This was based on a lack of information, as there was no other residential hotel in New Orleans, and so her lady friends were comparing Pontchartrain Hotel rates covering complete hotel service to the rent for an apartment. Since there was no other residential hotel, there was no way they could possibly make a true comparison.

"As it developed, this was probably the most important conversation in my life. The lady was paying $180 a month for a complete apartment—living room, bedroom, dressing room, bath, and a complete kitchen."

At the time, Mr. Aschaffenburg pointed out to the lady, "Ducky, you are paying approximately $6 a day for a 3-room apartment, or approximately $2 a day per room, a rate much lower than you could get in a flophouse in New Orleans."

An idea had been planted in the hotel owner's mind and during the night he awakened. "From my knowledge of the space," he continued, "I drew a crude arrangement incorporating in the same space three hotel rooms, each with a bath. The following morning I called a young friend, a Cornell graduate and architect, and told him what I was planning to do. I assured him I knew the space was there, but, since I didn't know about pipes, shafts, and other possible structural obstacles, I asked him to send up one of his men to inspect the area and, if possible, draw a plan that took structural factors into consideration but that could incorporate the three bedrooms and three baths in the space now occupied by one apartment."

A few days later the plans were delivered. When the architect was asked what he thought the job would cost for 9 floors, changing 9 apartments into 27 rooms, each with bath, the architect replied, $20,000. "Then," recounted Mr. Aschaffenburg, "I asked him if he would gamble and draw the plans, because if the job could be done for $20,000, I would proceed with it."

The architect asked for a 10 percent leeway and, when the plans had been completed, proceeded with the remodeling. The timing could not have been better—the job was completed and the rooms available for sale two weeks before Pearl Harbor. Almost immediately New Orleans hotels became so busy that, by general agreement, guests were told when they registered that they could have a room for only five days. Rates for the new Pontchartrain rooms were set at $10, $8, and $6 per room, so instead of returning $6 a day, the space was returning $24. This was the first step in the complete renovation of the Pontchartrain into a transient hotel.

It was in 1948 that IVY Award winner Lysle Aschaffenburg imple-

PONTCHARTRAIN HOTEL, NEW ORLEANS

Lysle Aschaffenburg
Chairman of the Board
and Owner

Albert Aschaffenburg
President

mented his idea that one of the most important services a hotel can offer is fine foodservice. Using space that had formerly been a parlor, the Caribbean Room was designed and launched. In a very short time it had developed a reputation as a fine dining room. A little later, because of its success, the size of the room was tripled by taking in space that had been a patio and garden. Today the Caribbean Room is rated among the finest in New Orleans. It has been a *Holiday* award winner for the past 15 years.

Among the specialties at the Caribbean Room are Oyster Broth, Trout Veronique with Hollandaise, and Crepe Souffle.

One of the most dramatic items on the Pontchartrain menu is the Mile High Ice Cream Pie served with a sauceboat of Chocolate Sauce. Faced for the first time with this seemingly insurmountable triumph, one male patron of the Pontchartrain buried his head briefly in his hands. A slim and charming lady at an adjoining table leaned over and said encouragingly, "Go ahead, you can do it. I did." And he did, finding it delectable to the last bite.

Fine dining and fine service are equal assets of the Pontchartrain. President and co-IVY Award winner Albert Aschaffenburg explained the approach to service that is presented to the employees. Actually, standards set by father and son have become ingrained in the employees, many of whom have been with the hotel 25 years.

Albert Aschaffenburg states, "It's my conviction that a hotel should be a lot more than just a bed to sleep in, or a place to shower, or a room in which food is served.

"Our staff is schooled not only in service but also in the *spirit* of service. Guests prefer us because they don't feel like a number on the door. We have the largest board of directors in the world—the people of New Orleans!"

Illustrating his point, Aschaffenburg commented, "One man, a regular customer here, described the Pontchartrain as his 'personal bastion against the commonplace'.

In the final analysis, we don't own the hotel. The hotel owns us!"

(Bruce McFarland who became an IVY Award winner while general manager of the Pontchartrain Hotel, has been general manager of the Quail Hollow Inn and Golf Club, Painesville, Ohio, since November, 1974.)

The weekly buffet at the Caribbean Room of New Orleans' Pontchartrain Hotel is always a beautiful blend of food and flowers, a display that is a spectacular showcase for the culinary prowess of the hotel's "great kitchen."

Anthony Athanas

In addition to being a fine restaurant which features excellent cuisine, Anthony's Pier 4 in Boston has been described by some people as a minor operating miracle. It combines a unique and exciting atmosphere for large numbers of people with excellently prepared food which is the result of a complex production operation.

What makes Anthony's Pier 4 work?—the planning and personal supervision of owner and operator Anthony Athanas, an IVY Award winner who also owns four other fine dining operations. An Albanian immigrant, he started at the bottom of the restaurant business and went on to achieve outstanding success.

In 1971, while taking primary responsibility for the success of Pier 4, Athanas was working 10 to 12 hours a day, he seemed to be everywhere from the kitchen to the cab stand. Throughout all of this, Athanas remained a cool, calm ringmaster. Moreover, he made it a point to greet Pier 4 guests personally. At the same time waiters and waitresses were carefully trained to meet the needs of patrons. He was also keeping a sharp eye on his 3 other operations.

Pier 4 itself is a massive building at the end of a 1,000-foot pier. Appropriately enough, based on this setting, the restaurant has many niches filled with nautical antiques, and the waiters and waitresses wear Colonial and nautical costumes.

To pay tribute to the past in a sea motif and, at the same time, attract new business, Athanas has moored the Peter Stuyvesant, a former Hudson River steamboat, next to his pier. The old steamboat, which is connected to the restaurant by a covered passageway, serves special parties and as a cocktail lounge, an attraction in itself.

A popular restaurant, Pier 4 has more than 300 employees. Sales for this facility have continually mounted, currently are at the $10 million annual level.

Pier 4 has achieved outstanding success; in addition to being recognized by customers, it has also been honored by the experts. In fact, it was the first single restaurant operation in the country to qualify for the INSTITUTIONS 400.

Athanas continues to strive for perfection. He not only tries to make certain that the food is excellent, the service good, and the personnel well trained, but also he tries to make every effort to create an atmos-

ANTHONY'S PIER 4, BOSTON

The sommelier at Anthony's Pier 4 wears a special costume; here owner Athanas checks a wine selection.

phere that is conducive to comfort and friendliness, and to provide an intimate experience for his patrons.

In spite of his hectic schedule, however, Athanas has never thought of standing still. Assets to his progress have been his four sons, Anthony, Jr., Michael, Robert, and Paul, who provide capable management as needed in the several Athanas restaurants. The other restaurants are Anthony's Hawthorne, Lynn, Mass.; Hawthorne by the Sea, Swampscott, and General Glover House, Marblehead.

This freed Athanas Sr. to plan, and open in June, 1975, Anthony's Cummaquid Inn on Rt. 6A in Yarmouthport near Hyannis on Cape Cod. There he has restored and expanded the dining area of an early inn, adding the most modern of kitchen facilities. Located on an elevation, the inn's handsomely appointed dining facilities have a sweeping view of Cape Cod Bay.

In keeping with the interest generated by the Bicentennial year, the new operation has its own historical interest in that it is located on what was originally the land of the Cummaquid Indians whose sachem, Iyanough, befriended the Pilgrims in 1620 and 1621. In keeping with Athanas' reputation for business acumen, the year-round restaurant has had impressive numbers of customers since its opening.

While Pier 4 comes to mind first, there are four other operations in Anthony Athanas' fine dining group.

Dominique Beauchard,
Jean-Claude Fardeau

As 1975 IVY Award winners, the talents of Dominique Beauchard and Jean-Claude Fardeau, plus a skilled and highly trained staff, combined to make dining at the Ninety-Fifth Restaurant something akin to eating on a cloud. Beauchard was manager of operations and Fardeau, the catering director at that time; they have since left the operation. Dominique Beauchard has become food and beverage manager, and Jean-Claude Fardeau, catering manager of Chicago's new Ritz Carlton Hotel.

The Ninety-Fifth sits high atop Chicago's John Hancock Center. From a plush seat inside you can, on a clear day, see 48 miles into the distance.

Although customers are treated to a breathtaking view from the Ninety-Fifth, Beauchard and Fardeau believed that it was in spite of the spectacular view, rather than because of it, that the Ninety-Fifth was one of "Davre's" most profitable restaurants. Their views of the restaurant as stated at that time follow:

He also emphasizes the importance of the fact that he offers a French menu prepared, of course, entirely from scratch. "I think we're serving a better product at a lower price," he says.

To illustrate his point and back up the reasons for his belief, Beauchard explained that competition among French restaurants in Chicago is very keen. Moreover, he admits that the Ninety-Fifth's reliance on a small kitchen, as well as a dependence upon elevators to reach its lofty heights, places the restaurant at a distinct disadvantage. Yet Beauchard is firmly convinced that, during the entire five years he has been at the Ninety-Fifth, he has outdone the competition.

Beauchard is in an excellent position to make his assessment of the operation, because he has been with the restaurant since it opened in August, 1970. He started as assistant to the general manager and was named manager of operations in January, 1974.

"Another big difference between us and the other French restaurants in Chicago is the number of people we serve." Noting that total seating for the entire floor of the Ninety-Fifth is 475 persons, Beauchard pointed out that on a good Saturday evening, there may well be 550 to 600 people served at the restaurant. He also stated that the Ninety-Fifth's average check of $15.50 helps to boost its annual sales to more than $3 million each year.

While the able talents of Beauchard have been used most constructively at the Ninety-Fifth, they have been complemented, and very effectively, by those of Jean-Claude Fardeau.

Catering director Fardeau stresses that quality control is first in everyone's mind. He says, "I would say it has been the consistent level of quality 365 days a year that has made the Ninety-Fifth the great restaurant it is."

Fardeau handles between 15 and 20 banquets a week and applies the same exacting standards for a party of 200 as Beauchard does for a party of two. Fardeau's staff of 50 is trained to handle parties of many sizes, although the average banquet size is usually 50 to 150 people.

A candid man, Beauchard freely admits that initially the restaurant had its problems. When it first opened, the Ninety-Fifth tended to

**THEN AT THE
NINETY-FIFTH, CHICAGO**

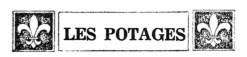

LES POTAGES

GRATINEE MONTAGNARDE 2.75
Baked Tureen of Onion Soup
BISQUE DE HOMARD 3.00
Cream of Lobster
PETITE MARMITE HENRY IV 2.00
Beef Broth with a garniture of Beef,
Chicken, Marrow and Vegetables
VICHYSSOISE 1.75
Chilled Blend of Leek and Potato Soup
VELOUTE BONGA-BONGA 2.50
Cream of Oysters, Hawaiian Style

cater only to the elite, thus intentionally restricting its market, as well as its appeal. That concept, however, did not work and was changed by an astute management.

Beauchard recalled the situation, saying, "We found we couldn't afford to serve only the upper level of society." Then, expressing his own belief, which would no doubt be confirmed by sociologists, he says, "That strata (of society) doesn't exist in the numbers it used to, in my opinion. Besides, we need a broader base of support—since we require at least three times the patronage of any other French restaurant in Chicago."

Many, including Beauchard himself, also now agree that the Ninety-Fifth no longer deserves the stinging appraisal once given it by a local restaurant critic, who said: "Service not commensurate with price."

For no matter how large or small the party or request, Dominique Beauchard and Jean-Claude Fardeau take special pains to make the Ninety-Fifth the brightest star in "Davre's"—and Chicago's—heaven.

Food as elegant as the surroundings shown here was the goal attained at the Ninety-Fifth Restaurant, Chicago by Dominique Beauchard, Jean-manager of operations, and Claude Fardeau, catering director. For an example of Ninety-Fifth menu offerings, see preceding page.

Jerome Berkman

Combine in one person a tireless, natural desire to build a better mousetrap with an equally strong dislike for the traditional hospital-tray assembly line and the result almost inevitably becomes Jerome Berkman's approach to foodservice at Cedars-Sinai Medical Center in Los Angeles. Berkman has been foodservice director at the hospital since 1968 and became an IVY Award winner in 1975.

Berkman has developed at Cedars-Sinai a system which eliminates the tray line. It not only makes a la carte menus possible, but also enables foodservice department "stewardesses" to serve food readied in one of the modular kitchens located near patients' rooms on each floor.

To do this requires a large production kitchen where the food is prepared in advance. It is then frozen or chilled and appropriate amounts are transported to each floor, where it can be reconstituted and available whenever the patient wants it, instead of being "a half hour and three rings away." It also means "hot food hot and cold food cold," a special treat for captive patrons.

Shortly, Berkman's department will be moving into this new $1 million kitchen, engineered to mesh with a highly centralized preparation procedure that is decentralized in the final preparation.

The chief contributing factor in his search for new approaches to hospital feeding was Berkman's first job in a northeastern hospital. It all started when a winter blizzard prevented employees from getting to work. With no personnel available to man the tray line, there was such chaos that Berkman began to question the effectiveness of the system. He reasoned that there had to be a better, more efficient way.

"Faced with that tunnel of confusion," Berkman comments, referring to the tray line, "there is no one, unless it's the checker, who is accountable for each tray and sees that it contains every item it should." He indicated that even when a checker has this responsibility, "Too many times I've seen her just run off and cry because the whole thing gets out of control. There is so much chance for human error."

Never forgetting this early lesson, he continued his study of alternate solutions at Glendale Hospital, where he conducted research into the freezing of foods made on the premises, and subsequently at Cedars-Sinai Medical Center in Los Angeles, where entirely new worlds of research and experimentation opened up for him.

When he went to Cedars in 1968, Berkman recognized that, because of the 1961 merger with Mt. Sinai Hospital, an impressive potential existed. This merger had been executed as the initial step in the development of a prestigious medical center.

The growth has equalled his anticipation. Later this year, the two progressive health care establishments plan to open a 1,120-bed, $100 million medical center. When completed, it will be the largest community hospital in the West.

Because of the hospital's progressive atmosphere, Berkman was an excellent choice for the job. He was hired with the understanding that he would develop a foodservice program that would be equal to other developments in the innovative center. He is certainly fulfilling these original terms.

Berkman's innovative and daring spirit will also pay financial dividends. His system is expected to realize, as was originally projected in

CEDARS – SINAI MEDICAL CENTER LOS ANGELES

Jerome Berkman, R. D. Foodservice Director Cedars-Sinai Medical Center

1972, a savings of from $300 to $600 per bed each year over the conventional tray-line method.

In addition to his patient-feeding system, Berkman has also devised a compact kitchen for the Thalians' Community Mental Health Center. Based almost entirely on convenience items, the cafeteria scramble unit and patient foodservice are operated by just six employees, including the manager, although the operation serves the center's 85 beds, all of its employees, medical staff, as well as visitors, it is also designed to undertake catering activity. It is proof that Berkman really makes his motto work, "The way to think big is to think small."

Currently, Berkman is experimenting with a scientific method of determining how well or how little people like specific foods. A dish is judged on five different weighted criteria. If it scores high enough, it is then considered for possible inclusion in menus at Cedars-Sinai. Apparently, the method is both successful and accurate because, during 1974, employee cafeteria business increased by 10 percent.

As an outstanding man in an unusual hospital, Berkman can be counted on for continuing foodservice improvements.

At Cedars-Sinai, there is a climate of innovation, with an administration that has encouraged him to improve the foodservice system. It is the best possible vantage point for a pioneer who is challenged by the untried, and comes up with unexpected solutions that work.

Management concerns about sanitation emphasizes its importance to personnel at Cedars-Sinai Medical Center. Jerome Berkman, R.D., foodservice director, conducts a sample inspection to demonstrate his belief that the only sound basis for full-flavored food is a sanitary production center.

Bruno Bernabo

Although Mamma Leone's Restaurant is located in New York City, going there is a total Italian experience.

When a guest calls Mamma Leone's for a dinner reservation, the person who answers the phone at the restaurant answers with a warm and hearty Italian greeting.

From first impression to last, this restaurant is Italian—in flavor, style, atmosphere, decor, and cuisine.

"Mamma Leone's," as described by one patron, "is what everybody thinks Italian is. It is certainly Italian, more so than any place I've seen, even in Italy."

To create just such an effect was the goal of the plan carefully followed by management. To illustrate, Italian artifacts, which have been valued at close to $1 million, fill the spacious dining rooms of this restaurant that brings Italy to New York.

In addition to its famous atmosphere, Mamma Leone's is also well known for its excellent food, which is served in heaping, generous portions. The size of the portions led one of the operation's regular customers to describe them as the restaurant's "orgy of food."

The cost of dinner at this establishment, despite inflation and high food prices, remains relatively reasonable. For example, Mamma Leone's, which is open to the public only for dinner—although it is available to private parties for lunch—offers meals of many courses, each a bountiful serving, for as little as $7.50.

But what Mamma Leone's really does best is market itself to a national audience. Significantly, the restaurant won its greatest support for the Ivy Award from out-of-town colleagues.

One of the Italian paintings which create the "more Italian than Italy" interiors cited by a delighted patron at Mamma Leone's is shown by the restaurant's managing director.

The restaurant carries on a continuing effort to attract this trade and concentrates on making the dining experience one that out-of-towners will want to repeat. To reach groups within the travel market, Mamma Leone's hosts theater parties and dinners prior to and/or following sports events. As a result of these marketing efforts, the restaurant has been the recipient of national attention and publicity.

Noting this major emphasis, Mamma Leone's IVY Award winning managing director Bruno Bernabo pointed out that it is, and has been, part of the history of the restaurant. He then went on to explain the history of Mamma Leone's, which began nearly 70 years ago.

In 1906, Mamma Leone, an Italian immigrant, started her own restaurant in New York City. She herself operated the eating establishment for nearly 40 years; however, when she died in 1945, she left the facility to her three sons.

The brothers owned and operated the restaurant for a number of years, but one, Gene Leone, eventually bought out the interests of his two brothers and became the sole owner. Subsequently, however, Gene Leone also relinquished his interest in the family business. In 1959, Mamma Leone's was sold to Restaurant Associates.

Despite changes in ownership, Mamma Leone's has retained its distinctive character. Restaurant Associates has, since acquiring the facility, constantly striven to maintain the restaurant's individuality. Thus, since the purchase of Mamma Leone's 16 years ago, the organization has given Bernabo a free hand to operate the fine restaurant within the style and flavor of its own grand Italian tradition.

Consequently, Mamma Leone's continues to be a popular and highly successful operation. This situation is the result of a combination of several factors. These include: (1) the wise and enlightened policies of Restaurant Associates; (2) the operating skill of managing director Bruno Bernabo; (3) the able assistance of a dedicated and well-trained staff, and (4), of primary importance, the excellent cuisine and generous portions which it serves.

Careful attention to portion size and presentation assures patrons they will have the same hearty servings of Italian favorites each time they come to Mamma Leone's. Managing director Bernabo's many years of supervision stand him in good stead in keeping the cuisine up to anticipated standards.

Vincent and Anthony Bommarito

The effectiveness of making dining out an exciting experience, one with a touch of theatrical suspense, is nowhere better illustrated than at Tony's in St. Louis. People who dine there enjoy not only superlative food specialties, but also the excitement of a "first night" in the theatre.

This highly successful formula has been developed over the years by two brothers, Vincent and Anthony Bommarito, joint winners of the IVY Award. Essential to making the formula work is the "family of 70 workers."

Vincent Bommarito, the older of the brothers, admits this is a high ratio, but Bommarito stresses the fact that 30 members of that employee family have been a part of Tony's for 15 years or more. Furthermore, Bommarito contends that these two figures, when viewed together offer a clear explanation of how he and his brother Anthony have been able to develop the foremost restaurant in St. Louis, as well as one of the country's finest evening spots.

Employee interest and cooperation at Tony's was developed and maintained in the early days by regularly scheduled meetings held by the Bommarito brothers, and by the example of the brothers themselves.

The kind of devoted attention they gave to guests set a standard that all the employees tried to reach.

"People make a place," Vincent Bommarito believes. "You need their involvement, as well as their labor of love and dedication. You can't have employees who keep watching the clock to see when they can go home. Atmosphere is fine, but it's the people who give you the feeling that somebody cared that you remember after you leave."

Vincent Bommarito checks the preparation of the Italian food specialties that have earned the description "foremost" for Tony's.

Having employees out front who could be counted on to provide the cared-for feeling and a kitchen staff organized and trained by Anthony made it possible for Anthony himself to open a second restaurant about three years ago. He did not take over his new place until the kitchen staff could be counted on to produce steaks and Italian specialties at Tony's of the same high degree of excellence each evening.

In his new restaurant known as Anthony's, Bommarito (Anthony) serves French and seafood specialties. Designed in contemporary style, the new restaurant, Anthony's, is located eight blocks away, and has been a success from the start.

Tony's continues on its successful way with Vincent Bommarito keeping a close watch over service and stepping in at key points to add his own special type of fanfare to the presentation of a meal. Basic to the restaurant's success is Vincent Bommarito's comment, "Tony's has been my life." This statement is true of both brothers. Known today as Tony's, the establishment was started by their late father in small quarters known as Tony's Spaghetti House. When the father died in 1948, the family decided to keep the restaurant. Thus, immediately after his graduation from high school, Vincent went to work there as a waiter and a few years later, Anthony joined him.

The brothers undertook the effort with enthusiasm and caution, making changes and improvements little by little. Gradually, Tony's Spaghetti House evolved into Tony's and, in the process, earned a reputation as a great restaurant.

This is apparent from the fact that it has been honored by *Esquire* Magazine and is consistently recognized by *Holiday* Magazine with a Distinctive Dining award. Such recognition has not changed Vincent Bommarito's approach; he continues to make dining at Tony's a gala occasion. He is still a greeter of his guests and tends to their needs as he moves through the dining rooms.

Tony's is a thriving business, but a dinner-only operation, a switch that was made in 1958. Explaining this decision, Vincent said, "One of the reasons we quit serving lunch was that we'd be serving lunch and worrying, at the same time, about dinner. You can't do both right."

Because of Vincent's conviction that dining out should be a unique experience, with much of the pleasure coming from people-to-people encounters, there are no special rooms at Tony's. As he explains, "We don't have banquet or private rooms. This way we get to see the people."

What Tony's has to offer St. Louis diners has been communicated primarily by word of mouth. No formal advertising campaign has ever been conducted, although gestures similar to an ad in the St. Louis Symphony's program—it simply says Tony's—do remind the public that an unforgettable experience in dining out is available to them.

Anthony Bommarito, pictured while still at Tony's where he formulated recipes and supervised production for many years. He has since opened his own restaurant, which serves French and seafood specialties and is known as Anthony's.

Edwin L. Brashears, Jr.

Under the watchful eye of owner and IVY Award winner Edwin L. Brashears, Jr., the graceful, 700-room Drake Hotel on Chicago's Near North Side maintains its reputation for unparalleled excellence. One of the last great independents, it has been described as ". . .unquestionably the most wonderful hotel in the world, one which will not soon be imitated."

A large, old hotel that caters to a quality clientele, The Drake retains a fresh appearance with the aid of 97 full-time tradesmen, a resident interior decorator, and a three-step battle plan for replacements and repairs.

It not only remains current, but also is a leader. It was the first Chicago hotel to have (central) air conditioning in all guest rooms and the first with alternating current. It is one of the few hotels serving bottled water, as well as having its own purifying system.

Another of The Drake's famous trademarks is the Cape Cod Room, consistently named as one of America's top restaurants and on *Holiday* magazine's list of distinctive dining places for 22 consecutive years.

Quietly achieved excellence is apparent here, and while high-style seafood restaurants come and go, the Cape Cod Room, an institution at The Drake, retains its original image. The 135-seat restaurant, which serves an average of 600 patrons from noon to midnight, is in a class by itself. Moreover, it realizes the highest profit of any dining room or restaurant area in the hotel.

Combining excellent personnel, fine service, and modern equipment— new ovens and a completely updated kitchen– the restaurant's success gets extra impetus from owner Brashears, who insists on high standards of food purchasing and preparation excellence. He has a reputation among Chicago wholesalers for buying the best produce, meat, and fish available. Certainly the quality and freshness of the food are prime factors in its success.

Weathered artifacts from seashores decorate this first-rate seafood house. The decor comes across as old, secure, and familiar, because its large clientele of regular patrons insist that it remain that way. The room still looks as it did years ago. When repairs or replacements are required, they are made when the operation is closed between serving periods. There can be no obvious indication that "the best seafood room in the country" is in any way being changed.

This devotion is based on the superior food and service that the Cape Cod Room is noted for. The restaurant serves the choice catches from lakes, streams, and oceans. They arrive fresh and flavorful each day and are prepared and served in an unusual and distinctive style.

"We've maintained this hotel in unusual fashion," says Brashears, who feels that this is essential where design and location, construction, equipment, and furnishings are of consistently high quality.

The Drake is equally concerned with its service, which is widely regarded as the best to be found anywhere. Maids still turn down sheets at night and lay out bedclothes, and letters/phone messages are neatly and promptly clipped to guests' doors. Also, for the convenience of guests, the hotel still has its own barber shop, in-house laundry, and is the only Chicago hotel that still has elevator operators.

Because The Drake management clearly recognizes that the quality of its service is highly dependent on its employees, their surroundings

THE DRAKE, CHICAGO

**It takes six hours to make the soup.
Thirty minutes to press your suit.
And two minutes to get
to the beach.**

*E. L. Brashears, Jr.
President, The Drake*

are upgraded as needed. The employee cafeteria, which overlooks the lake, has one of the best views in the house and is completely air-conditioned for comfort.

As part of its continuing effort to maintain high employee morale, The Drake recently completed a $70,000 renovation of employee locker rooms. "While this investment produces no revenue," said Patrick Kane, Drake executive vice-president, "it contributes measurably to the attitude of the employees and to the service they provide."

This approach to employees is credited with assuring excellent service and an unusual record for retaining good employees. In fact, 450 of the 1,100 employees have been with the hotel more than five years, 36 for 30 years or more, and some have even achieved 55 years of service. But average length of service of those who have been awarded over-5-year pins is 18 years.

Patrons are extravagant in their praise of the Cape Cod Room's superb cuisine. Among particular menu favorites, according to William T. Burns, Jr., The Drake's assistant general manager, are: the famous Bookbinder Red Snapper Soup, served with imported sherry; Pompano Papillote, a fillet enclosed in parchment with lobster and mushrooms in a red wine sauce; and Broiled Imported (French) Turbot.

The Cape Cod Room is doing a thriving, booming business, as is The Drake Hotel itself. And despite persistent recurrent rumors to the effect that Edwin Brashears plans to divest himself of the property, he doesn't plan to give up the struggle. The Cape Cod Room and The Drake are alive, well, and doing beautifully, and Edwin Brashears intends to see that they stay that way.

Renewal of the furnishings in The Drake's Cape Cod Room can only be done when guests are not there. Patron devotion to its outstanding fish and seafood cuisine is matched only by resistance to any change in this long-time favorite!

Mike and Lee Comisar

At La Maisonette, located in a midwestern city, guests tend to favor beef; in fact, Beef Wellington is the restaurant's single most popular item. However, to acquaint guests with other menu items and widen the appeal of the restaurant, if new or unfamiliar items are encountered by a guest, a dollop of the item is served for the guest to try.

In addition to adventures in eating, warmth and friendliness are synonymous with La Maisonette. While these qualities aptly describe the atmosphere of this highly rated Cincinnati restaurant, they are equally descriptive of Mike and Lee Comisar, the two brothers who own and operate it.

These qualities are being passed down by the brothers Comisar, the second generation of restaurateurs, to a new generation. As Michael Comisar explained, his brother's son, Michael E., has joined the operation, becoming a new and vital part of La Maisonette's management team.

The effort to create this comfortable atmosphere is not lost on guests, who are both aware and appreciative of it. As one visitor to the restaurant remarked, "At the others (distinguished Cincinnati restaurants), you're conscious that you're in top-rated French restaurants. But La Maisonette makes you feel at home."

Statements like that must be music to the ears of Mike and Lee Comisar, because this is what they strive to achieve. Describing their approach, Lee Comisar says, "At La Maisonette, we do not have customers or clients; we have guests." Every attempt is made to make guests feel relaxed and at ease, just as if they were dining in their own homes.

The Comisars concentrate on putting young guests at ease, just as they do their older, more sophisticated guests. Their successful policy for young diners-out is especially effective with those who visit their less expensive restaurant, Le Normandie. Located on a lower level in the same building as La Maisonette, it is extremely popular with young adults on a limited budget.

Frequently, the young people are curious about what is upstairs. When they indicate interest, they are encouraged to visit La Maisonette and see for themselves.

Upon arriving upstairs, they are treated cordially and respectfully by members of La Maisonette's staff who welcome them and freely answer their questions. This practice seems to work to La Maisonette's advantage, because frequently the "visitors" return for dinner as regular customers.

Young and/or inexperienced diners are encouraged to look around and when they come to dine are subtly and discreetly given assistance when they need it.

"When we see a young couple or group poring over the menu," says brother Mike Comisar, "we quietly send someone over to help. We don't want a waiter laughing at them."

Undoubtedly, attitudes such as these help to explain the popularity of La Maisonette, as does their inventory of fine wines, valued at between $70,000 and $80,000, the excellence of the food that is served, and the well-trained staff.

Realizing that employees can spell the difference between an operation's success or failure, the Comisars make every effort to treat employees properly and to recognize their achievements. To implement

LA MAISONETTE, CINCINNATI

Elegant settings for small dinners in private rooms are personally supervised by the Comisar brothers who firmly believe "fine food deserves fine presentation."

their efforts, the Comisars hold what they call the "5:20" meeting, where employees are urged to taste new dishes or wines, discuss problems, or simply air gripes—before they get to be major stumbling blocks. These meetings have been highly successful in developing an especially dedicated and loyal staff at La Maisonette.

Apparently, the Comisars have found the right key. For, in addition to the elegant La Maisonette, they also own the less expensive Le Normandie (previously mentioned), as well as the Golden Lamb.

In October, 1972, they opened Chester's Road House. An urban restaurant in the greater Cincinnati area, it features a salad bar operation and an adjacent greenhouse.

The Comisars are also contemplating opening another restaurant. To be located behind La Maisonette in what was formerly an electric power plant, it will be known as the Gano Street Power Station.

It will, in all probability, be as successful as the other Comisar operations. For in this impersonal age, often characterized by indifference, the Comisars have learned that providing an outstanding cuisine and serving it with warmth, courtesy, friendliness, and respect produces satisfied guests and results in a successful business as well as qualifying them to be IVY Award winners.

Mike and Lee Comisar, owner/ operators, La Maisonette, talk over a new menu idea.

James and Charles Doulos

At Jimmy's Harborside, Charles "Jimmy Jr." Doulos and his father, the original Jimmy, have successfully bridged the generation gap. They own and operate the restaurant, opened in 1955 and located on Boston's bustling pier.

The Harborside seats 400 in the restaurant and 100 in the lounge, and serves 1,500 meals a day. It is the Harborside's spectacular food that accounts for the 2- to 3-time turnover. The food and beverage checks average $4 to $5 for lunch and $10 to $11 for dinner.

Charlie lives by the maxim: "You can't run an absentee restaurant." He says "I went into the business voluntarily. . . no coercion, no filial obligation thing, nothing forced me to."

Explaining his start, Charlie added, "I began sweeping floors, making strawberry shortcake, shaking ice coffees. I knew what I was getting into. . . the hours, the work. But it was what I wanted. So, now, I more or less handle the administration part and the front of the house. But dad? He's boss in the kitchen.

"We have a wonderful rapport; I guess our close feelings are transferred to the staff and our guests. One of us always tries to be around for lunch or dinner. People expect it and, well, we kind of look forward to seeing them ourselves.

"I've been here professionally, so to speak, since 1956. I started the day after I got my degree in principles of management from Harvard. My father told me, 'If you want to be in this business, work, work, work!' He wouldn't even let me take a vacation. He finally agreed to give me six months off—for the Army reserves!

"I'd be willing to expand the present operation but would not want to go beyond that. Another place would cost us the intimacy we've created here. It's important not to spread yourself. Money isn't everything. I love this business, and I hope my kids will want to come into it. If they don't, I won't be able to retire! My father doesn't know the meaning of the word, and I can't imagine Harborside without him. The Harborside—it's his life and the word 'stop' isn't in his vocabulary.

"What fascinates me about running a restaurant is seeing how raw produce—like meat, fish, vegetables—is cut, scaled, popped in a broiler or fryer, or put through all those processes of preservation, storage, and preparation before it finally reaches the customer. I relish details. The more the merrier. The finer they are, the better I like it," Charlie concluded.

Joining the conversation, Jimmy the original said, "My son was, and still is, my inspiration. He deserves all the credit. The only area I want for myself is the kitchen. If he loves details, he can have them.

"At one time, I used to be very fussy—if you're not, you won't succeed—but the business is much more complex behind the scenes than it ever was before. One thing I've found. You never stop learning. There are always new ideas. My son teaches me much, but it's become too sophisticated for me.

"To me, this business will always be people. Now it's complicated with paper work, machines, payrolls, purchasing, red tape. I prefer to be with our customers or prepare something special for them in the kitchen. I don't know how Charlie does it all! He still spends as much time with the guests as I do!"

Describing some of the important elements of the Harborside, Jimmy

The original "Jimmy" Doulos against a background of mementos, products of a lifetime spent satisfying customers.

Charles "Jimmy Jr." Doulos, working with his father, neatly divides his time between business details and making guests feel especially welcome.

said, "We're family-oriented. Our wives come down and help out because they want to share our work and be a part of what we do. (I tell Charlie it's because they want to keep an eye on us!) Our staff is our family. They've been with us a long time. We were one of the first places to set up profit-sharing for our employees. Harborside belongs to them as much as it does to us.

"I know of very few professions which permit you to meet so many people from all walks of life. I've been in this one 50 years. It's been a privilege to serve presidents, film stars, sports celebrities. I'll never retire. I've met and know them all, and they know who I am and who Charlie is. The trouble with so many restaurants today is that you seldom know who the boss is!"

A Boston cab driver summed it up as he delivered luncheon guests at the Harborside's location at the end of a bustling Boston pier: "I can tell you one thing about Jimmy's. The food's spectacular. If it's not, Jimmy sends it right into the garbage, and if he doesn't, little Jimmy will."

Richard N. Frank

"You won't get better service anywhere else," said one knowledgeable individual, speaking of Lawry's Prime Rib in Los Angeles. Continuing, the expert noted that he felt this way about Lawry's "not because it's in the old-line tradition but because of its modern, informal, California-type service."

The idea for the contemporary, California-style of eating was introduced in 1938 by Lawry's co-founder, Lawrence L. Frank, when he revolutionized the restaurant business by developing a one-entree specialty house. The concept drew "won't work" warnings from traditionalists, but the Lawry's offering of prime rib and baked potato, preceded by a green salad in a spinning bowl, has been a lasting success, widely copied across the country.

While the unusually well-prepared, single item menu is an important part of the restaurant's success, Lawrence L. Frank also stressed the idea of exceptional presentation for fine food. He realized that this was vital in developing favorable patron response.

To put proper stress on presentation, Frank introduced unique food and service methods, for example, the serving of a tossed green salad prior to the entree, a concept that originated at Lawry's which has since become a part of the American dining tradition. He embellished this idea with the spinning salad service mentioned earlier and tableside service of roast beef from a cart, allowing the diner to specify exactly what he prefers—and get it. The beef itself is roasted by a special method that preserves prime flavor and moistness, and the specially designed, lighted carts keep the beef at the peak of perfection during serving.

Over the years this concept has achieved remarkable success for the restaurant, as well as wide acceptance by the general public. In recent years, Lawry's president and IVY Award winner Richard N. Frank, son of Lawrence, has carried Lawry's concept of exceptional service and showmanship to a number of additional locations—the newest of which is Lawry's Prime Rib in Chicago.

Lawry's restaurant experience began in the '20s with a restaurant near Glendale, California, called the Tam O'Shanter Inn. The name has been changed in recent years to The Great Scot. It is a gold mine of merchandising ideas. One of the Great Scot specialties is the Toad-in-the-Hole, a best-selling meat and mushroom "pie" using Yorkshire Pudding as the pie shell.

Their next venture was Mediterrania, which features decorative elements and foods from all countries bordering the Mediterranean. It was also the first restaurant in America to serve wine by the liter.

Others of the older restaurants in the Lawry's group include The Five Crowns, an exact replica of an English inn, also located near Los Angeles —and the Ben Jonson, one of San Francisco's leading restaurants. Its interior is furnished with one-of-a-kind authentic pieces appropriate to the period, and its food specialties and attentive service drew from one critic a new application for the phrase, "O Rare Ben Jonson."

In addition to these operations, Lawry's boasts four newer establishments. Casey's Bar, a hideaway in the basement under a bank building in downtown Los Angeles, reflects the personality of a mythical, unpolished, lovable Irishman. It has a menu of simple Irish recipes with The County Cork (corned beef and cabbage with potato dumplings) as a staple. A second similar Casey's Bar has recently been opened in Westwood, California.

Richard N. Frank
President
Lawry's

The English Cut

As traditionally served in England — and gaining in popularity here. ■ A generous portion of prime rib deftly carved in thinner slices. This method of carving tends to further enhance the rich, natural beefy goodness of the meat — you'll love it........

A new Great Scot is a remodeled seven-level inn in Arcadia, where lassies who serve the food and drink wear Scottish plaid costumes to complete the carefully evolved design theme of this restaurant.

In Lawry's Foods Company's own beautiful backyard is La Cocina, a Mexican styled, self-service restaurant located in a garden setting. Started as a public relations gesture, this operation has turned into a beautiful and prosperous attraction. This new California Center also includes a gift shop, wine shop, and garden shop. Mexican furniture, colorful tiles, bright canopies, lavish landscaping, and plenty of parking in a flower-packed lot all have helped make this a popular weekday luncheon spot (no dinners; closed weekends). Sangria is a favorite luncheon beverage, but the nicely garnished, fresh lemonade is an even more unusual meal beverage.

At Lawry's, it has always been recognized that presentation depended to a great extent on the persons doing the presenting or serving of the meal. To ensure success in this area, the California based organization developed and implemented a broad policy of rigorous personnel selection and training.

Lawry's not only remains a highly successful operation, but also one that has been a pace-setter at home and throughout the industry. Lawry's has introduced a variety of foods to Californians and a variety of foodservice presentation and preparation techniques that have served as inspiration for many foodservice designers and operators. Lawry's has also effectively demonstrated that food and its presentation can be spectacular and still be products of an efficient system.

The pioneering prime rib service at Lawry's, pictured in 1971, is just as popular in 1975. Their belief in the exceptional presentation of fine food has had many successful applications since '71. The careful choice of a theme and a decorative scheme and menu that will dramatize it are other important elements in their approach to foodservice.

Peter Goldman

Situated atop Nob Hill in romantic San Francisco is the Fairmont Hotel and Tower, which for seven decades has continued to adhere to a tradition of luxury that can be traced to its opening day. This tradition becomes evident the moment one enters the hotel and steps into its lavish lobby. Long recognized as one of the most beautiful in the world, it is considered symbolic of the grace, charm, and dignity that San Francisco conveys to visitors and inhabitants alike. Luxury is also the keynote in the spacious rooms and suites, many of which have private balconies overlooking the beautiful flower gardens. Decor and furnishings are both custom-designed and alive with color. A roof garden, with stately terraces and promenades, is resplendent with flowers and contains a magnificent fountain, all of which contribute to its semi-tropical atmosphere.

How does the Fairmont, which has received the Mobil Five-Star award for 15 consecutive years, and whose former general manager Peter Goldman was an IVY Award winner, manage to maintain such excellence?

One of four top-rated hotels whose president is Richard L. Swig, the Fairmont's reputation as a luxurious hotel has been due, in part, no doubt, to its decor, atmosphere and excellent service. It is a reputation carefully maintained by thorough and unchanging attention to personal care.

Amply demonstrating this are these extra touches that are an integral part of each of the Fairmont's 700 rooms: two pillows—one soft, one firm—for each bed; super percale sheets; Irish linen hand towels; am/fm radio and background music; an electric shoe buffer; a personal alarm clock; color television; a walk-in closet; evening maid service, and fingertip temperature tuning.

The Fairmont, however, is equally noted for its wide assortment of fine restaurants: the Squire, which serves continental cuisine; the Fairmont Crown, which overlooks the city and is reached by a glass-enclosed elevator, features an elaborate buffet daily; the Brasserie is open 24 hours a day and serves specialty dishes from around the world; the Tonga, which serves Chinese food in an exotic Polynesian setting; Canlis', which has an international menu, and the Venetian Room, which is a supper club featuring continental cuisine and topflight entertainment.

Proof positive of their popularity is the fact that the Fairmont is one of the few hotels where food and beverage sales even top the room sales.

Contributing to the Fairmont's reputation for fine foodservice is the belief, shared by IVY Award winner Peter Goldman, then Fairmont general manager, now managing director of all Fairmont Hotels, and current Fairmont general manager Herman Wiener, that a hotel needs a mix of restaurants, as well as good banquet facilities, to attract additional business.

That the Fairmont's banquet business excels is due largely to Goldman who, for many years, was catering manager at the San Francisco hotel.

Goldman built up the area by re-booking meetings before they adjourned and by meeting with the executives who were responsible for arranging group functions. Even after he became general manager of the Fairmont in San Francisco, Goldman continued to see convention executives—based on friendship, as well as good business sense.

Another reason for the Fairmont's outstanding position is a loyal and

Peter Goldman
Managing Director
Fairmont Hotel Company

long-tenured staff. One valet, for example, has been a hotel employee for 50 years, while many maids have been there for more than 20 years; most department heads have been Fairmont employees for 15 to 20 years.

Reasons for employee loyalty and longevity are often complex, as well as vague. But Herman Wiener, general manager of the San Francisco Fairmont, feels that with his employees it is due to a combination of factors. He includes a sense of belonging, a feeling of being part of a team effort working toward a common goal, and the knowledge that they are respected and appreciated.

While employees have certainly contributed to the hotel's success, another important reason is also present. It is management's refusal to let a rigid organization get in the way of customer satisfaction, a policy instituted some years ago by Peter Goldman.

This policy is also strongly endorsed and actively pursued by Herman Wiener. Explaining the reasoning behind the policy, Goldman says, "Everybody in the hotel should take care of each guest's needs. We don't make a guest go through 'the proper channel'."

Fine food may be the prime contribution of an IVY Award winner but, as Peter Goldman demonstrates, the dedication needed to assure the best in cuisine is usually accompanied by equally strong attention to the operation's total performance.

The Carriage Entrance of San Francisco's Fairmont hotel where distinguished visitors from all over the world arrive daily to enjoy the menu offerings of their favorite among the hotel's several restaurants.

Roland and Victor Gotti

Described by discriminating persons as "the most elegant restaurant in the world," Ernie's has gained an international reputation for the excellence of its French cuisine, its wine, its impeccable service, and for the authenticity of its Victorian decor.

Located in San Francisco, Ernie's occupies an historic site, which was known as the Frisco Dance Hall prior to its destruction during the 1906 earthquake and fire. Later rebuilt, the name of the structure was changed to Il Trovatore.

The birth of the current restaurant took place in the early 1930s, when Ernie Carlesso and Ambrogio Gotti purchased Il Trovatore, and a few years later, rechristened it Ernie's. The two men operated the restaurant jointly until Carlesso's death in 1946, when Gotti assumed sole ownership.

The year following Carlesso's death, Gotti retired from the business, turning over the ownership and control of the restaurant to his two sons, Victor and Roland, who have operated it ever since.

The Gotti brothers immediately took their responsibilities seriously and began looking for ways to improve the restaurant. In 1951, they undertook a massive redecoration program at Ernie's. Since then, they have set aside annually a two-week period for general freshening and refurbishing. Victor and Roland Gotti have spared no expense in creating

ERNIE'S, SAN FRANCISCO

Pictured at a 1970 Harvest Luncheon held at Ernie's, are (left to right) Victor Gotti, one of the owners, Alfred Fromm, President, Fromm and Sichel, Inc., San Francisco, world-wide distributor of the wines, champagne, and brandy of The Christian Brothers, Brother Timothy, F.S.C., famed Cellarmaster of The Christian Brothers, and Capt. Joseph Svatos of Ernie's staff.

at Ernie's both an outstanding restaurant and a Victorian-age monument to San Francisco's past.

But Ernie's is more than just decor. It is an award-winning restaurant whose menu selections have drawn patrons with educated and discriminating tastes. The veal entrees have a well-deserved reputation for excellence and a devoted following among regular patrons.

For 20 consecutive years, Ernie's has earned *Holiday* Magazine's award for distinctive dining. The restaurant has also been the recipient of the coveted five-star rating from Mobil Guide for the entire nine years the rating has been in existence. Ernie's is one of the very few U. S. restaurants to have received recognition from France's prestigious *Guide Michelin.*

In addition to excellent food, Ernie's serves a wide array of the finest wines. The wine cellar is especially well stocked, having a constant inventory of $50,000 in imported wines and approximately $20,000 in California wines. Its wine list may well be the most extensive of any restaurant in the United States since customers may choose from more than 200 imported and domestic wines.

To maintain the excellence of Ernie's wine selections, one of the Gotti brothers spends a month or more each year touring European vineyards and wineries to make selections for the Northern California restaurant.

No detail escapes the attention of the owners at Ernie's; food, wine, and decor are under constant scrutiny. It is this that makes dining there an unforgettable experience.

Ernie's now contains three elegant dining rooms—the Montgomery Room, the Elysian Room, and the Ambrosia Room, seating a total of 180 persons—with silk brocade wall coverings, fine antique paintings, plush red carpeting, and rich red velvet upholstered chairs.

The restaurant also has a small additional room, the Bacchus Cellar, which seats from 12 to 28 persons. This room has become increasingly popular with some of the Bay Area's distinguished hosts as the setting for their more impressive entertaining.

Most of the accessories at Ernie's have been purchased from the famous San Francisco mansions of the Flood and Spreckels families. However, its elaborate mahogany bar with stained glass and antique mirrors was part of Il Trovatore, Ernie's predecessor. The bar was shipped around the Horn at the turn of the century on a clipper ship from Chicago.

The elegant decor at Ernie's often has made it the setting for motion pictures. Scenes from the movie "Vertigo," starring James Stewart and Kim Novak, were filmed at Ernie's, and it was mentioned frequently in "The High and the Mighty." Ernie's was also a picturesque part of both "The Days of Wine and Roses" and "Take the Money and Run."

Elegant decor, an outstanding wine cellar, and excellent cuisine are important factors in Ernie's success, but there are other areas on which the management also concentrates. According to the Gotti brothers, these include constant attention to every detail, no matter how minute, that will ensure customer satisfaction, plus unceasing care in maintaining the highest standards of quality.

Fred Graczyk

"It is nice to have a good thing going. But it's even nicer to know that I can still operate a fine restaurant and have a happy home life." That is the philosophy of Fred Graczyk, owner and operator of the Vineyards in Southfield, Mich. "Without that balance, Vineyards wouldn't mean a thing to me, because although I'm devoted to my restaurant, I'm not wed to the business."

Graczyk, the former busboy in a large Detroit hotel who liked food-service so well that he decided to make it his life work, does not believe in being a part-time restaurateur. "You can't give your all to two places; something's got to give. I'd rather do a good job with one."

Perched in the middle of a 20-acre vineyard and located in a French Normandy building with touches of Old English style, the Vineyards has a main dining room, two small intimate and secluded rooms, and a piano/entertainment bar. Recently added, but located separately from the restaurant, is a cabaret-style cocktail lounge called the Annex.

The Vineyards, which serves as a culinary mecca for Detroit area residents and visitors alike, draws local crowds and is also nationally known for the excellence of its cuisine.

The restaurant's favorite menu item, and the one for which it gets the most recipe requests, is its sweet and sour pork roast, which is roasted for three hours. However, other popular specialties of the house include boneless chicken a la chantilly, pike dumplings, roast duckling, shepherd's pie and roulades of veal in white wine.

Fred Graczyk bought the Vineyards in 1965. He has since turned it into a nearly $1-million-a-year operation and, what has been described as "one of Detroit's most beautiful eating places." Says Graczyk, "It took us six years before we had the place the way we wanted it, but it was a labor of love."

Speaking of the remodeling and restoration, IVY Award winner Graczyk praises his brother's tireless efforts. "My brother Lou is a mechanical and electrical genius," he says. "Without him, I'd still be at it."

He also praises his wife Diane. "She's a dietitian, so she helps plan menus and test recipes. Originally, she handled the payroll, too, but that's in the past. Now she tells everyone I replaced her with a computer."

The Southfield restaurateur also speaks highly of his staff. "My people knock themselves out for me. They know what to do and what's expected of them. And I stay out of their way."

Graczyk, who fully trusts his staff, feels sorry for restaurant owners who do not. "My attitude about it is: don't hire incompetents and don't hire people who will steal you blind."

In selecting employees, Graczyk does not emphasize experience. He looks for people who are willing to work and who can get along with others. "If the staff doesn't get along, that affects the service, the morale, and the general ambience. Eventually," he reasons, "it touches the guests; when that happens, everything will start going downhill."

He also relies on the competency of his trustworthy employees to free him for speaking engagements, to take part in various events, to give demonstrations, and to do ice carvings. Being able to do these, he feels, is important because, "It impresses people, and I think it helps to

THE VINEYARDS, SOUTHFIELD, MICH.

Fred Graczyk, owner/operator

Diane Graczyk, dietitian, who does recipe testing and menu planning at the Vineyards.

merchandise the restaurant—because word of mouth is still the biggest drawing card.''

The Vineyards is also highly regarded by those who know how to judge restaurant quality, and experts. Molly Abraham, news entertainment writer for *The Detroit News*, rated it among the Detroit metropolitan area's ''Ten Top Restaurants.'' And Jeanne and Richard Findlater in their guide to Detroit dining, *Eats*, selected it as one of their two favorite restaurants. They said, ''It's survived the test on several counts: the food choices offered and a combination of equal parts of quality food (excellently prepared in a clean kitchen) and enthusiastic service.''

To what does Graczyk attribute his success? He believes it is due to his personal philosophy of having fun in one's work (which he feels he and his employees do), of owning just one restaurant at a time, and of putting trust in the staff to help run the operation.

But the regional monthly publication *Southfield Magazine* explains the success from the customer's point of view. ''With the lovely atmosphere, superb food and great service, there's another bonus—prices are absolutely moderate. The Vineyards—that is what fine dining is all about.''

The exciting prospect of an excellent dining experience is conveyed to Vineyard patrons as they approach the table through both the surroundings and the care taken in table arrangement.

Louise Hatch

Massachusetts General Hospital, the oldest hospital in New England, is the third oldest voluntary, nonprofit hospital in the U. S.

Three primary functions which have remained constant at the hospital since its doors opened in 1821 are: caring for the sick; teaching, and research.

Louise Hatch, R.D., director of dietary services and IVY Award winner, explains the prevailing philosophy. One element she considers basic is the evident spirit of cooperation pervading the hospital. "The hospital has grown fantastically," she said, "but we have managed to continue some of the things that were special about it when it was smaller. For instance, we cook from scratch both kitchen and bakery products."

Since Miss Hatch has been with MGH for 30 years, she has played an important part in implementing this approach. As she details the policy in concrete terms, "We enjoy good intra- and inter-departmental cooperation, and committees work smoothly in accomplishing their goals."

The dietary department is an extremely active and busy unit. The foodservice operation is generally considered outstanding. Census counts last year totalled 2,475,021: 1,060,086 patients and 1,414,935 patrons. Procurement experts purchase $1,500,000 worth of food annually.

In spite of the hectic pace required, the department remains progressive. Recently, it increased the usage and number of special diet items. This innovation was in direct response to requests for yogurt, bran muffins, low-calorie salad dressings, and other items that today's patients expect to find available.

The dietary department at Massachusetts General Hospital feels privileged to participate in a 12-month American Dietetic Association-approved internship that offers opportunities and experience which prepare a student to qualify either as a professional in management or as a member of the health care team.

MASSACHUSETTS GENERAL HOSPITAL, BOSTON

In guiding her department, Miss Hatch is assisted by a staff of 36 graduate dietitians and 300 personnel in other foodservice positions.

Although a smooth-running operation, the dietary department is not exempt from problems and difficulties. Cost and size factors, according to Louise Hatch, are the areas that require constant observation if controls are to be effective. These difficulties are more than offset by the satisfaction of serving the patients and their caretakers.

In many ways, Miss Hatch's comment is typical of the attitude of the hospital, which offers fine service and a unique atmosphere. A basic philosophy of keeping the special things associated with smallness, with the use of participative management to encourage personnel cooperation, and with a record for high morale and low turnover, the Massachusetts General Hospital has built an environment conducive to the well-being of patients and personnel.

Personnel at MGH are made to feel an important part of the hospital team because they are kept informed about the various phases of the operation.

Samuel L. Huff

"If there is a secret to success in foodservice endeavors, it must include WORK: Willingness, Organization, Responsibility and Knowledge." This is the belief of Samuel L. Huff, foodservice director at Washington State University in Pullman, Wash. An observer of his operating methods would be inclined to add, "All this and a creative approach to students and staff, too."

Despite suffering from the effects of declining residence hall occupancy from 1972 through 1973-74, Huff was able to reorganize his foodservice operation to avoid an overall deficit. The 1972 IVY Award winner notes that he and his department have continued to communicate and work with student customers, refining menus and providing variety as much as possible.

To better serve students, Huff works with them to find out what they want. One way he does this is via food committees, which serve both dining hall members and management in an advisory, nondecision-making capacity. These members are either appointed or elected by a representative group (dorm, section, or floor) and serve as an important communications link.

Based on input from the various food committees, as well as his own and his staff's ideas, Huff also adjusts menus to meet changing student preferences, makes special diet items available, provides for guest meals, and, in general, tries to offer as much variety as possible.

Among his student customers, steak with french fries is the most popular item. However, because of student requests, even when steak is served, Huff offers another entree, usually a fish item, such as fried shrimp or fish fillet. Casserole dishes are quite popular at WSU, also.

To perform effectively and efficiently is not an easy task because of the operation's scope. To illustrate, Huff and his department operate six dining rooms—Rotunda, Rogers-Orton, Stephenson, Regents, Streit-Perham and Davis-Wilmer—having a total seating capacity of 4,040 with a 6,200-plus feeding capacity. The department serves about 2,500,000 meals per year. A cost differential (up or down) of only one cent per meal served adds up to $25,000.

The department also runs a vending services operation, administered from a central foodservice building that provides purchasing, warehousing, delivery, and clerical assistance to the operating units.

Flexibility and concern for students is apparent in Huff's approach to providing sack lunches for home games in Pullman Stadium. Huff and his staff always keep one of the dining halls open for late dinners when football games are played in Spokane. While Huff wants students to get a good dinner, his basic concern is their safety. "Since students know that dinner will be available on their return, we hope they will be less inclined to rush back and will drive at safer speeds."

Huff runs an efficient and successful operation, in no small part the result of his concern for staff as well as students. He puts a high priority on achieving recognition and compensation for staff a difficult task in a state institution where working hours and salaries are largely established by others. He has found that compliments on work well done and promotions from within do help. To facilitate the latter, he keeps employees informed of ways in which they can improve and encourages them in all efforts that will make them eligible for advancement.

Obviously, Huff has a difficult job at WSU, but he enjoys it and finds

WASHINGTON STATE UNIVERSITY, PULLMAN, WASH.

Sam Huff, Food Service Manager, with typical menu where yogurt and salad offerings reflect ready response to student wishes.

it challenging. "The most challenging aspect of my job is providing an environment where management personnel can and will do their best to satisfy student customers, while observing good business practices. But our staff *does* accept our students as customers who are paying board without which we would not exist as a foodservice operation at Washington State University."

WSU's foodservice director's genuine liking for young people is the reason that he entered the field of campus feeding. "I feel that college students usually are a pleasure to work with if approached openly and honestly in matters relevant to their foodservice. We communicate and attempt to be agreeable or, at least, disagree agreeably."

No doubt this is why WSU students have accepted the increases in meal costs that have been necessary. They have been kept aware of the rise in food and operating costs, and they react cooperatively.

"I hope that any credit given to Washington State University Food Service will be to dining hall managers. They are the ones who deal most closely with our student customers and they are the ones that make the system work."

—Sam Huff, Food Service Manager

Frank Kessler

In 1968, Frank Kessler took over the helm as the man at Arizona State University who represented Saga Administrative Corporation, longtime managers of foodservice at ASU. In 1975, he became orientation director for Saga at the same university.

Why did Kessler, an ex-Marine, a former football player, and a psychology major choose a career in institutional foodservice, turning in a performance that five years later, in 1973, won him an IVY Award? In 1973, he described his career choice and performance as follows:

"I guess you'd say it was an offshoot of my part-time job with Saga," he said. "They operated the foodservice at Idaho State when I was a student there. I started as a dishwasher, working my way up to waiter status, and, by my senior year, was managing the dining unit.

"Working at ASU, or at any university for that matter, keeps you on your toes. Did you ever try to stay one jump ahead of 40,000 kids?" Explaining some of his difficulties, Kessler stressed, "We want students to eat on campus. But quick-food places in this area doubled in the three years (1970-73), and they attract young people like magnets.

"It's our job to tap the pulse of the campus and initiate changes."

ARIZONA STATE UNIVERSITY, TEMPE

Frank Kessler
Orientation Director
Saga Administrative Corp.
at Arizona State University

To illustrate these changes, Kessler said, "We've enlarged concessions; expanded boarding operations; established a sandwich counter out front; put in a bake-and-take area, and reduced the 21-meal plan to 15. This is what students want, and we have to make them happy. Giving kids what they want is important."

Kessler explained that some people feel that the university caters too much to the whims of students and that you must draw the line somewhere. Commenting on this criticism, he said, "Well, that depends on the administration. Sooner or later, there has to be a stopping point. When? I don't know. I'm convinced, though, that it will be the kids themselves who draw the line. They get caught up in so many things, and they can't follow through on half of them because they don't have the time. They're here to study.

"That isn't to say they shouldn't question us when something upsets them. They *should!* We'll listen. The big thing is *how* you question. In our business, we face people who are out to toy with the world—with the intention of fouling it up. Ten percenters we call them—there are a few kids like this, but only a few. The point is *ask.* Don't *demand.*"

Speaking about his operation, Kessler pointed out in 1973, "We try to emphasize quality, service, and price. Because we're a contract catering firm, we must provide continuous management and assume cost risks. We're out to make ASU the best foodservice operation in the country. We don't stress inter-unit competition. Here, everyone pulls for everyone else. If there's a problem in one cafeteria, the manager sends out an SOS, and the others jump in to help out."

Reporting on his continuing efforts in interesting workers in foodservice, Kessler noted, "I'm always looking for recruits for our field. Saga is large enough so that it can train within its own divisions. We've got our own training area at ASU. Youngsters working with us find noncommercial foodservice a challenge, feeding the same people day after day. Much the same as I did when I was a student. The people in the business are fun folk and *that's* a prime drawing card."

Looking to the future, the ASU foodservice manager said, "We'd like to do other things—put in a deli, a grocery store, a candy shop, and possibly a smoke shop. If the administration agrees to go along with the program," Kessler added, "we'll do it. The important thing is thinking ahead. The kids know what we've done and are trying to do. And they honestly appreciate it. That's what makes us tick—knowing *they* have noticed our changes and that they don't take our efforts for granted."

Paul Kovi, Tom Margittai

"A study in elegance" is the phrase often used to describe the Four Seasons, which is owned and operated by IVY Award winners Paul Kovi and his partner, Tom Margittai.

Since 1966, Kovi has served as director of the establishment. However, in March of 1974, he and Margittai acquired the restaurant, a New York landmark, from Restaurant Associates. Few dining rooms can boast the excellence of architecture and design of the Four Seasons.

Central to the structure's architecture and design is the restaurant's unique theme, in which everything revolves around the seasons of the year. As Kovi points out, "The most important thing in maintaining allegiance to the seasons is the food: the beauty of the food; the purity of the approach to the food of that particular season, and the fact that our menu completely changes with each season."

Referring to the seasonal menu changes, Kovi remarked, "This is a great challenge and a very poetic expression. It is also true that because of these changes, the Four Seasons will always remain a 'new' restaurant."

Continuing, the co-owners of the Four Seasons noted that the restau-

THE FOUR SEASONS, NEW YORK CITY

Food and decor that changes to suit the seasons makes dining at New York's Four Seasons Restaurant an exceptional experience. Paul Kovi and Tom Margittai, co-owners who concentrate on creating this special climate are agreed that when "things are going right, it's a fantastic feeling."

rant has no special allegiance to any type of ethnic cooking. "We take the best we can from all cooking and present it to our patrons. It may depend on a new food or a new style, but the expression of each season is always new."

Mr. Margittai feels that this formula is successful. The 300-seat restaurant, which is divided into two rooms, does a thriving business that in 1974 was in excess of $2.5 million a year. Three private dining rooms, which seat up to 150 persons, also bring in a big business.

The annual revenue of the Four Seasons is additionally aided by subsidiary operations. Mr. Margittai listed their wine symposium, which has more than 2,000 graduates, and a cooking school, whose graduates number over 6,000 persons—plus the *Four Seasons Cookbook*, published in 1970.

But the real pride of the Four Seasons, they agree, is its kitchen.

"Each station," they say, "is a battle station. It's a classic kitchen and one of the best we've ever seen. We have units which steam vegetables in 10 seconds, an electric souffle machine, and even a cotton candy machine (used for making decorations)."

Obviously, Paul Kovi and Tom Margittai are multi-faceted men, men for all seasons. For, in addition to numerous career activities, they also enjoy a wide range of cultural interests. They are devotees of opera, the theater, and the city of New York.

But in spite of all these extra activities and interests, there is no mistaking the fact that their first love is their restaurant.

They like the independence of owning their own place, but also recognize the problems and responsibilities that this situation entails. "Now, there is more concern and more work to do. And you tear your hearts out if there is anything not up to your personal standards."

Searching for words to sum up their feelings, Kovi and Margittai agreed: "The great pleasure is when things are going right; it's an absolutely fantastic feeling."

Ropes of twisted baked bread dough form a dramatic frame for fall centerpieces at a Four Seasons' table.

Bob* and Peter Kriendler, Jerry Berns, Sheldon Tannen

Dining at New York's 21 Club may represent the pinnacle for many upward-mobile Americans for whom it is the sign of "arriving." Its reputation, however, has been built by a clientele made up of a tightly knit group of knowledgeable New Yorkers, whose allegiance often covers three generations.

"21" has a strong and ongoing tradition of fine dining, one that goes back many years, including a time—during Prohibition—when a speakeasy was located behind a door that was bricked up to look like a wall. The IVY Award won in 1972 by its four principals—Bob Kriendler, since deceased, Pete Kriendler, Jerry Berns, and Sheldon Tannen—was well-deserved recognition for that accomplishment.

In this age of transience and impermanence, adherence to tradition is extremely rare. But for The 21 Club, it is a valued and sought-after element, and one which is accorded the utmost care and attention.

The three principal owners of "21," Pete Kriendler, Jerry Berns, and Sheldon Tannen, would undoubtedly agree with Jerry Berns' observation: "We're like the bird who's not supposed to fly but does. Nobody ever told us that the day of fine dining and club atmosphere is dead. So, we just go on about our business."

A club-like atmosphere and special courtesies add to the diner's enjoyment of the food. Elegant presentation, calculated to please even the most jaded eye, is the hallmark of The 21 Club's cuisine. While the presentation emphasizes elegance, simplicity is stressed in preparation. "No obfuscated dishes at The 21 Club," states Jerry Berns. Simplicity is the keynote as far as meal preparation is concerned.

Luncheon favorites at this famed New York establishment include fish and emince dishes, particularly chicken. The emince entrees, which are on a two-week cycle, vary slightly, but vegetable purees, rice, and potatoes rotate daily. The "21" Burger, served with Sauce Maison, is another luncheon favorite. Named by popular demand, it is the frequent choice of great and near-great alike.

Dinner favorites are game bird and meat entrees. Veau Charleroi is a typical specialty of the house. The veal, prepared to retain its delicate flavor, is served with asparagus tips and a puree of carrots on an artichoke bottom, a simple yet well-balanced combination.

Such simplicity has its own elegance, an important part of the charm of "21," a 550-seat facility, which includes a bar, a main dining room, and four private dining rooms.

The tradition at "21" and the fact that the restaurant maintains a close relationship with its customers accounts for the continuing allegiance of its patrons. Parents and grandparents still set aside bottles of wine for an heir's 21st birthday. Among them is cartoonist Charles Schulz, who has some Jack Daniel's put away in The 21 Club's prestigious and world-renowned wine cellar for his grandson's 21st birthday.

Keeping a tradition alive is no easy task; at "21" it is the result of continuous building of personal relations with each new generation. The "21" management exerts every effort to make certain that this is done. Helping to maintain and develop relationships is Sheldon Tannen, the youngest of the three partners, who takes special care to act as a liaison between young and old.

*Deceased

Known as Jack and Charlie's 21 in its early days, it was the place frequented by celebrities— whether writers and artists, members of the acting profession, or leaders in the world of sports. They entered through a wrought iron gate that later became the logo of The 21 Club.

*A legend among Manhattan
wine lovers, the "21"
wine cellar holds a 5-year supply
of red wines in storage.
Preference in reds is for Bordeaux;
in whites, it is Burgundies.
Jerry Berns has found that making
Pinot Chardonnay and Rhone
available by the glass has
encouraged many patrons to
substitute it for whiskey
and cocktails.*

Partner Jerry Berns is also an experienced practitioner of the fine art of personal attention at "21," which is one of only six restaurants to have received *Holiday* Magazine's Distinctive Dining Award each year—without interruption—since the program was first instituted in 1952. Berns keeps track of patrons, as well as their careers, their friends, and their likes and dislikes. His own warm greeting is a prime part of the "21" experience for old and young alike.

According to Berns, another reason for The 21 Club's continuing success is the fact that at least one of the three principal owners is always on hand to assure the continuance of the unique personal approach to patrons. Members of the staff are continually aware of the example of management.

Berns also believes that the desire of Kriendler, Tannen, and himself, as well as manager Tony Berns and co-hosts Bruce Snyder and Terry Dinan, to assure consistency in management policies is a vital ingredient in their success.

Summing up the restaurant's focus on meeting the needs of its patrons, Berns said, "My prime concern is not price or cost. It's what I'm giving the guest and how well I'm serving his/her needs."

Although maintaining tradition is important, The 21 Club must also progress, and that is assured with "new ideas in our kitchen that come from attention to trade magazines and newspapers, together with guest suggestions. We also attempt," Berns added, "to keep up with today's informality, and yet maintain standards of dress, decorum, and quality."

Jean Lapuyade

Mastery over "The little things that make the difference between a fine restaurant and one that's merely a place to eat" have resulted in 2-time turnover and an $18 to $20 check average for 1973 IVY Award winner Jean Lapuyade's La Bourgogne in San Francisco.

"La Bourgogne may easily be one of the finest restaurants in the country," volunteered a knowledgeable customer. "I like the way it's run, and if it were up to me, I'd give it six stars; no less!"

At that time, owner/operator Lapuyade had had La Bourgogne 14 years. "I've also opened and operated other restaurants, usually with partners. They were successful," he explained, "but nothing like this one. I bought out my partners in La Bourgogne in 1961 because I wanted to operate this one alone.

"I've run into the usual combination of problems, though. We get bigger as we go along and I prefer to think that we also move ahead by striving to obtain the best of the produce and offer the finest of service."

While superb French cuisine, excellent service and growth have contributed to the restaurant's success, Lapuyade believes much of the credit should also go to his 38 employees, "I've had very little turnover. This year (1973) some staff members have been with me for 16 years and others for 11 years, none less than 4 years. Those who leave go off to try a place on their own."

If a good staff contributes to the success of a restaurant, how does Lapuyade select potential employees and how does he assure competency?

Commenting on his employment practices, Lapuyade explained, "I'll only hire experienced people. They *must* be qualified to do 'their thing'."

Lapuyade then went on to explain his background and exactly how he became involved in the restaurant business. "I have always been around places where food has been prepared since my family owned a small bistro in a farming community in southwestern France. Then from 1943-45 I was in charge of an officers' mess hall for a Free French Air Force Squadron, stationed near London. It was at this time I decided to go into the business.

"In 1947, I came to the United States and worked as a waiter until 1958 when I opened my first restaurant in San Francisco. In 1961, I opened La Bourgogne and have remained there ever since.

"During this past 14 years, I have observed the existence of many opportunities for the establishment of fine dining places. The clientele who enjoy it is there, the only problem is that to hire qualified help is becoming more difficult, and for this reason I wonder how long we can survive."

Although Lapuyade is very successful, it has not been easy and he deliberately seeks diversion to renew his enthusiasm; he skis, hikes, fishes, and hunts, enjoying the exhilaration of the clean mountain air. He also owns land in France which he wants to put into production, and he is planning to open a gourmet shop in San Francisco.

"My dream," he said, "is that the demands will lessen so that I can spend half my time in France harvesting my own land and the other half running the gourmet shop. Right now, this is only a dream."

While Jean Lapuyade has a dream for the future, he does not overlook the present; he appreciates his success, and understands how it was achieved. "I've been exceptionally lucky in this business. But hard work has been a must."

Stunning objets d'art and collector's china on display, crystal chandeliers and fresh flowers establish La Bourgogne as a "Restaurant Francais." The surroundings were created as a subtle setting where the haute cuisine would always hold the center of the stage.

Ella Brennan Martin

Creating dining excitement has always been the genius of the first generation Brennan family of restaurateurs—Ella, Adelaide, Dick, and John. Mrs. Ella Brennan Martin was one of the original IVY Award winners in 1971 while with Brennan's of New Orleans. These first-generation Brennans have since sold their interest in that restaurant and now operate the famous Commander's Palace in New Orleans, as well as Brennan's restaurants in Atlanta, Houston, and Dallas; the Chez Francais restaurant in Metairie, La., and the Friendship House restaurant on the Mississippi Gulf Coast.

The Brennans assumed ownership of the 200-seat Commander's Palace in 1974. The site had been selected because, as Mrs. Martin explained, "It was a very beautiful physical plant, and was exactly where we could put the kind of restaurant we wanted to operate."

Housed in an 1880 Victorian mansion that is a New Orleans landmark, Commander's Palace is in the city's Garden District. This lovely area, filled with large, beautiful homes (many antebellum) is the city's most prestigious residential area.

The restaurant itself is equal to its location. It contains an enchanting Garden Room, overlooking a beautiful patio, and bright and colorful main dining rooms. Patrons may dine indoors in casual elegance or outdoors in the flowery patio and around the fountain.

But lovely atmosphere is just one part of the Brennan formula for

THEN AT BRENNAN'S — NOW AT COMMANDER'S PALACE, NEW ORLEANS

Ella Brennan Martin at Commander's Palace in "the kind of restaurant we wanted to operate."

success: it also includes good wine/liquor, excellent cuisine, and a comfortable, unpretentious ambience.

In addition to good wine and liquor at affordable prices, Commander's Palace generates fun and excitement at dinner, luncheon, and brunch. A lovely and leisurely Garden District Brunch is served during the week and, on weekends, the restaurant "turns on" with Jazz Brunch—a Commander's original. At Jazz Brunch, old-time jazz "greats" play Dixieland music. The special menu, and balloons, add to the gaiety of guests who enjoy great music and food.

The evolution of the Jazz Brunch was logical for the area. It was compounded of the city's jazz heritage, the many fine old-time jazz musicians in New Orleans, and Ella Brennan Martin's previous use of jazz bands and entertainment.

Patrons at Commander's Palace certainly appreciate this event and have made it very successful. It was started on Sundays about a year ago and has since been expanded to include Saturdays. Now two bands play on each day, and there is muted, "jazzy" music all over the restaurant.

However, one of the best known features of the restaurant is its excellent cuisine, emphasizing Louisiana Creole cooking. As a result, the restaurant is widely acclaimed; *Women's Wear Daily* recently rated Commander's Palace as one of the top 60 restaurants in the world.

Among the most popular menu items in this New Orleans showplace is Crabmeat Imperial. It is a luscious combination of backfin lump crabmeat with pimientos and the restaurant's own special mixture of mayonnaise and delicate seasonings.

Reflecting the French touch is Veal Lafayette, done in the style of a veal dish originally served at Laserre in Paris. (It also happens to be the personal favorite of Ella Brennan Martin. "It brings back memories of that lovely restaurant," she says.) In essence, the Veal Lafayette is the finest white veal, sauteed with ham, mushrooms, and green onions, and then folded into a crepe and glazed with gruyere cheese.

While excellent food draws patrons to Commander's Palace, so does its warmth and friendliness. Explaining this feeling, which is all part of Mrs. Martin's philosophy of the "Innkeeper's Obligation," she notes, "People like to be treated on a familiar basis. When a customer walks in the door, we approach him/her as a guest in our home. Most people enjoy it when we talk to them, join them for a drink, get to know them and what they like."

This is precisely what the Brennans do. They insist on knowing their guests. And a stranger to Commander's Palace certainly will not be a stranger for long.

Explains Mrs. Martin, "When one of us is working (which is most of the time), we go over the reservation sheet. If none of us knows a person, we go over and introduce ourselves. By the time a customer walks out the door, we know that person and we'll remember him or her the next time he/she comes in."

Guests do return because they know the Brennans care—even about such things as the cost to customers. "We don't like to shock people with the check," says Mrs. Martin. "We like to see people pay the check and be willing to come back later in the week."

Such concern for the customer is typical of Commander's Palace and probably explains why it remains popular with its clientele. Perhaps its success is best summed up by Ella Brennan Martin, who says, "If you like people and you're not just out for a buck, the customers are going to come."

Marie Marinkovich

Marie Marinkovich, foodservice systems consultant in 1973 for the Northern California-Kaiser Foundation Hospital, upon becoming an IVY Award winner, provided an affirmative answer to the question: "Can a quiet, serious, soft-spoken, small-town girl (Ms. Marinkovich is from Skamakawa, located in Wahkiakum County in the state of Washington), be a success in the complex world of institutional foodservice?"

On the job, Ms. Marinkovich was an undisguised professional—a perfectionist with strong convictions in her own beliefs and with the ability to articulate them. In 1975, she became a consultant involved in the establishment of foodservice systems on an international basis. The ideas that worked so well at Kaiser are being adapted to meet the food needs in other parts of the world.

In 1973, however, in describing what had led to her choice of a foodservice career, Ms. Marinkovich said, "I guess I come from a foodservice background. Before they came here, my family owned an anchovy factory.

"My first job, which I got through a fluke, was working for the bar manager in a hotel. My first chore was a liquor inventory; there were 10,000 bottles in those cabinets—rows and rows of them!"

She laughed, "I didn't know *anything* about liquor. They don't teach you those things in Skamakawa; in fact, they make their own there." To compound this situation, Ms. Marinkovich indicated that her boss was no help because he did not drink.

To learn how much was in the bottles, Ms. Marinkovich explained, "I'd sneak some home at night and practice pouring shots till I was bleary-eyed; eventually, I got that down pat. I spent lunch hours memorizing brand names, but I still don't know scotch from bourbon. Initially, I thought Old Grand Dad was maple syrup!"

However, if that part of the inventory was bad, another part was even worse. "The worst was totaling up everything on the adding machine," said Ms. Marinkovich. "I'd close my eyes, pull the lever, and pray for all I was worth. Talk about your moments of truth; I don't know how I lasted!"

She then explained what she felt had helped her through that period and others that followed. "It takes a sense of humor," adding, "I think it's the key to enjoying hard work, particularly in a hospital. There's such a slim margin for error, and we're constantly exposed to outside scrutiny, which we have to learn to tolerate."

Ms. Marinkovich did not believe in the one-woman show; she spread credit around. "It's the dietitian who keeps things going in our hospitals," she noted. "If a location ticks, it's because of her, not because of me. Perhaps, I was instrumental in getting her in there, but the rest is, and has to be, up to her.

"It takes a long time to organize a system. But you can be certain it will work because the women running it are behind it. They pool all their ideas and tell me what they'd like to do. If they feel it can work, I say 'let's go do it' because they know what's going on.

"It's still a people thing, even in hospital feeding. You have to trust your people, and they must trust you. You can give some direction without really calling all the shots, because dietitians don't need someone checking on them all the time. They're not second-class citizens and shouldn't be regarded as such. Many people are surprised that a group

THEN AT KAISER FOUNDATION HOSPITALS, OAKLAND

of women can work compatibly together, but there's no secret. If we advance, we do it together.

"As for me? My responsibility, after a system has been evolved, is to be careful things are evened out, that each employee has what she needs to do a good job. Sometimes trying to get what you need is like trying to find water with a divining rod. It's an uphill struggle. There are other priorities besides foodservice within a hospital."

But for Ms. Marinkovich, who indicated she was a loner by nature, the hardest part of her job was the interruptions. To compensate she arrived at the office two hours early in order to make certain that the necessary pre-planning was completed for the production of the 10,000 to 12,000 meals for which she was responsible daily.

This picture taken in 1972 at a Kaiser Foundation hospital shows the snacks, all in pretty disposable packs, that helped make the five-meal day a reality. The interesting variety includes: left, 8 oz. ades, 4 oz. juices; instant bullion; cheese and crackers. Top center, milkshake with Kaiser Foundation Hospital name; chocolate pudding; gelatin; vanilla pudding. In the foreground is cottage cheese with pineapple in custom-labeled paper container; cold cereal in manufacturer's plastic bowl; cinnamon roll; 8 oz. milk in plastic bottle; fruit cup; tomato juice (only item which still came in a metal container and had to be poured). Top right, ice cream sundaes and sherbets; vanilla ice cream and cookies.

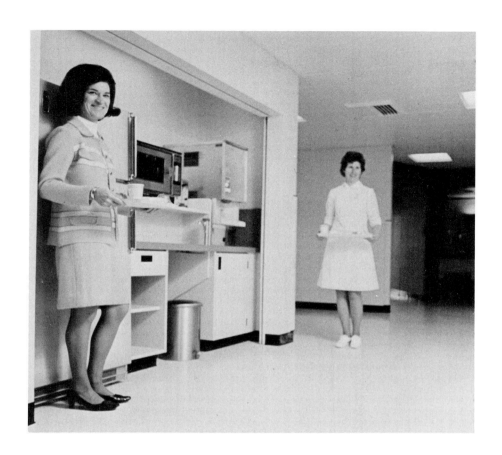

Marie Marinkovich was food-service systems consultant for Kaiser Foundation Hospitals-North when she became an IVY Award winner. Shown left above and at right below she poses in situations that demonstrate the preparation and service she has devised.

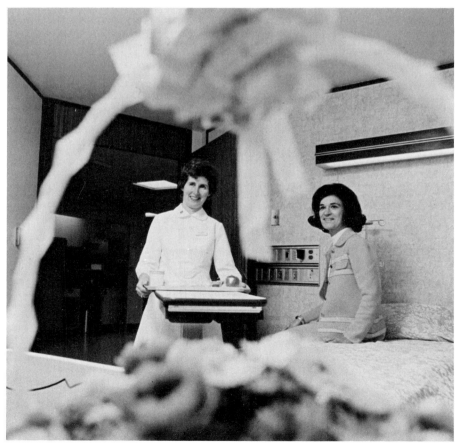

John Philson

**THEN AT KAISER
FOUNDATION
HOSPITALS,
LOS ANGELES**

While most of the working world was sipping its first cup of coffee, John Philson, then (in 1973) regional foodservice coordinator for the Southern California-Kaiser Foundation Hospital, was opening a can of cola. "I drink it straight with no cream or sugar," he quipped. "I'm a 'colaholic'. I drink it all day long. And I go through half a dozen at hockey games."

Philson then confessed that he's a "dyed-in-the-wool hockey nut." He said, "I gave up football for it, and my daughter, Mary, was weaned on it." He then told how he and his wife had taken their daughter to hockey games when she was still in the cradle.

Explaining more fully his interest in hockey and, another of his hobbies, coin collecting, IVY Award winner Philson stated, "The demands of our job here are hectic. You need an outlet. I've been in every conceivable facet of foodservice—except country clubs, railroads, and sea-going vessels—during the last 20-odd years. But I think I get more satisfaction in health care feeding than in any other area of foodservice."

"Hospital feeding is a very personal area unlike, for example, airline feeding. In our business, boredom can set in." To counteract that possibility, Philson indicated that Kaiser Foundation Hospital had followed the lead of the religious hospitals, which tend to be more employee-oriented. "We initiated more coffee breaks for our employees, as well as special events in the cafeterias.

"Employees were given hot meals and good value for their meal dollar. This also created better relationships, getting dietary employees out of the cellar. Additionally, other staff members began to see what was involved in foodservice and the extent of the foodservice staff's contribution."

Reflecting for a few moments, Philson went on to describe his own career beginnings. "My first big venture," he indicated, "was an ice cream drive-in in Omaha. That was 1948, and it looked like a big kick. We did all right, too, but we had a built-in location. We were right in the middle between two high schools."

Commenting further on the challenges of the health care field, Philson acknowledged, "We deal with what is, for lack of a better phrase, a 'captive audience'. Let's face it, patients aren't patients by choice." As a result of that fact, Philson said that the hospital staff tried doubly hard to make life more pleasant for the patients. "Because of that extra effort," said Philson, "we want to give our people a little more."

Explaining some of the ways that this had been accomplished, Philson noted, "A few years ago, West Los Angeles was the first Kaiser hospital to get a deep fryer and a grill. While it can be used for patient feeding, it's really for the employees. After all, they're here 250 days a year, while a patient's average stay is just five days. We want our cafeterias to impart aroma and eye-appeal. Our employees deserve that much!"

John Philson is a man who enjoys his work. "The past few years have been rewarding. Sure, there are setbacks, frustrations, disappointments. What job hasn't got them? Somehow, though, you cope."

Charles Masson*

**LA GRENOUILLE,
NEW YORK CITY**

*Charles Masson, restaurateur of distinction and IVY Award winner, died February 4, 1975 in New York City. The material that follows, based on an interview in 1973, sets forth the beliefs and approaches that contributed to Mr. Masson's stellar position among restaurateurs. Mrs. Masson is carrying on La Grenouille in the tradition described below with the help of her two sons and the staff that she and her husband had assembled.

Early morning in New York City's La Grenouille is faintly reminiscent of a scene from "An American in Paris." Amid cheerful "bon jours," and the bustle of a restaurant being readied for yet another day, the ear catches the pleasant cacophony of musical sounds. Everyone—from the man on his knees polishing the brass transom to the waiters setting up tables—is either humming, singing, or whistling.

Commenting on the prevailing mood among employees, owner/operator Charles Masson declares, "I guess it's because they enjoy their work."

Apparently, this is true, despite the fact that the employees are faced with a full schedule. As Masson explained, "Business has been good; we are getting a clientele that doesn't know where to go. Competition no longer exists since most good restaurants have closed. That doesn't please me because those restaurateurs were friends and colleagues."

When queried as to the reasons for the dwindling ranks of good restaurants, Masson replied, "Labor is the root of the problem. I'm also put out with columnists who pan restaurant operations. One critic lashed into mine not long ago, knocking everything and I mean everything—food, service, staff, wine, just everything."

Shaking his head in disbelief that such feelings could have been expressed, Masson said, "I'm proud of my kitchen (a compact, duplex arrangement). I have a spotless setup; why, you can eat off the floor. Working conditions are excellent, and our food is superb. The things said were not true. Yet I'd be out of business if it were not for my customers who rallied to us.

"However, I'm convinced that for every 'knocker', there's a 'doer'." On that note, he turned to the developments today that will have an important effect on fine dining in the future. "Our whole clientele is changing; diners are younger, more sophisticated, more adventurous."

Then Masson expressed concern about the potential for quality restaurants in the years ahead. "Young people," he indicated, "are not going to find superlative dining in years to come unless we start luring their generation into the business.

"Who is going to man the stores if young people are not made aware of the challenge and creativity and job opportunities in foodservice? All they ever see or hear is a small group of critics 'knocking' this or 'panning' that or always finding fault with something."

As evidence that creative and capable young people will enter the business if they have a chance to learn about the opportunities it offers, Masson mentioned one of his employees, a young man who had started out sweeping floors and had worked his way up to the position of hors d'oeuvre man. "He had no background, but he wanted to learn," said Masson. "Anyone who can think and *who wants to learn* can be taught. Today, that young man makes lovely trays of hors d'oeuvre, and he's a steady, meticulous worker who takes pride in his work."

Commenting on his restaurant, Masson noted that he and his wife had worked hard together to build La Grenouille into something they could be proud of, and that he considered it a monument to his wife. "It was her urgings, her efforts, her involvement. The table settings, decor, fresh flowers every day—I insist on that—it's all her doing." But he also praised his staff.

"They work as a team; performance is what matters. If you don't want to perform, don't get into this business. One mediocre musician can ruin an orchestra's performance. In a restaurant it's courtesy rather than music that counts. My staff represents itself as though the restaurant was theirs. As a Frenchman once wrote, 'The best aperitif is a smile'."

In summing up, Masson explained what he feels contributes to his success. "I believe in teaching my staff the 'niceties' of the business. Therein lies the future of foodservice. What I've learned, I've learned from others. My ambition is to teach others about running a restaurant, but time is an enemy.

"As it is, I live now with two meals a day, a roof over my head, and the love of one woman. It doesn't allow for much else at my age. But," added the 59-year-old restaurateur contentedly, "Truly, I don't want for much else!"

Karl W. Mehlmann

"The Brown Palace Hotel is located where the majestic Rocky Mountains cast their sunset shadows on 'The Queen City of the Plains', Denver, Colorado." This is the description in the brochure which commemorates the founding of this Mile-High City landmark 75 years ago.

Located in the downtown area and convenient to shopping areas, the business/financial district, theaters, entertainment, and points of local significance, The Brown Palace is known both for its Old World hospitality and its commitment to excellence. According to IVY Award winner Karl W. Mehlmann, president and general manager, this commitment is a well-established policy.

"If you're going to maintain an image, there are some things you must do. As an example, we have more than 600 employees for a 500-room house, which is way beyond the usual rule of thumb."

Recognizing the problems, especially those associated with cost, of maintaining such a standard, Mehlmann admits, "Our labor and operation costs are continually rising."

The Brown Palace executive wages a constant, strenuous battle with inflationary cost trends to maintain the hotel's reputation for unparalleled excellence. But, Mehlmann notes, "What we're trying to accomplish dictates what we can do to cut costs."

Sticking by old standards, even though compromise might be easier, is an integral part of The Brown Palace and typical of the standards set by all IVY Award winners.

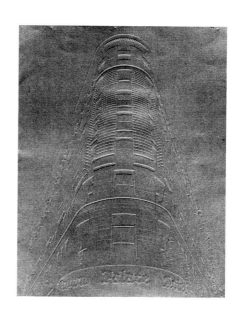

The Brown Palace is widely recognized for its superb cuisine. Contributing to this is the fact that the hotel maintains its own bake shop and still prepares most foods from scratch. Two of the most popular items on the dining room menus are prime rib and, the chef's specialty, Trout Saute Almondine. Guests may dine in any one of three fine restaurants—The Palace Arms, San Marco Room, and Ship Tavern.

The Palace Arms, decorated with authentic flag reproductions of the American Federal period, prior to 1830, and antique objects dating from 1670 to 1825, is designed for intimate luncheons and very special dinner parties. The award-winning food that has won an international reputation for the room is prepared in a highly efficient, separate kitchen. The wine cellar is stocked with the finest domestic and imported wines.

Decorated in Italian Renaissance style, the San Marco Room serves three meals daily and offers dancing/entertainment five nights a week. Adjoining it is The Gondola, a cocktail lounge, also decorated in an Italian Renaissance theme.

Karl Mehlmann
President and General Manager
The Brown Palace

For less formal, more relaxed dining there is the Ship Tavern. Filled with replicas of famous ships, it has solid chestnut woodwork, an authentically roped mast and crow's nest, and red leather chairs and booths.

To maintain the reputation of these restaurants, as well as that of The Brown Palace itself, would be a challenging job. However, it is a challenge relished by Karl Mehlmann, who has been at "this great institution" since 1940 (except for several years during World War II).

To guests, the hotel's standards of excellence are immediately obvious. Upon entering the hotel, they see The Brown Palace's most famous feature—its breathtaking and magnificent lobby, the Rotunda.

"People want to hold all sorts of functions in the lobby," Mehlmann said, noting that one group even wanted to hold a bull auction there.

Indeed, many functions are held in the Rotunda. One of these, an annual debutante ball, requires "stripping out the lobby and putting up a bandstand," said Mehlmann.

Describing his entry "into a most fascinating business which was to become my life's career," Mehlmann explained that he began in college. During summer vacations from the University of Denver, he worked in the Colorado vacation resorts of Estes Park.

"Various positions and responsibilities over the years with the hotel stimulated my interest in the food and restaurant business, which," says Mehlmann, "is a very important part of the overall daily business of a first-class property."

With dedication to excellence exemplified by its top management, the 500-unit Brown Palace is able to maintain its reputation for true hospitality, superb service, and fine cuisine. It is an establishment where gracious service and modern comforts and conveniences are combined with the elegance and beauty of yesterday.

Excellence in all aspects of fine dining has established a world-wide reputation for The Brown Palace. Table-side cookery adds its special drama during the dinner hour.

James A. Nassikas

Although the adjectives "elegant," "opulent," and "sumptuous" are often used to describe it, The Stanford Court Hotel makes an equally firm impression as a genuinely warm and inviting place. The achievement of this unique ambience in the luxurious hotel high atop Nob Hill in San Francisco grows out of the conviction of James A. Nassikas, president, that a hotel is "a sensitive, human institution, not a cold assemblage of bricks and concrete without heart or emotion. The Stanford Court is confronted with a remarkable opportunity to market tradition to a contemporary audience."

To achieve this, the hotel combines the luxury and convenience of the 20th century with the elegance and tradition of the 19th century. Active in hotel management and administration throughout his entire adult life, James A. Nassikas, a graduate of the University of New Hampshire, is the holder of service and cuisine certificates from the Ecole Hoteliere de la Societe Suisse des Hoteliers in Lausanne and has established a national and international reputation in the exacting field of foodservice.

In directing the operation of The Stanford Court, built at a cost of $18 million, IVY Award winner Nassikas has been able to innovate in his own way, avoid a mold, and set up a "total hotel" with a real residential

James A. Nassikas, president and managing director, checks ingredients for the day's specialties with Marcel Dragon, executive chef de cuisine at Fournou's Ovens, the restaurant at The Stanford Court.

feel. "The true birth of a total hotel," he explains, "takes place when it begins to assume its own personality and character."

Nassikas believes that if operating philosophies and principles are taken into consideration during the designing of the building, certain elements will be assured as part of the hotel's personality and character. These might include a design to motivate a high standard of achievement from staff members in caring for human needs, and/or a high standard of acceptance from guests.

One highly visible aspect of its personality is luxury. Guest accommodations in the 402-room, 34-suite hotel, built on the site of the famed Leland Stanford home, include a dressing room, French armoires, authentic etchings of old San Francisco, marble-topped tables, and canopied beds. Luxury is also apparent in the bathrooms, which have mini-screen TV's, towel warmers, and specially scented, hand-milled soap.

The hotel's individuality is apparent in the dining facilities Nassikas has created at Stanford Court. Cafe Potpourri is a blend of three intimate cafes in one. As he describes the Cafe, "It combines the most attractive elements of a Viennese coffee house and a Paris bistro."

The 150-seat Fournou's Ovens has a cocktail lounge with club-like sofas and armchairs, intimate dining areas on five levels, each fronted with a scrolled iron grille, and an extensive wine cellar. From its attractively decorated, open-hearth ovens come outstanding cuisine, as specialties from five continents make up its menu.

Diners at Fournou's may enjoy such San Francisco specialties as Cream of Artichoke Soup with Crushed Fresh Hazelnuts, Crab Claws in a Shallot Sauce (claws are removed from the shell, and there is a hint of tarragon in the sauce) as well as the oven specialties: roast lamb, beef, and duck. Chicken and veal dishes are other menu favorites.

The huge ovens are faced in provincial French tile. As guests await the service of Fournou specialties, they can study the 18th century French provincial armoires and chests, the antique metal wall brackets and light fixtures, and the exquisite paintings and wall panels, all of which help to establish the warm yet rich atmosphere created in this restaurant.

Physical surroundings are important, but employee attitude and performance are vital. Thus, Nassikas considers that it is (1) essential to know each of his 340 employees by name, and that it is (2) a wise investment of his time to chat with each at regular intervals. Thus he gains a real understanding of their problem-solving capabilities.

Proudly extolling the virtues of the executive housekeeper and building plant manager and their staffs, he says, "They're fanatics about the condition of the hotel." He is equally proud of service personnel who are also totally dedicated, a fact not unnoticed by guests. Nassikas notes, "I have piles of letters from guests who make no mention of the look of the hotel but dwell on the attitude of the people."

However, The Stanford Court's excellence has not escaped the experts. In 1974, the hotel received the Diplome de l'Excellence Europeenne, the coveted international prize of the Comite de l'Excellence Europeenne. And, this year, it was recognized as "one of the best hotels in the country," having received the Mobil Oil Corporation's *Travel Guide's* highest honor, the Five-Star award.

"My dream for more than 20 years," proclaims Nassikas, "was to exercise my own judgement and institute a great hotel with its own particular character." The many discriminating guests who recount its virtues and return regularly to enjoy its pleasures are ample testimony to the fulfillment of his dream.

Lobby area provides atmosphere of quiet luxury visible from cocktail area where leather upholstered sofas and chairs are grouped for conversation.

G. William Peffers

Because of his hotel background, G. William (Bill) Peffers, director of foodservice for Chicago's Michael Reese Hospital and Medical Center, has put the Center in the top echelon of hospital foodservice. A major contributing factor in its rise to such a prominent position is Peffers' menu, which is among the most selective of any hospital in the country operating on a cycle system.

"Hospital feeding and hotel feeding," says Peffers, "are totally parallel. The only difference is in dietetics and," he adds, "hospitals that aren't doing a good job are the ones that aren't applying those principles used commercially."

Peffers started out in the commercial segment of foodservice. A Michigan State graduate, he had, prior to joining Michael Reese, worked at the Palmer House in Chicago and, for five years, was associated with Harris, Kerr, Forster, and Company.

This was the experience that Peffers brought to Michael Reese in 1958. At that point the hospital's menus were mimeographed, containing just two choices on a 4-week cycle. Shortly after arriving, however, he started a 14-day cycle and greatly expanded the menu selection.

On the basis of this cycle, which took a year to complete, patients are able to choose from 12 entrees (three of which are rotating); five salads (two rotating), and 12 desserts (three rotating). On Saturday evenings, feature entrees might include a choice of broiled lobster tail, filet mignon, or roast Long Island Duckling with orange sauce.

A Wednesday evening meal might be Cantonese pepper steak, roast leg of veal and currant jelly, or sauteed chicken livers.

However, after five years spent developing and implementing the system at Michael Reese, Peffers decided to return to the hotel business. In 1964 he accepted the position of food/beverage manager for New York City's giant Americana hotel. However, after two years, he rejoined Michael Reese.

"I'm glad I went back to hospital foodservice," says Peffers. "I enjoy applying the principles of management and merchandising learned in commercial foodservice to hospital food operations."

He also mentions his people with considerable pride. "Once we work up the planning and the systems," he said, "I don't have to worry about patient feeding. We have an abundance of talented patient-service personnel and management staff."

As the result of this situation, Peffers is free to devote himself to doing and planning other things. One current project involves Michael Reese's three kitchens, which are soon to be centralized into one (20,000 sq. ft. in size) with some remodeled and some new nonpatient facilities. It will include a 200-seat table service restaurant which will meet fine dining standards.

By very definitive administrative policy Michael Reese Hospital and Medical Center gives full recognition to the importance of the food to its patients. In keeping with that policy, the staff works very hard to produce food that meets the highest standards of quality at all times.

A problem that Peffers faces, particularly in his efforts to maintain the quality and the type of menu items which he has instituted and for which Michael Reese Hospital and Medical Center has come to be known, is one all too familiar to today's foodservice operators.

"Our food costs have been affected by the inflationary trend of

MICHAEL REESE HOSPITAL AND MEDICAL CENTER, CHICAGO

This cartoon figure enlivens section of Michael Reese Hospital and Medical Center menus where choices are requested and directions given for making them.

food market prices." He also indicated that although prices leveled off in late 1974, they have soared and have shown drastic increases in 1975.

Consequently, this presents Peffers with what he defines as his most difficult recent problem—maintaining fiscal stability in light of inflationary trends. This applies not only to food market prices, but also to the prices paid for permanent serviceware and disposable items.

But the challenge of patient foodservice, particularly with patients constantly expressing approval, is well worth the effort. As Peffers concluded, "I am delighted to say that our patients, by and large, react favorably to our foodservice."

Menus at Michael Reese are 11 by 20 in. in size, divided into sections horizontally for the three meals. They are printed in large, easily read type, with plenty of space left to note choices. Special diet requirements are stamped in red across the menu for each meal.

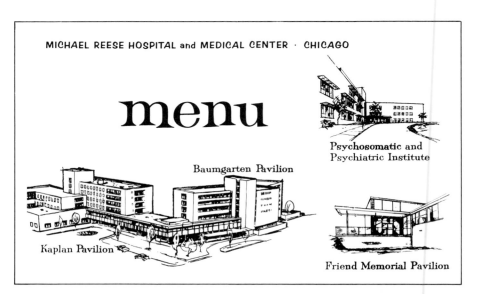

MICHAEL REESE HOSPITAL and MEDICAL CENTER · CHICAGO

menu

Psychosomatic and Psychiatric Institute

Baumgarten Pavilion

Kaplan Pavilion

Friend Memorial Pavilion

luncheon for WEDNESDAY noon

PATIENT_____

ROOM_____

calculated diet

soup	CREAM OF ASPARAGUS	BEEF CONSOMME

feature entree

    BROILED PETITE TENDERLOIN STEAK, MUSHROOM CAP

    FRESH FRUIT PLATE

standard

    COLD ROAST SIRLOIN OF BEEF   BROILED WHITEFISH

    GROUND BEEF PATTY   COTTAGE CHEESE, SOUR CREAM

    HOT SLICED TURKEY

    EGGS TO-ORDER: SCRAMBLED   SOFT COOKED

    HARD COOKED   PLAIN OMELET

potato   MASHED   BAKED IDAHO

vegetable   BRUSSEL SPROUTS   PEAS   SPINACH

salad   CHEF'S TOSSED

    CELERY AND CARROT STICKS

    SMALL DISH OF COTTAGE CHEESE

dressing   FRENCH   VINEGAR

    LOW CALORIE FRENCH

bread   WHITE   RYE   WHOLE WHEAT

    SALT STICK

dessert   W.P. APPLESAUCE

VANILLA ICE CREAM   ORANGE SHERBET

ANGEL FOOD CAKE   PLAIN JELLO   BAKED CUSTARD

VANILLA WAFERS   D-ZERTA

beverage   COFFEE   TEA   SANKA

    MILK   SKIMMED MILK

    BUTTERMILK

misc.   CREAM

    LEMON WEDGE   CRACKERS

SACCHARINE

Edwin and Robert Power, Mrs. Edwin I. Power, Sr., and Mary Helen Fairchild

"The Nut Tree is a celebration," applauds one customer. "It's a creative, festive environment with so much to interest everyone in the family that waiting an hour to eat is highly pleasurable."

Located midway between Sacramento and San Francisco, The Nut Tree is a family affair. Originally, it was the site of a family-owned fruit ranch, but in 1921, Helen Harbison Power and her husband, Edwin (Bunny) Power (since deceased), set up a fruit stand under a giant walnut tree.

"Within the first three weeks we had so many repeat customers that my husband decided we should set up a restaurant," Mrs. Power recalls. "We learned the restaurant business from our customers. They told us what they wanted and we served it."

In the fall of 1921, the first permanent restaurant building was constructed. It was then that Edwin (Bunny) Power's motto was first established as The Nut Tree standard: "Give service, quality, and courtesy."

By the mid-1930s, The Nut Tree had become an established western institution. Then, after WWII, the children of Edwin and Helen Power—sons Edwin, Jr. and Robert, and daughter Mary Helen Fairchild—all IVY Award winners, joined the operation.

Today, they all work closely with Dennis Gomes, the designated president of Nut Tree Associates, an affiliate which manages all the operational facilities of the complex, including The Coffee Tree restaurant operation located directly across Interstate 80.

Since those early days, The Nut Tree, which mixes shops, displays, and play areas, has grown. In 1952 The Nut Tree added a Toy Shop and The Nut Tree Railroad and in 1955 an airport was added. In addition to remodeling the dining room in 1958, the Nut Tree Plaza was added in 1960, The Coffee Tree in 1965, and, to celebrate its 50th anniversary in 1970-71, the new Bake Shop, customer/employee facilities, and a merchandise area for original products created at The Nut Tree.

In 1962, after many years of trying, The Nut Tree even got its own postal substation. This station is a stamp collector's dream where many past commemorative stamps are also available.

"Changes are constant, and there is a continuing effort to improve and refine the dining and gift shop areas," said Nut Tree Associates president Dennis Gomes. "To further ensure that only the finest of fresh ripe fruit is served," he added, "the partners recently acquired an apple and apricot orchard, with the fruit from each being served in both restaurants." He also pointed out that since 1972 the foodservice unit in the Plaza has been remodeled; it has new equipment, plants, colorful tablecloths, and a revised menu, and its name has been changed to The Sandwich Garden, which features delicious, unusual sandwich combinations.

During the growth and progress of the operation, the Power family has never forgotten that good food is of prime importance. Therefore, constant vigilance and painstaking experiments go into The Nut Tree's foodservice. Menus at The Nut Tree and The Coffee Tree are constantly

THE NUT TREE, NUT TREE, CALIF.

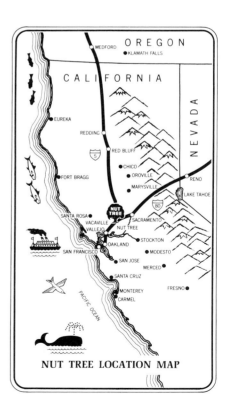

NUT TREE LOCATION MAP

being reviewed and evaluated, with items added or deleted as the season dictates. The goal at The Nut Tree is to make a masterpiece of every plate.

One of the most popular food items served is Tropical Fruit with Breast of Chicken (see cover picture) or Prawns—the customer's choice of hot breast of chicken, on wheat, or golden fried prawns—arranged on a plate with chilled fresh pineapple, papaya, avocado, banana, and tomato. Another menu favorite is the Fresh Fruit Plate—chilled fresh pineapple, papaya, melon, banana, coconut, orange, and other western fruits in season. Accompanying it are homemade nut breads and a choice of cottage cheese, sherbet, or ice cream.

"The success of our food presentation," Gomes believes, "has much to do with the fact that we use only top quality products in the preparation of our menu items." All entrees are prepared to order, as are the salads which, of course, contain fresh fruits and vegetables.

Gomes says "These factors, coupled with generous portions, exemplified by our fresh whole pineapple with marshmallow sauce, and service in delightfully relaxed surroundings contribute to the enjoyment of food presentations at The Nut Tree and to the reputation it has gained for extraordinary foodservice."

Robert Power poses with some specialties that were featured at The Nut Tree in 1972 when he, his brother Edwin, his mother Mrs. Edwin I. Power, Sr., and Mary Helen Fairchild became joint IVY Award winners.

William G. Quinn

It takes time to build tradition, but tradition has long been the main-stay of the St. Francis Hotel in San Francisco. "We've been on Union Square since 1904 and, needless to say, we've seen, and been part of, a lot of history," said William G. Quinn, then vice-president and general manager when he became an IVY Award winner in 1974. He has since become vice-president and general manager of the Bonaventure Hotel in Los Angeles.

The following is based on an interview in which Quinn related his approach and philosophy in regard to the St. Francis; it was recorded in 1974 while he was still active in the hotel's operation:

While Quinn is proud of the St. Francis' long-time reputation as a lively and romantic pace-setter, he is even more enthusiastic about the modernization efforts at the 1,200-room St. Francis, which were begun in early 1969. Western International Hotels, now the parent company, undertook the program, intent on surpassing past glories. Their efforts were successful.

Every detail of construction and decor was considered so that the new facilities would blend with the old, further enhancing the worldwide reputation of the Hotel St. Francis as a leader in San Francisco's tradition of gracious hospitality. Complete air conditioning was installed; every bathroom was modernized at a cost of $2,500 each.

Western International spent $28 million on the project. Among the additions was the 520-room, 32-story Tower, with bay windows in the guest rooms; a carriage entrance; a 6,000-sq. ft. lobby; a four-level parking area at the base of the Tower, and five exterior glass elevators offering guests a stunning view of the city.

Crowning the three-year-old Tower is a magnificent restaurant, Victor's, named for the hotel's famed chef Victor Hirtzler (1906-1925), which offers formal, highly-acclaimed continental dining from an a la carte menu.

Decorated in an ochre-caramel-gold color scheme, beautifully carpeted, and expertly staffed, Victor's is a 120-seat, dinner-only operation averaging 178.3 covers per night, with a food check average of $13.

The restaurant, Quinn indicated, was established because Western International felt it was essential to provide St. Francis' guests with a first-rate restaurant *in* the hotel. Despite the strong competition within the San Francisco area, the restaurant is thriving.

Victor's even pleased the hypercritical San Francisco restaurant critic, Jack Shelton. He says the restaurant produces the city's best continental cuisine. A favorite on the menu is the Silver Cart Service, which varies daily. An outstanding California wine list is also available.

Other specialties include Quenelles Victor, feathery balls of souffleed fish in lobster sauce; rich French onion soup crusted with cheese; pepper steak flambeed with cognac, and crab legs Voltaire, fresh crab in a wine sauce with chives and mushrooms, served over fluffy rice.

The restaurant is just one of the facilities in Bill Quinn's domain. Quinn, a veteran hotelier who has a strong food/beverage background and a graduate of Denver's hotel school, maintains a watchful eye on every aspect of the hotel's operation. It is a labor of love because he enjoys his work.

"I've never considered any other business; I've relied on it all my life," he says. "I was bellhopping at age 13, and throughout college I

The Silver Cart
Our Complete Dinner
Choice of Soup or Bay Shrimp Salad
~
The Specialty of the Evening on our Silver Cart
~
Selection of Sweets from the Pastry Wagon
Ice Cream or Sherbet
Beverage
15.00

always turned to the food and beverage business where I could be a waiter or a cook.''

It's easy to understand Quinn's devotion to the St. Francis. When it opened in 1904, the hotel immediately became the center of the city's social, literary, and artistic life. This was the beginning of the traditional position of the St. Francis—as the gathering place for the city's leaders, a tradition that is still much in evidence today.

Quinn considers this tradition to be a major attraction for employees as well as guests.

"Tradition is of prime importance for our employees," says Quinn. "The backbone of our staff has been here more than 40 years, with every department having a nucleus of people deeply steeped in the tradition of the St. Francis. Employees take pride in the tradition, and it doesn't take long for this feeling to wear off on new employees.

Table appointments at Victor's in the Hotel St. Francis provide the proper setting for the elegant cuisine to come.

Gerald Ramsey

Server of what is generally agreed to be "the best food in academe" is the not unexpected reputation of Gerald Ramsey, noted for his creative, artistic, and dedicated approach to student foodservice.

A 1972 IVY Award winner, Ramsey, director of foodservice, who has served Southern Methodist University in this capacity since 1950, is a highly regarded professional, a member/officer of numerous industry and trade organizations, and a winner of many awards.

Ramsey recognizes the real challenge of university foodservice: "The students are here from one to four years, and we must do as much as we can to eliminate boredom." Ramsey is always ready to listen to students. Both he and his staff feel that students are their prime concern and are always looking for ways to make things better and more pleasant for them. To encourage students to submit their ideas and comments, there is a suggestion box. In response to suggestions, he has instituted a make-your-own salad bar, which was warmly received, and also has developed special Chinese, Chicano, and Soul Food meals.

The SMU food director also likes to add extra special touches, things like monthly birthday parties, toasters and an assortment of breads at breakfast, and smooth and crunchy peanut butter with crackers, an especially popular gesture. Ramsey is convinced that such efforts not only make students "feel at home," but also remind them that the university cares about each of them as individuals.

"We're not like a restaurant where customers change all the time. Little things mean something to the students. These little things let them know that we know they're here, and that they are not just a number."

Ramsey's considerable talents and abilities can also be seen in SMU's catering operations. The catering activities have been so successful that many organizations in the area try to hold at least one function a year at SMU in order to enable their members to partake of what is generally acknowledged to be a very special food presentation.

Part of Ramsey's success is due to his imaginative approach to the planning of banquet menus. He also keeps careful track of what each group has been served previously so that they will have something different if they re-book. As a result, his customers can be sure of a fine food adventure and, generally, do come back for return engagements.

Ramsey's ability to continually please outside groups, as well as students, is based on a high degree of dedication and a vital creativity. However, these activities also contribute to the growth of SMU's foodservice operation. To illustrate, his department has an annual food budget of $2 million and serves more than 600,000 covers in two main dining rooms. This does not take into account the extra revenue generated from numerous banquets and educational workshops held on campus.

For Jerry Ramsey, a graduate of Texas Tech University with a B. S. in institutional management who has also done graduate work at the University of Chicago, foodservice is an art that involves more than preparing food.

In 1974, Dr. Wm. Heroy, SMU vice-president and treasurer, underscored this when he said, "Gerald Ramsey is a good manager with both his budget and his personnel. He's well organized—a good planner who always has an alternate plan in case a shipment doesn't arrive on time—

and he's very strict about cleanliness. His meals are balanced, and he works hard to make them appetizing."

SMU's foodservice operation is equally highly regarded by persons from off campus. Following a tour of SMU kitchens, one leading restaurant operator exclaimed that it was the finest operation she had ever seen. In addition, Ramsey is the only university foodservice director to have won the coveted Golden Plate award as Food Service Operator of the Year from the International Foodservice Manufacturers Association of America. He received this in 1967.

But despite these honors, Ramsey remains a modest, unassuming man with a delightful sense of humor. "Years ago," he quips, "all my customers were 18. Today they're still 18, and I'm the one who's grown old."

Gerald Ramsay displays one of his salad specials.

Karl Ratzsch

An exterior of colored windows and bright medieval crests sets the stage for patrons of Karl Ratzsch's restaurant in downtown Milwaukee—a favorite of residents and visitors for nearly half a century.

Inside the famous landmark, the guest is surrounded by authentic antiques, German and Bohemian relics, and other appropriate art objects. Included in the collection are such items as pewter platters, English copper mugs with elk horn handles, wooden carvings, and a set of green-shaded glassware that is more than 300 years old and once belonged to the Emperor Franz Josef of Austria. The glassware bears the Hapsburg court's coat of arms and the double eagle.

Ratzsch's also offers cuisine that combines New World Favorites (American dishes) and Old World Suggestions (German dishes). The restaurant's reputation for the preparation of dishes in either category is unexcelled. Among the "Old World" items are kassler rippchen, schnitzel a la Holstein, and the two most popular items, sauerbraten and wiener schnitzel.

To complement and enhance its fine food, Ratzsch's stresses attention to detail and fulfillment of patrons' psychological needs. This sounds like a tall order, and one wonders how Karl Ratzsch does it. "Simple," he states, "the guest is everything."

Explaining how this is achieved, Ratzsch advises that employee training at the restaurant is geared totally to the customer. "We concentrate on the attitude of service personnel, not on past restaurant experience or the technical aspects of the job. And the first line is our service personnel. A waitress can, at any time, reject an order if it doesn't look right, or if something seems wrong."

In his operation, Ratzsch focuses on and attempts to please the once-a-year customer, the customer who has saved up and goes out to a restaurant for that special occasion dinner.

Ratzsch reasons that the individual who is a frequent guest will understand if one meal is not up to the restaurant's usual high standards. "But," he says, "the once-a-year customer doesn't. You can ruin his entire year!"

To avoid such experiences, Ratzsch goes to considerable length to make sure that customers receive careful and personal attention, and he never ceases to be gratified on learning that patrons have had a pleasurable dinner and outing.

"I stand out on the front steps of the restaurant," he says, "because I love to hear people talking as they leave—about the enjoyment of the meal."

The restaurant business for IVY Award winner Karl Ratzsch has been an integral part of his life; he grew up with it. His father, the famed Karl "Papa" Ratzsch, Sr., immigrated to the U. S. from Hertzberg, Germany, a town about 60 miles south of Berlin.

Following his arrival in the U. S., Ratzsch senior worked briefly as a busboy, then as a waiter for seven years, ultimately marrying the owner's daughter. In 1929, he opened the present restaurant, having been forced by a building development a year earlier to close the restaurant he and his father-in-law, Otto Hermmann, operated since 1904.

After founding the restaurant, his parents worked hard to build its reputation. Then in 1962, Karl junior bought it from his parents. Now

This colorful figure appears on the cover of the menu used in Karl Ratzsch's, Milwaukee's famous Old World restaurant.

in his late forties, he has turned managerial responsitilities over to *his* only son, Karl III, but he is at the restaurant every night as always.

Remembering the early days when there were very few restaurants in Milwaukee, Ratzsch recalls that, "Everything was terribly competitive and everyone secretive about his business." However, Ratzsch reversed the trend to secrecy, willingly helping other restaurateurs, as well as chefs in other operations "because good meals encourage guests to continue going out.

"Enough bad experiences," Ratzsch believes, "turn people off to the point where they either stop going out to dine entirely or stop trying places they haven't been to before."

Ratzsch's has an enviable reputation, having received a four-star ("outstanding—or worth special effort to reach") rating from the Mobil Oil Corporation's *Travel Guide.* In addition, *Holiday* Magazine has rated it among the top restaurants in the country by honoring Ratzsch's with an award each year since the program was first instituted nearly 25 years ago.

Karl Ratzsch, an industry leader who is the former president of the Wisconsin Restaurant Association and a current member of the National Restaurant Association's board of directors, is proud of his restaurant's heritage. He is especially proud that its traditional excellence is being undergirded by modern business methods and "attitudinal" training.

Karl Ratzsch with a display of some of the Old World cuisine for which his Milwaukee establishment is noted.

Don Roth

Don Roth of the Blackhawk Restaurant in Chicago is a master of merchandising. A reflection of his ability, as well as his promotional know-how, is the fact that the Blackhawk has continued to be successful; it is one of the few surviving long-time restaurants in the city's downtown area.

IVY Award winner Roth may not have invented all the merchandising ideas in the book, but he certainly knows them, and knows how to use them well. To be sure, dreaming up promotional ideas comes naturally and rather easily for Roth. His original goals included a career in the field of advertising. Obviously, of course, he chose a different path and began working in the Blackhawk, the restaurant his father had founded in 1920.

From 1920 to 1952 the Blackhawk featured some of the countrys' most famous orchestras which broadcast each night over the 50,000 watt radio station WGN. Featured bands included the Coon-Sanders Nighthawks, Hal Kemp, Kay Kyser, Bob Crosby, Les Brown, and even Chico Marx with Mel Torme.

With the big band era petering out in the early 50s, live entertainment was terminated, and Roth turned to the service of top quality food, but using his knowledge of showmanship in its presentation to the public. A large roast beef cart and the now famous Spinning Salad Bowl replaced musical entertainment at the Blackhawk, and to this day these merchandising techniques are still being successfully employed. In addition to prime rib, steaks and a very special salad, customers in the three Blackhawk restaurants consume about 1,000 pounds of fresh scrod each week.

A Don Roth Restaurant was opened in the suburb of Wheeling in 1969, followed by another Blackhawk on the near north side of Chicago, three years ago. This newest Blackhawk on Pearson, just off Michigan Avenue's miracle mile, is an exciting contribution to this extremely busy shopping and dining area. Featuring a sumptuous salad bar and an expanded Blackhawk menu, this restaurant has waiting lines, at both lunch and dinner, almost every day.

Of course, the flagship of the small chain of three restaurants is still the original downtown Blackhawk. Some of the unusual merchandising ideas employed over the years include a Blackhawk Restaurant dinner flight on American Airlines; a French food festival featuring Raymond Oliver of the three star Grand Vefour Restaurant in Paris, with six of his chefs; package dinner-theatre programs with downtown shows; and today they operate a "Show Shuttle" which takes customers to opera, concerts, and sporting events. All-evening parking is available a few steps away for $1.00. In addition, the restaurant develops a "new look" every six weeks with a change of art exhibits, displayed by many cooperating galleries in Chicago.

As a consequence of careful and effective management, for example, the restaurant's menu prices have escaped the outsized increases experienced by most businesses as a result of inflation. While the menu prices have risen, they have done so at only a nominal rate. Thus, customers are still able to enjoy an affordable meal at the Blackhawk, and, even more important, the restaurant is still able to maintain the quality and excellence for which it is known.

In the Chicago area, the Blackhawk is not only acclaimed for its reputation as a restaurant that serves superb food and offers excellent

**THE BLACKHAWK,
CHICAGO**

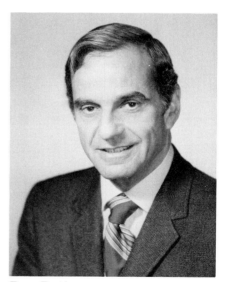

*Don Roth
Owner
Blackhawk
Restaurants*

service, but also it is recognized as an institution that has a faithful following developed over the years, with a satisfactory quotient of new patrons added each year.

The same excellent cuisine, service, and imaginative merchandising helped to quickly establish Don Roth's on Pearson, opened in 1973 in Chicago's North Michigan Avenue area, proving that his successful formula is sufficiently flexible to work in many locations.

The salad bar is a real test of showmanship and it is one passed with flying colors in Blackhawk operations. Contents and containers are equally innovative.

Hermann G. Rusch

The Greenbrier, run in a highly organized manner, its operation modern, streamlined and efficient, is, in every sense, of the present time. Yet the Greenbrier also reflects life as it once was; it has the unhurried style of a more charming and elegant time.

Nestled securely in a secluded valley of the Allegheny Mountains in White Sulphur Springs, W. Va., the Greenbrier is a sprawling, 6,500-acre resort that, like a charming Southern belle, is warm, gracious, and alluring.

Behind much of the resort's Southern hospitality stands one man—Hermann G. Rusch, the executive food director. IVY Award winner Rusch, who joined the staff of the Greenbrier in 1955 as its executive chief steward, is a man whose abilities are recognized the world over. He is one of the 12 world-famous chefs selected to receive the prestigious Order of the Golden Dozen.

The Swiss-born and Swiss-trained Rusch presides over what is essentially a formal European kitchen. It is ably manned by 50 chefs and 25 apprentices who prepare the exquisite cuisine, basis of the Greenbrier's reputation for famous food.

A poll of guest preferences would list as leading menu favorites Beef Wellington, Rack of Lamb Persillade, Souffle Grand Marnier, Quiche Lorraine, and the cookies that accompany many of the desserts. Many people can attest to the considerable skill and abilities of Greenbrier's chefs and apprentices, in 1974 alone, 66,000 guests were visitors at the Greenbrier.

THE GREENBRIER, WHITE SULPHUR SPRINGS, W. VA.

Herman G. Rusch
Executive Food Director
The Greenbrier

At the White Sulphur Springs resort, nothing is left to whim or chance. To achieve the quality standards that have been set, the resort conducts its own apprentice training program, strongly emphasizing culinary excellence. Credit for the consistently high standards of this now-famous training program must be given to Rusch who, with E. Truman Wright, recently retired managing director, established it in 1957.

The training program is just one measure of the performance both given and required by Rusch. His motto, which is known by all employees in the Greenbrier's kitchen, is: "Punctuality, obedience, and respect."

What results from his direction is clearly demonstrated by gourmet dining amid fresh flowers, with soft music, fine wine, and unsurpassed service.

What underlies it was once expressed by the executive food director when addressing a group of apprentices. He told them, "The delight of eating is the only enjoyment that belongs to all weathers, to all conditions, and to all ages."

"Planning a menu," Rusch has also said, "is a creative process into which the culinarian puts his entire soul, art, and culinary knowledge in order to attain a masterpiece worthy of presentation at the table. The object of this process can conceivably be no other than to increase the happiness of mankind."

Hermann Rusch is a remarkable individual whose philosophy undoubtedly contributes greatly to the tremendous success experienced by the Greenbrier.

Guests who are fortunate enough to visit the Greenbrier, where Southern tradition lives on at its very best, will certainly be treated to a bountiful menu, flawless service, and the finest of recreational activities.

A display piece designed for pheasant is arranged on a silver platter surrounded by silver sauceboats. The cooked birds are placed around a base of a mound filled with tiny white flowers and ivy. Perched atop it is a pheasant in full plumage. Vegetables are placed in front of the cooked birds with just the right crisp green garnish to show the foods to full advantage.

Louise Saunders

Charlie's Cafe Exceptionale, housed in a large, white brick, English Tudor structure in Minneapolis, adheres to the standard of excellence typical of IVY Award winners. This standard has been maintained by Louise Saunders, who took over the operation in 1964 following the death of her husband.

When she first began, Mrs. Saunders knew almost nothing about the restaurant business. But with organizational skills developed in her professional capacity as a lawyer, with expertise supplied by many loyal employees, by attending Cornell University and many seminars, and by traveling extensively throughout the world in search of knowledge applicable to the restaurant industry, she has mastered the art.

As she encounters new influences and ideas, she continues to apply them to changing/improving Charlie's. "I never forget about Charlie's when I leave at six o'clock," she says. "It's with me all the time, but I love it."

Explaining her commitment, she states, "A restaurateur totally commits himself/herself to the gracious service of cuisine, wine, and liquors of the highest quality in an atmosphere relaxing to the customers."

Further evidence that her approach is successful are receipt of a *Holiday* Magazine award for 25 consecutive years, (an honor accorded to only six restaurants); the Silver Spoon award, and the Business Executive's Dining award.

What may also partially explain this success is the fact that Mrs. Saunders is always trying to make Charlie's cuisine and service exciting and different. A few innovations made in 1974 include: a phonetic wine list; fresh Atlantic fish daily; oysters flown in live from Boston and shucked to order; and Slim 'n Trim lunch/dinner entrees, different each day and made from recipes prepared by registered, consulting dietitians.

Other measures designed to help the dieter "enjoy yet comply" are hors d'oeuvre trays available by order so that four people may order only two trays if they are cutting calories; Charlie's own slim and trim dressing; margarine always available, and fresh fruit featured on the menu as a regular dessert offering.

A consistent leader among the top five best sellers is, however, Charlie's Peppered Ribeye of Beef Roast which is listed both as a Duke and Duchess portion.

On the main floor there are four dining rooms: The Hunt, Oak, and Coach Rooms (for formal dining), and the Dub Room (informal dining room). The first three rooms have large, persimmon leather swivel chairs; the Dub Room has black leather captain's chairs and banquettes. There is also the Fireside Cocktail Lounge. On the second floor there are three banquet rooms, each with individual decor.

Mrs. Saunders is sensitive to the expressed needs of customers and tries to anticipate desires that may develop. She reads periodicals about the economic climate of the country, encourages customers to discuss their wishes, and listens to what she terms the "drum beats" of the community.

Listening to the latter resulted in Charlie's instituting bus transportation to and from Minnesota Orchestra and Metropolitan Opera performances and introducing menu items to meet the needs of the persons who are watching their diets, eating less or differently.

Typical of the celebration luncheons hosted by Charlie's Cafe Exceptionale is the menu below. These special menus are part of a monthly newsletter sent to her customers by Mrs. Louise H. Saunders, owner of Charlie's.

St. Patrick's Luncheon

IRISH LAMB STEW
with assorted vegetables

Choice of one:
Shamrock Salad (pineapple-lime, cottage cheese, coconut — whipped)

or choice of luncheon salad

or vegetable du jour

Charlie's bread basket — butter

$3.25

Of course, Charlie's potato salad and marinated herring

Mrs. Saunders not only combines organizational skill with good management/business techniques, but also applies an equal amount of human understanding.   Illustrating this is her belief that an executive must meet the needs of the public but stay in the background, permitting employees to share the limelight and know the pride of accomplishment that it fosters.

To encourage and motivate her 175 employees, she holds weekly staff meetings; provides total communication on all facets of the business; takes a personal interest in the welfare of her employees, and, in general, tries to create a "good family" relationship.

Louise Saunders seems to have found the key to building not only a superb restaurant, but also a dedicated, loyal staff. For example, while her executive chef is a relative newcomer with only 18 years of service, one bartender has been there for 31 years and two others for 25 and 20 years, respectively.

But one man at Charlie's (now in its 41st year) holds the record. He is beverage manager Joe Peterson who, earlier this year, celebrated his 40th service anniversary.

Perhaps employees' feelings for Charlie's are summed up best in Peterson's words. "In the morning," he said, "I never feel as if I'm going to work. It's different at Charlie's; you're on your own. I hope I'm here for another 40 years."

When such employee loyalty is combined with excellence, it is easily understandable why Charlie's Cafe Exceptionale is a restaurant of unquestioned distinction, where everybody adheres to the guiding principle. . . "at Charlie's, there is no compromise with quality."

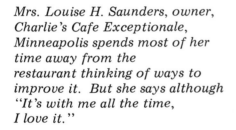

Mrs. Louise H. Saunders, owner, Charlie's Cafe Exceptionale, Minneapolis spends most of her time away from the restaurant thinking of ways to improve it. But she says although "It's with me all the time, I love it."

Win Schuler

A belief in consistency of quality and flavor in food served, the offering of a generous assortment of appetizers presented as soon as the patron is seated, and an atmosphere marked by cordiality and friendly smiles are all elements in the formula for success of Michigan restaurateur and IVY Award winner Win Schuler.

For the 64-year-old Schuler, now chairman of the board of Win Schuler's, Inc., the restaurant business has represented a major portion of his life. He began working as a morning cook at the 40-room Royal Hotel and Restaurant shortly after his father purchased that Marshall, Mich. hotel in 1924.

Following graduation from Albion College in 1930, Schuler taught history and coached football at a small high school in Wakefield, Mich. But after four years, he was looking for new challenges and took over the 20-seat restaurant in his father's hotel.

Not only was it the start of a lifelong career, but it was also the start of an empire. For the restaurant, now known as Win Schuler's Centennial Room, was the first of his eight establishments in Michigan and Indiana, all within a 200-mile radius.

An energetic, progressive young man, Schuler immediately began to think ahead. Believing that good food was not enough, he decided that "to stand out, you need something extra."

While Schuler gave high priority to producing the very finest in food, he also felt it was important to know his patrons' names. With the help of a fine memory, concentrated effort, and the use of association techniques, he successfully mastered this feat, much to the delight and amazement of customers and friends alike.

Their reputation for excellent food was built on such American and English dishes as steaks, chops, and beef, as well as prime ribs, London broil, and rack of lamb, the special favorites of Schuler customers. Seafood specials include shrimp filled with crabmeat and mariner's sole stuffed with crab and shrimp.

Also part of the standard fare are the famous Bar-Scheeze with crackers, coleslaw, casseroles of hot Swedish meatballs, served in a kettle over a hot flame, and individual loaves of warm, freshly baked bread.

Moving forward rapidly, he took over ownership of the restaurant in 1936 and expanded it in 1940. Although interrupted by a stint in military service during World War II, Schuler quickly resumed dynamic leadership upon his return in 1945.

In the space of eight years, he opened four new Win Schuler's, beginning an expansion program that continues to this day. Together with the Marshall facility and the most recent one in West Bloomfield, Schuler has, over the years, added restaurants in Benton Harbor, Jackson, Stevensville, East Lansing, and two in conjunction with the Marriott Inn—one in Fort Wayne (Ind.), the other in Ann Arbor.

To provide food of the uniform excellence he wanted to serve in all his restaurants, Schuler decided to set up a commissary-type operation. Located in Marshall, Quality Restaurant Suppliers, the distribution center, prepares and packages foods for the Schuler restaurants. "This," says Schuler, "reduces costs, and central purchasing allows us to maintain an unusually high degree of quality control on our products."

Schuler also discovered early in his career that people like to munch on something while they wait, so crackers and crocks of cheese are

WIN SCHULER'S, MARSHALL, MICH.

Some of the dishes credited with creating Schuler's dining tradition are shown below:

The Innkeeper Recommends

Turkey Combination
An open faced broiled combination of turkey, tomato and a crisp bacon strip. Served in casserole on homemade toast and topped with cheese sauce. 2.55

Seafood Rosellini
Delicate seafood simmered in a Schuler white sauce. Topped with tomato and cheese and browned under the broiler. Crisp green salad. 2.95

Strip Sirloin Sandwich
Strip sirloin steak . . . . a beefeater's delight. Tossed green salad. 4.95

Knocs 'n Brats
Milwaukee's finest sausages accompanied by hot German potato salad and served with a tossed green salad. 2.95

Sole of the Fleet
Delicate sole oven broiled to perfection and served with a crisp green salad. Deep fried on request. 3.25

The Sweets
Cheesecake 85
Caramel Ice Cream Pie 75
Coconut Snowball 65
Grasshopper Pie 85
Wine Pie 75
Peppermint Ribbon Pie 85
Fresh Strawberry Shortcake . .85
Fresh Melon 85
Ice Cream Sherbet 55
Sundaes — Chocolate,
   Hot Judge 65

WE HONOR
THE FOLLOWING CREDIT CARDS:
American Express,
Bank Americard, Diners Club,
Master Charge
and Win Schulers Charge.

Beverages
Coffee
Tea (hot or iced)
Milk
Soft Drinks
.25

among the items placed on every table. The cheese, which is extremely popular, comes from a recipe developed by Schuler himself and is merchandised aggressively in all his operations and in supermarkets in 13 states.

Schuler restaurants are noted for their Old English decor, low-beamed ceilings, rough-hewn wood, fireplaces, and memorabilia and artifacts from the lives of English literary figures—all of which reflect the former history teacher's personal interests.

Among awards which have been presented to Schuler are the Business Executives' Dining Award; for 23 consecutive years Win Schuler's Restaurant in Marshall has received *Holiday* Magazine's annual Distinctive Dining award.

Although board chairman Win Schuler has turned the presidency and day-to-day administration of Win Schuler's, Inc., over to his oldest son Hans, he is still very much involved in the business. He takes great care to be certain that customers receive the very best of food and service in a pleasant atmosphere.

Carved on a beam in one of Schuler's restaurants is the saying, "Man thinks not well with an empty stomach." Win Schuler has made it a certainty that none of his patrons will ever have that problem after dining at one of his restaurants.

Win Schuler samples one of the soups listed on his menu as "A Jolly Beginning."

Mavis and Hans Skalle

Hans Skalle not only believes in dreams, he turns them into reality. Camelot, a 15th-century castle that recreates a romantic legend, is just such a dream come true.

Speaking of his dream, Camelot owner Skalle says, "I felt Minneapolis needed something it had never had—a fine restaurant serving fine continental cuisine. It was long overdue. People were ready for it; I just knew."

Skalle, a former head waiter at the Waldorf, where he met his wife Mavis, who was then a vice-president of a Milwaukee steel company, decided to put this idea into action. It is the successful culmination of their venture that won a joint IVY Award for Hans and Mavis Skalle.

Finally, in September of 1965, after spending $1 million and devoting one year of their lives to the project, the Skalles opened the Camelot. The distinguished, gray-haired, Norwegian-born Skalle had indeed accurately taken the pulse of the public. The people in the Minneapolis area were more than ready for Camelot; they came, and continue to come, in impressive numbers, despite increasing competition in recent years.

Patrons remain enthusiastic because, whether it is food, furnishings or atmosphere, excellence is the key word at Camelot. The restaurant's continental menu is extensive and yet carefully assembled with an eye toward gourmet tastes. Specialties of the "castle" include scampi, fresh river trout, prime rib, pheasant, and young partridge.

"Though prime rib is the largest seller by volume," reports Mrs. Skalle, "everyone thinks of us for fish." Camelot serves nine tempting fish entrees, ranging from a delicate Dover sole to Gulf red snapper to mildly flavored walleyed pike from Northern Minnesota, all of which are flown in fresh daily.

Each dish is prepared by one of two working chefs, an American and a Frenchman, who perform their culinary wonders in a very compact kitchen. The American chef prepares luncheon menu items, and the French chef prepares items for the evening menu. Skalle himself, on occasion, may head for the kitchen to skillfully fillet a Dover sole, or take over at tableside to prepare his dramatic version of Steak Diane.

Complementing the menu is a leather-bound wine book. It displays the labels of more than 100 imported and domestic wines, including 1966 Chateau Lafite-Rothschild.

"We were an instant success," Skalle remembers proudly, noting that there was an avalanche of customers. In fact, for months after the opening, the banner-bedecked castle caused traffic jams on the nearby expressway as motorists pulled off to the side of the road to take a closer look. And, as Skalle points out, "We didn't even advertise for the first five years."

While the public raved over the merits of the castle, the local press was less than enthusiastic. Members of the press criticized Camelot as too expensive and called it out of place and time for suburban Minneap-

Camelot RESTAURANT OF DISTINCTION

olis, "A continental restaurant in steak and potatoes country just won't wash."

The local press was over-ruled in the very first year of Camelot's operation (and has been every year since), for the restaurant has received a *Holiday* Magazine award. There was also practical proof of the wisdom of the Skalles' decision; last year Camelot grossed $2 million in food and beverage sales.

Occasional talk of menu prices continues even today. (The average check—without liquor—is $10.75.) But that doesn't bother Skalle anymore.

"People say we're expensive. But," he contends, "I think for what they get we're very reasonable."

In carrying out their theme in furnishings, Camelot has expertly combined dark natural woods, rich red and black decor, and an extensive collection of pewter that set the mood for an evening of elegant food and drink. Authentic medieval weapons and armor attract considerable attention. High-backed, hand-carved, chestnut chairs and huge round tables placed in the six, intimate, hexagonal dining rooms that make up the castle, provide an "Old World" atmosphere.

"The idea of Camelot is important," Skalle notes, "not just the name. We wanted to create the image, so chose the hexagonal shape, as well as using other elements reminiscent of the romantic King Arthur legend."

"We still tend to be stuffy and formal in the front rooms," Mrs. Skalle says firmly. "We're a special occasion place, and a place that young people graduate into; we really don't ever want to change that."

Scandinavians and non-Scandinavians alike enjoy this annual buffet. The authentic Juleboard gives food preparation workers an opportuinty to demonstrate their versatility.

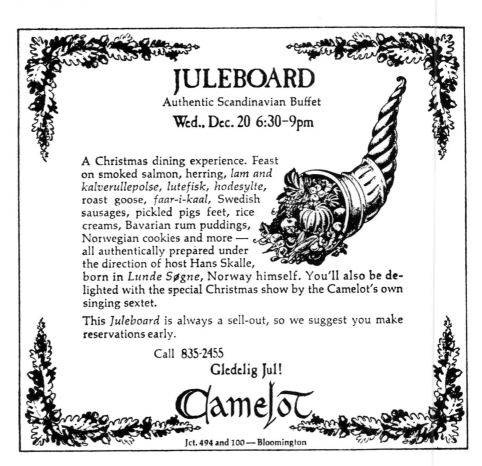

JULEBOARD
Authentic Scandinavian Buffet
Wed., Dec. 20 6:30-9pm

A Christmas dining experience. Feast on smoked salmon, herring, *lam and kalverullepolse, lutefisk, hodesylte,* roast goose, *faar-i-kaal,* Swedish sausages, pickled pigs feet, rice creams, Bavarian rum puddings, Norwegian cookies and more — all authentically prepared under the direction of host Hans Skalle, born in *Lunde Søgne,* Norway himself. You'll also be delighted with the special Christmas show by the Camelot's own singing sextet.

This *Juleboard* is always a sell-out, so we suggest you make reservations early.

Call 835-2455
Gledelig Jul!

Camelot

Jct. 494 and 100 — Bloomington

John C. Smalley

"Modernize, update, and keep the Union contemporary." These are three ways of stating the dominant goal of John C. Smalley, director of university residences and the Memorial Union at Purdue University, West Lafayette, Ind.

IVY Award winner Smalley is a man with great natural presence; he immediately commands respect. Smalley exudes the quiet, assured confidence of a man who not only is in command, but knows it. With his head held high and his shoulders set squarely, he presents a rather military bearing.

Nor is his manner pure coincidence. Smalley is a retired artillery officer whose spit-and-polish attitude, combined with a natural attentiveness to detail, are evident in all the things he does, as well as all the areas under his control at the university.

As an employee, Smalley has been associated with Purdue University for 29 years. However, Purdue has been a constant factor all of his life: he is a graduate of the university, as was his father before him; in fact, he was born the proverbial stone's throw away from the campus. Except for the interruption of World War II, moreover, he has lived his whole life in the community of West Lafayette, Ind.

Smalley began his career at Purdue in 1946, starting as assistant manager of the residence hall. During the intervening years, he had numerous responsibilities, while serving in six different positions. In 1961, he was named to his present position—director of university residences and the Memorial Union and in November, 1975, to his present position of vice-president for housing and foodservices.

In this capacity, his responsibilities are impressive. They include 12 residence halls, which house approximately 10,000 undergraduates; two

PURDUE UNIVERSITY, W. LAFAYETTE, IND.

J. C. Smalley, left, presents an award to Laura Weismantel, a member of Purdue's Student Union Board. Student views are carefully considered and as a consequence student cooperation is impressive.

resident houses for 1,500 graduate students; 1,700 married-student apartments; one of the largest college union buildings in the world, and a 254-room (hotel-type) operation to accommodate university guests and alumni.

Also under Smalley's direction are the university's food facilities, which include 21 production kitchens, 40 dining rooms, and 7 snack bars.

Between the foodservice and housing operations, Smalley is responsible for $17.1 million in gross annual revenue. Although Purdue is a state-related school, its foodservice operation is entirely self-supporting, with its operations running well in the black.

Smalley is the first to admit that such growth and development have been a team effort. "In an operation this wide and varied," he says, "the key to success is a coordinated team effort. I merely set the goals."

Smalley speaks highly of his people. In particular, he lavishes words of high praise on his tightly knit and knowledgeable staff. Members of the staff mentioned by him include: Helen M. Townsend, assistant director of residence hall foodservice; Charles E. Dunn, director of foodservice, Purdue Memorial Union; Robert L. Page, director of residence halls, and Edgar R. Park, director of purchasing.

While recognizing the importance of quality and an excellent staff, Smalley believes Purdue can only stay contemporary if it concentrates on providing a complete food program, not just a "foodservice operation." Recently, for example, while discussing an off-campus fast-food unit, he said, "We don't compete with them. We just fill the voids they can't."

Illustrating the special events Purdue's facilities can provide are the formal dinner dances with gourmet food, buffets, ethnic dinners, picnics, recognition banquets, faculty dinners, parent receptions, etiquette dinners, and guest luncheons—all of which are a normal complement of activities for one year.

His bearing may lead those who meet him to consider saluting him; these accomplishments make it clear that he deserves a salute.

Banquets are well planned and plans are well carried out at Purdue. This function was arranged in honor of a retiring staff member.

Don Smith

"The IVY Award was one of the most outstanding honors I have ever received," says Don Smith, former owner of Chateau Louise, Dundee, Ill., which he sold to the Gaslight Group in 1970.

Smith's entry into the restaurant business is an unusual story in itself. The ex-Big Ten footballer chucked his football coaching career at the urging of a friend, who had inherited a bankrupt restaurant business from his father. Persuaded by his friend to join in the venture, Smith left coaching, moving, as he puts it, "from gridiron to the griddle."

Shortly afterward, in the fall of 1962, Smith headed for Michigan and the kitchens of Win Schuler, the famed restaurateur, himself an IVY Award winner. Armed only with a thirst for knowledge, he took a six-week crash course in the restaurant business from this successful restaurateur. Schuler proved to be an exceptional teacher, and Smith was an unusually apt pupil.

Recalling his early learning experience, Smith says, "First, I cracked lobsters until my hands were bleeding. I worked every station," he added. "In 27 days I lost 21 pounds and went through a pair of shoes."

Less than a year later, Smith opened Chateau Louise and scored his first victory in the restaurant business, winning the coveted Northern Illinois Wine and Food Society Gourmet Dinner of the Year award. He also instituted a building program which, subsequently, was a continuous and ongoing project.

At first glance, it must have seemed incongruous for a former Big Ten guard and high school football coach to create and open an elegant French restaurant with motel facilities. But Smith, who served as general manager of Chateau Louise from its opening in 1963 until becoming the primary partner and president of the corporation in 1969, knew precisely what he was doing and how he wanted to run the operation.

As his staff soon discovered, Smith directed Chateau Louise personnel with the same techniques required for a well-coached football squad, frequently incorporating tactics that had been taught to him by his coach at the University of Illinois.

In some ways, his attitude reflected this background. For example, he believed that while profits may substitute for applause, the presentation is at least as important as the preparation in foodservice. Like any good showman, he felt that the restaurateur must mask the hard work required with professional grace in order to transport his patrons from daily cares to a pleasurable atmosphere.

During his tenure at Chateau Louise, Smith once said, "We're the greatest actors in the world; we put on a play. Our audience—our customers—don't see the production costs, the direction, and the problems, for instance when you have to send in an under-trained understudy because one of the regular waiters didn't appear. The restaurant business is theater."

But at Chateau Louise, Smith combined good hard business sense with human effort. As he put it, "I frequently served as a catalyst, bringing together the ideas of my staff, my guests and a lot of my competition."

To lure more business—especially meetings—to the Chicago-area location, Smith added shops, motel rooms, recreation facilities, and a swimming pool complete with a sunken ship and pads on which guests were served cocktails.

THEN AT CHATEAU LOUISE, DUNDEE, ILL., NOW AT CONRAD N. HILTON SCHOOL OF HOTEL AND RESTAURANT MANAGEMENT

Donald I. Smith, named an IVY Award winner while he was president of Chateau Louise, has since sold the operation and is now assistant professor, Conrad N. Hilton School of Hotel and Restaurant Management, University of Houston.

"While I didn't want a hokey place," Smith says, "I did want to give people something interesting." He then pointed out that, ultimately, Chateau Louise was not just a restaurant. It was shops, a health club, a place to go. It was more than a foodservice/lodging complex; it created a state of mind for patrons who came there.

While he was at Chateau Louise, Don Smith's operation was noted for its appetizing food, served in a delightful setting. Baked Stuffed Lobster was one of the elegant items he offered to his midwestern guests, who were sometimes reluctant to tackle lobster plain and unadorned. The most popular item on his menu, however, was prime rib, which realized approximately 17 percent of the business from a 26-item product mix. Smith's own personal favorite was the Lobster in Beer Batter because of its unusual flavor and texture.

But, in 1970, Smith sold the Chateau Louise to realize yet another ambition. "The hospitality business has been marvelous to me," he said, "but I am now fulfilling a dream that I have had for a long time—that is teaching (in the Conrad N. Hilton School of Hotel and Restaurant Management at the University of Houston), consulting, and also traveling."

This arrangement of colorful raw ingredients was arranged by Don Smith to be photographed for a postcard that was used to build interest among prospective patrons in Lobster and Crabmeat Thermidor.

Justine and Dayton Smith

Self-confidence, determination, and a need for challenge is a combination that characterizes Justine Smith, explaining why she entered the restaurant business. These same qualities, coupled with a vibrant, outgoing personality and dedication to quality when added to her husband Dayton's management expertise, account for the highly successful fine dining establishment they operate as Justine's.

Located in Memphis, Tenn., where it is housed in a Memphis landmark beautifully restored to its original state in 1958, Justine's is recognized as one of the country's leading restaurants. Not only does it regularly make the prestigious *Holiday* Magazine list of distinguished restaurants, but it has been described as "conceivably the best restaurant in the South."

The Justine's of today is a far cry from the one that started it all. Aware 30 years ago of the need in Memphis for a place to dine away from home that would meet the traditions of Southern hospitality and elegance, IVY Award winner Smith decided to establish a restaurant. Although she had attended the University of Tennessee, she had not had any practical experience in foodservice operation. Borrowing the money, she rented a narrow warehouse near Beale St. and opened her doors in November, 1948. Operating on a shoestring, she purchased second-hand kitchen equipment, made draperies, and brought crystal and silverware from her own home. She opened with two cooks, three waiters, and reservations for a party of ten. Twenty other guests came too, and Justine's was off to a fine beginning.

Justine worked around the clock to build her business, but the hard work and long hours paid off very soon. Within a few weeks, the 86-seat restaurant was serving to capacity, and, after a scant two months, she was able to pay off her loans. It was quite an achievement, since Justine's used no advertising except word of mouth—not even a sign out front. These practices are still followed at Justine's.

The discovery of the beautiful quarters they now occupy occurred in 1956 when the Smiths decided to move into surroundings more befitting Justine's classic French cuisine. "Dayton and I came across this marvelous old house and decided it would be a good spot to relocate the original Justine's."

Like many old but elegant structures, the stately home on Coward Street needed considerable work. IVY Award winner Dayton Smith, a retired management engineer with an intense interest in authentic restorations, was more than equal to the task. However, as Mrs. Smith noted, "It was a slow process."

After 14 months of tireless effort, the Memphis landmark was restored to its 1843 stature—an elegant old plantation which had hosted debut parties for the society belles of the Civil War period. It was well worth the effort. For, when Justine's opened at its new location, guests were delighted and highly complimentary. As one customer noted, it was like "finding the perfect frame for a fine old painting." With a capacity of 185, the restaurant serves 200 dinners nightly.

The former Southern mansion is a handsome dining establishment where delectable appetizers such as Crab Justine, a lightly glazed creamed crab seasoned with sherry; Crab Suzette, with a light mornay sauce; Oysters Rockefeller, or Oysters Bienville set the stage for epicurean

Justine Smith
Owner
Justine's

delights to follow. Patrons often find it difficult to select just one entree.

The basic cuisine at Justine's is French with Creole overtones, with the New Orleans influence readily apparent in dishes such as Shrimp Remoulade and Eggs Sardou. Charcoal-broiled steaks of the finest quality and oysters en brochette are also popular but, notes Mrs. Smith, "Seafood rather than meat is the most popular item."

In crediting Justine's achievements, Mrs. Smith explains, "Much of our success is due to our staff, especially if you consider longevity a key." As examples of their long-time employees, she listed 2 waiters who have been there for 24 years, 6 employees for at least 20 years, and 2 chefs who started acquiring their skills at Justine's when they were teenagers. All of these employees make a special contribution in creating the atmosphere of Southern hospitality which makes dining at Justine's a special pleasure.

With Justine's a showplace of herringbone brick walks, a Napoleonic-era chandelier, white marble steps, a massive 1881 wrought iron gate, and a graceful colonial stairway, and complemented not only by the antique Georgian silver and the precious Baccarat crystal treasures, but also by a garden teeming with boxwoods, magnolias, camellias, and scores of other plants and trees, Justine Smith has no thought of slowing her pace.

Mrs. Smith continues to find Justine's "a real challenge. And I *like* a challenge." With equal fervor, Memphians say, "We like Justine's." That's the kind of reaction the Smiths say makes all the work, worry, and care they put into their restaurant well worth it.

Likened by one of Justine's customers to "the perfect frame for a fine old painting," this Memphis landmark was restored to its former state as an elegant plantation in 1958. Dayton Smith spent 14 months supervising the authentic restoration of Justine's present establishment.

Lloyd and Les Stephenson

Located on Highway 40 just 30 minutes from downtown Kansas City, Stephenson's Apple Farm is an establishment known for its fine food and country-style atmosphere that make customers feel that they are back in the "good old days."

Stephenson's, which got its name from the fact that the family had a reputation for selling quality orchard products from its small farm, was originally a fruit stand and grocery store. However, when IVY Award winners and twin sons Lloyd and Les Stephenson returned from military service in 1946 and wanted to go into business for themselves, they felt that their father's spot was an ideal location. It took more than a little persuasion to convince him of the soundness of their decision. He finally gave in with the provision that they build a new fruit stand for their dad.

With a cash outlay of $3,000 and the help of neighbors skilled in carpentry work, they built and opened the restaurant. A 40-seat, one-room cafe in the rural countryside, it featured, and still does, meats prepared in a smoke oven, a cooking method learned by the twins while working part-time at a small drive-in during their school years.

Recalling that early period, Lloyd Stephenson said, "We *had* to be perfect in those days. The food had to be excellent, the service perfect. If a guest came back a second time," he added, "he was like one of the family. We made sure he knew us and we knew him."

Those initial years were especially difficult—ones of hard, driving effort, but the effort was shared. Lloyd took responsibility for the front of the house, greeting guests and seeing to their needs. Les, on the other hand, took charge of the kitchen, where he developed recipes in which apples, of course, figured prominently.

Today although the menu has expanded, some elements of it are the same as they were in the early days. For example, the restaurant's line of meats—chicken, ham, pork, and beef—are smoked rather than cooked, true even of chicken gizzards, made tender by seven hours smoking time. The one lone exception to this role is the restaurant's specialty—Baked Chicken 'N Butter and Cream, Les's most popular creation.

In addition, food offerings are still of a regional character—prepared, with the care of a housewife readying an entry for a county fair, by loyal, long-time employees. Les has worked out ways to present Apple Farm dishes that will capture and/or preserve the image of a country-based operation.

STEPHENSON'S APPLE FARM RESTAURANT, KANSAS CITY

Les and Lloyd Stephenson check the menu at one of the colorful tables that provides an appropriate background for the country style cuisine their patrons enjoy.

Stephenson's Apple Farm Restaurant of today bears little resemblance to the original structure or operation. Although still located in the same spot, it is now a smart-looking countryside inn composed of a series of rustic and not-so-rustic dining areas; a country store filled with jams, jellies, preserves, relishes, and pickles from the restaurant's kitchen; a unique cocktail lounge containing an apple press filled with real apples; three banquet rooms—The Quilting Room, The Closet, and The Attic—and a magnificent, modern $150,000 kitchen. Yet guests entering the lobby are still greeted by a welcome sign and a keg of cider for free tapping.

Across the lobby there is a colorful Country Store stocked with antiques (also displayed in other parts of the restaurant) that have been collected during the Stephenson's travels throughout the Midwest.

The desire on the part of "folks who *really* care to do a good job" helps to explain the brothers' success. Their ability to make their people care is another asset. As Lloyd also says, "This business depends on people who want it to happen—who want to have a good place—and money comes second. But if you're good, the money will come."

As proof of his point, Stephenson's now grosses $2.6 million a year and serves an average of 1,200 covers per day. It employs 100 full-time persons and an equal number of part-time employees, including six local retirees who do part-time work and, according to Lloyd Stephenson, "love the opportunity and are excellent employees."

Lloyd and Les Stephenson have achieved success with their restaurant which has become career, hobby, recreation, and way of life, all rolled into one.

Dining out country style is frequently a family occasion so children's menus that will help hold children's interest as they wait for a meal to be served are an important element. Stephenson's Apple Farm Restaurant found this to be a successful format.

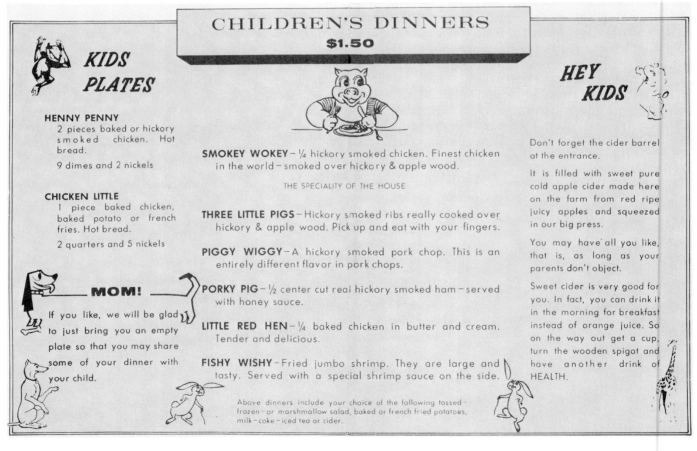

CHILDREN'S DINNERS
$1.50

KIDS PLATES

HENNY PENNY
2 pieces baked or hickory smoked chicken. Hot bread.

9 dimes and 2 nickels

CHICKEN LITTLE
1 piece baked chicken, baked potato or french fries. Hot bread.

2 quarters and 5 nickels

_____ MOM! _____
If you like, we will be glad to just bring you an empty plate so that you may share some of your dinner with your child.

SMOKEY WOKEY – ¼ hickory smoked chicken. Finest chicken in the world – smoked over hickory & apple wood.

THE SPECIALITY OF THE HOUSE

THREE LITTLE PIGS – Hickory smoked ribs really cooked over hickory & apple wood. Pick up and eat with your fingers.

PIGGY WIGGY – A hickory smoked pork chop. This is an entirely different flavor in pork chops.

PORKY PIG – ½ center cut real hickory smoked ham – served with honey sauce.

LITTLE RED HEN – ¼ baked chicken in butter and cream. Tender and delicious.

FISHY WISHY – Fried jumbo shrimp. They are large and tasty. Served with a special shrimp sauce on the side.

Above dinners include your choice of the following tossed – frozen – or marshmallow salad, baked or french fried potatoes, milk – coke – iced tea or cider.

HEY KIDS

Don't forget the cider barrel at the entrance.

It is filled with sweet pure cold apple cider made here on the farm from red ripe juicy apples and squeezed in our big press.

You may have all you like, that is, as long as your parents don't object.

Sweet cider is very good for you. In fact, you can drink it in the morning for breakfast instead of orange juice. So on the way out get a cup, turn the wooden spigot and have another drink of HEALTH.

Lyle A. Thorburn

Adapting to changing times is the hallmark of Michigan State University, believes Lyle Thorburn, manager of dormitories and foodservice at MSU. A 28-year industry veteran, he became interested in the field during WWII, courtesy of the U. S. Navy and its Sub Chaser Training Center in Miami, Fla.

IVY Award winner Thorburn heads an impressive operation. Based on most recent statistics (June 30, 1974) MSU's annual figures show: foodservice volume—$15.2 million; meals per day—65,000 to 70,000; units—25 dining rooms and 16 snack bars; lodging volume—$10.3 million in room sales and $3 million in apartment rent; number of rooms—9,100; number of beds—17,600, and miscellaneous income items—$4 million.

"One thing about us," said Thorburn, "we're open to, and willing to try, new ideas." Illustrating this, he pointed to the foodservice facilities provided in the residence halls and to the offering of hero-type sandwiches. "These sandwiches are extremely popular with today's young people," Thorburn said, explaining that they are specially made by the inch and can be as long as one foot, depending on student preference. However, at dinner time, the foodservice/dormitories director noted, standard foods such as roast beef and fried chicken remain the most popular items on campus menus.

Thorburn speaks with considerable enthusiasm about MSU operations, saying, "There are many things we're proud of. Our central commissary, which we developed from scratch and where we do meat cutting and salad items, is one. The concession department, which handles all athletic events and various campus activities, is another.

"Another fine facility is our food store. It serves as a purchasing, receiving, storage, and delivery facility for every one of our 16 kitchens and is comparable to a large wholesaler/meat supplier combined.

"We also have catering departments that operate out of the Student Union and the Kellogg Center for Continuing Study. In all, we have about 1,000 full-time employees and close to 3,000 student employees. So, you see, we've got a lot going on."

Acknowledging that many changes have taken place since he started, Thorburn noted that MSU was a pioneer in many areas. "We put in a telephone system that lets students direct-dial; are building rooms with connecting baths, and have, since 1960, constructed buildings with suite arrangements." Thorburn also pointed out that MSU furnishes linens on a weekly basis and has carpeted hallways in dining areas, as well as in some residences.

In spite of the fact that MSU has been on top of the situation, Thorburn admits that trying to predict what changes will be needed in the future is difficult because today's students are more sophisticated.

He also indicated that they know what they want, specifically mentioning private rooms and apartments, coed visiting privileges in dorms, and, in some cases, liquor on campus. "They're free to pick and choose," he says, "but, frankly, those sorts of things put more responsibility on them."

In addition to lodging and social activities, students are also more vocal about meals. Responding to their requests, MSU has implemented a 20-meal plan which is more economical for students; has expanded

MICHIGAN STATE UNIVERSITY, EAST LANSING

MSU has a decentralized management system, with each unit manager responsible for all aspects of foodservice and lodging in his hall. Each one tries to come up with the kind of special events—buffets, banana split parties, that will make his hall the most popular.

meal hours; has established a number of small dining areas, and offers continuous foodservice in snack shops.

Thorburn also mentioned that MSU has 2,468 married-student apartments, a total lodging capacity of 17,600, and an on-campus hotel, the Kellogg Center, which has 193 guest rooms, 23 meeting rooms, and seven private dining rooms which can accommodate anywhere from 12 to 900 people.

MSU wasn't always like this, as Thorburn points out, "In my early days, campus foodservice consisted of a few vending machines and sandwich lines!"

Reflecting on the many changes/improvements over the years, Thorburn said, "It's come a long way, hasn't it?"

Lyle Thorburn, far right, gives MSU students as many choices as possible. Here, students study condiment selection on cafeteria line.

Hans Weishaupt

A quiet, luxurious retreat in paradise that maintains an unusually high productivity rate—the operation that answers to that description is the Kahala Hilton. Located in Honolulu (Island of Oahu), Hawaii, the 10-story hotel, operated by the Hilton International Co., recaptures the graceful living of the period when Hawaii was a monarchy. It is stunning proof that good architecture and good business go hand in hand.

The 130-foot high main structure, which uses straight and slender design to produce a delicate and graceful building, the two-story cottage-like lagoon terrace, and the three-room Kawbata Cottage that adjoins it, are run by general manager and IVY Award winner Hans Weishaupt.

Weishaupt, who is responsible for the unusually high productivity rate, is a spirited, outgoing gentleman who has demonstrated during his two years in charge that he is singularly suited to the hotel. He was graduated from Cornell and attended Ecole Hotelier in Lausanne, Switzerland. Weishaupt says, "If I'd not had the Cornell training, I would have been dazzled by running the Kahala."

Despite its exquisite beauty, the Kahala Hilton is also an efficient operation. For example, one air-conditioned kitchen, which runs the entire width of the building, serves two restaurants—the Hala Terrace and the Maile. There is also the Maile Terrace that is available for private parties. It can accommodate up to 220 persons for cocktail parties and meetings and 174 for dining. The hotel itself requires only 200 employees for 372 rooms, with a usual occupancy level of 90 percent.

This formula of beauty and efficiency has spelled success, for the Kahala is one of Hawaii's most profitable hotels. Its design, which is built around the food, has more than paid off—nearly 50 percent of the hotel's $13 million annual revenue is derived from food and beverage sales. Unlike most resort hotels, it is frequented by the local people; 50 percent of the restaurant patrons are Hawaii residents.

Weishaupt is frankly enthusiastic about the Kahala. "We have the best hamburgers on the island, the best Hukilau (Hawaiian fishing festival), and have a seven-time *Holiday* Magazine award-winning restaurant, the Maile."

In the Maile, operated under Weishaupt's direction, by 26-year-old maitresse Charlene (Charlie) Goodness, the menu is a meld of continental cuisine and distinctive Hawaiian flair and flavor. Fountains, ponds, and hanging baskets of orchids also give an island touch, while the graciousness of the Orient is reflected by waitresses in kimonos.

Several elements, according to Ms. Goodness, make the Maile a great restaurant. They include a good kitchen staff, good waitresses, and good staff training through the pre-meal meetings each day that provide direct daily communication between the restaurant staff and herself.

In addition to forecasting the number of guests to be served, and staffing for them in the 200-seat restaurant, the necessity of planning for the future is recognized as being as crucial to successful restaurant management as preparing for the present is.

"We're always thinking of ways to improve the Maile and to enhance the beauty and comfort of the room. We do not take our business for granted; we try our best every night of the year," Ms. Goodness says proudly.

The changes that have taken place since the restaurant opened in 1964 are many: its mood has been tempered, gradually evolving from

Hans Weishaupt
General Manager
Kahala Hilton, Honolulu

strictly continental and very formal atmosphere and food into relaxed sophistication; gracious Oriental waitresses were introduced in 1968; and, a year later, a table d'hote menu of international, island, and oriental favorites was substituted for the more formal, earlier cuisine.

Each year since then has brought additional improvements—new glassware, more romantic lighting, greater use of flowers, brighter tablecloths, more contemporary music, and new wallcovering, uniforms, and carpeting.

With quality food, fine service, and outstanding atmosphere, it is small wonder that guests and tourists alike eagerly anticipate their visit to the award winning Maile Restaurant, where they dine elegantly amid lush orchids and lighted fountains.

Not only the Maile, but the entire atmosphere of this tropical hotel is inviting, relaxing, and reflective of the spirit that underlies the charm of Hawaii, the "Paradise of the Pacific."

Charlene "Charlie" Goodness, manager of the Maile Restaurant, credits exceptional cuisine, kitchen staff, and waitresses for its success.

IVY Award Winner Recipes

Appetizers

Cream of Mushroom Soup

YIELD: 1-1/2 quarts

INGREDIENTS

Butter	3 tablespoons
Fresh Mushrooms, finely chopped	1/2 pound
Flour	3 tablespoons
Cream, warmed	2 cups
Milk, warmed	1 quart
Salt	1 tablespoon
Monosodium Glutamate	1 teaspoon
Yellow Food Coloring	1 teaspoon

Melt butter in saucepot. Add mushrooms and cook until tender. Stir in flour until smoothly mixed. Add warmed cream and milk, stirring constantly until smooth. Add seasonings and coloring. Stir until hot.

Karl Ratzsch's

Lobster Bisque

YIELD: 12 cups (3 quarts)

INGREDIENTS

Lobsters, 1 pound each	2
Oil	1/4 cup
Mirepoix	1-1/2 cups
Garlic Cloves	2
Brandy	2 ounces
White Wine	2 ounces
Fish Stock	2 quarts
Tarragon Sprigs	1-1/2
Tomatoes, cut up	6
Tomato Puree	1/4 cup
Salt	to taste
Cayenne Pepper	to taste
Rice, Raw	1 cup
Heavy Cream	1-1/2 cups
Butter	1 ounce

Elegantly styled service of such specialties as Lobster Bisque gets full patron attention at La Bourgogne where interiors were deliberately kept simple.

Saute lobsters in oil over high heat until shells turn red. Add the mirepoix; cook 5 minutes, then add garlic. Flame with warmed brandy. Add wine and next 6 ingredients. Boil 15 minutes, then take out lobsters. Remove shells from lobsters, retaining the tails. Pound lobster shells in a mortar until fine; put into soup with rice. Simmer 1-1/2 hours. Press through a fine wire sieve; heat again. Add cream and butter. Dice lobster tail meat and add to soup. Serve hot.

La Bourgogne

Brown Palace French Onion Soup

YIELD: 1 gallon

Characteristic of the French
influence that marks
The Brown Palace Hotel cuisine
is their French Onion Soup
with special cheese croutons.

INGREDIENTS

Butter, melted	1/2 cup
Salad Oil	1/2 cup
Onions, Medium-sized, thinly sliced	12
Consomme	1/2 gallon
Water	1/2 gallon
Salt	to taste
Whole Black Pepper, crushed	1/2 teaspoon
CHEESE CROUTONS	
Hard Rolls	6
Butter, melted	1/2 cup
Parmesan Cheese	1 cup

Combine butter and salad oil in heavy kettle and heat to approximately 350°F. Add sliced onions and fry to a golden brown. Add consomme, water, salt, and pepper. Simmer for 1-1/2 hours. Serve with Cheese Croutons.

CHEESE CROUTONS
Slice hard rolls 1/4 inch thick. Place on a cookie sheet. Toast under broiler until golden brown on one side. Remove; dip untoasted side in butter, then in the parmesan cheese. Return to broiler until cheese melts.

The Brown Palace Hotel

Cold Cucumber Soup

YIELD: Approximately 1 quart

INGREDIENTS

Cucumbers, peeled	3
Butter	2 tablespoons
Leek, white part only, sliced	1
Bay Leaf	1
Flour	1 tablespoon
Chicken Stock	3 cups
Salt	3/4 teaspoon
Pepper	1/4 teaspoon
Cream	1 cup
Lemon, juice of	1/2
Fresh Dill *or* Mint	1 teaspoon
Sour Cream	to garnish

Saute 2 cucumbers gently in butter with leek and bay leaf for 20 minutes, or until tender but not brown. Stir in flour. Add chicken stock, salt, and pepper; simmer 30 minutes. Put mixture through a food mill, or blend, half at a time, in electric blender and strain through a fine sieve. Chill. When cold, add remaining cucumber which has been seeded and grated, cream, and lemon juice. Stir in fresh dill. Correct seasoning with salt and pepper. Chill at least 30 minutes. Serve "icy cold" in chilled cups with a dab of sour cream on top.

Victor's, The Penthouse, Hotel St. Francis

Essence of Tomato Soup

YIELD: 2 gallons

INGREDIENTS

Tomatoes	4 No. 10 cans
Diced Celery	3-1/4 pounds
Diced Carrots	1-1/2 pounds
Diced Green Pepper	1 pound
Diced Onion	1-1/4 pounds
Chopped Parsley	1-1/4 cups
Bay Leaves	4
Salt	1 cup
Pepper	1/2 teaspoon
Tomato Juice	2 46-ounce cans
Whipping Cream	1 pint

Soup is a daily offering in many student foodservices. This MSU soup is served with one of three luxury touches.

Mix first 9 ingredients in soup pot. Simmer for 2-1/2 to 3 hours. Force through sieve; add tomato juice. Serve hot, garnished with whipped cream.

VARIATIONS

Salted Whipped Cream: Season whipped cream with salt.
Chive Cream: Add chopped fresh or frozen chives after cream is whipped.

Michigan State University

Savarin Vegetable Soup

YIELD: 3 gallons

INGREDIENTS

Sliced Carrots	5 ounces
Sliced Turnips	5 ounces
Sliced Leeks	2 ounces
Sliced Onion	5 ounces
Cut String Beans	5 ounces
Butter	8 ounces
Stock	1-1/4 gallons
Chicken Broth	1-1/4 gallons
Salt	3-1/2 tablespoons
Peas	5 ounces
Lima Beans	5 ounces
Sliced Potatoes	5 ounces
Corn	1/2 ear (1/4 cup)
Cauliflower	1/4 head (8 ounces)
Crushed Tomatoes	5 ounces
Flour	5 tablespoons
Parsley, chopped	1/2 bunch

A vegetable soup with a hearty homemade flavor is a chilly day favorite at Purdue.

Saute carrots, turnips, leeks, onion, and string beans in butter a few minutes. Add stock, salt, peas, and limas; simmer 45 minutes. Add sliced potatoes, corn, and cauliflower. Cook 15 minutes. Add tomatoes, crushed and blended with flour, and parsley. Simmer 15 minutes.

Purdue University

Navy Bean Soup

YIELD: 40 to 50 servings

*Navy Bean Soup is a popular
Potage Dyuers, soup of the day,
on Camelot luncheon menus. It
is often featured as part of
the Soup 'n Sandwich Special
of the Day.*

INGREDIENTS

Navy Beans	3-3/4 quarts
Cold Water	10 quarts
Salt Pork	2-1/2 pounds
Ham Hocks	10 to 12 pounds
Diced Onions, Small	10
Diced Celery	5 cups
Diced Carrots	10
Milk	6-1/4 quarts
Salt	6-2/3 tablespoons
Pepper	2-1/2 teaspoons
Paprika	5 teaspoons

Wash and clean beans. Cover with cold water and soak overnight. Add salt pork and ham hocks. Cover. Bring to a boil, then simmer for 2 hours. Remove ham hocks and pork. Cut in 1/4-inch cubes and set aside. Add vegetables to the stock and cook slowly until beans are soft (about 1 hour). Stir in milk, salt, pepper, paprika, ham, and salt pork cubes heat to serving temperature.

Camelot

Soupe de Poissons

YIELD: Approximately 1 quart

INGREDIENTS

Saltwater Fish (6 different varieties)	1-1/2 pounds
Olive Oil	4 ounces
Assorted Shellfish (shells removed)	1 pint
Onions, chopped	4
Bay Leaf	1
Thyme	1/4 teaspoon
Fennel	1/4 teaspoon
Salt	to taste
Pepper	to taste
Water	1 quart
Bread, 1/2-inch slices	4
Garlic Cloves	8
Mayonnaise	1 cup

Cut fish in large chunks. Saute in oil with shellfish and onions. Add seasonings and water. Cook, uncovered, for 15 minutes. Strain the bouillon; set the fish aside for another use. Toast enough bread to line 4 individual tureens. Moisten each slice with some of the bouillon. Peel, chop, then pulverize garlic with a mortar and pestle. Add mayonnaise, and blend. Pour strained bouillon into the tureens. Add a dollop of garlic mayonnaise (aioli) to each and stir in lightly.

Fairmont Hotel

Onion Soup

YIELD: 4 to 6 servings

INGREDIENTS

White Onions, Small	6
Butter	1/3 cup
Sugar	1 teaspoon
Beef Stock	6 cups
Cognac	1/4 cup
Salt	to taste
Pepper, freshly ground	to taste
Toasted French Bread	4 to 6 rounds
Gruyere Cheese, grated	to garnish

Cognac adds a New Orleans touch to Onion Soup served by the Brennans at Commander's Palace.

Peel and slice onions thinly. Heat butter in a large saucepan with a little sugar; add the onion rings and cook them very, very gently over low heat, stirring constantly with a wooden spoon, until the rings are an even golden brown. Add beef stock gradually, stirring constantly, until the soup begins to boil. Then lower the heat, cover the pan, and simmer gently for about 1 hour. Just before serving, add cognac, salt, and pepper. Ladle into individual ovenproof bowls. Place toasted buttered rounds of french bread heaped with grated gruyere cheese in each bowl. Run under broiler briefly to brown cheese.

Commander's Palace Restaurant

Tomato Soup Supreme

YIELD: 40 to 50 servings

INGREDIENTS

Butter *or* Margarine	2-1/2 cups
Diced Celery	2-1/2 cups
Diced Onion	2-1/2 cups
Diced Carrots	2-1/2 cups
All-Purpose Flour	2-1/2 cups
Black Peppercorns	30
Bay Leaves	10
Cloves, Whole	20
Crumbled Tarragon Leaves	2-1/2 teaspoons
Tomatoes, Canned *or* Tomato Puree	6-1/4 quarts
Rich Beef *or* Chicken Stock	10 quarts

Melt butter or margarine in saucepan. Slowly saute the celery, onion, and carrots until lightly browned. Blend in flour, whole black pepper, bay leaves, cloves, and tarragon. Cook over low heat until ingredients are well blended. Add tomatoes and continue to cook over very low heat for about one hour. (It will be necessary to stir this mixture occasionally.) Strain through a fine sieve. Add brown soup stock and bring to the boiling point. Add salt and pepper if necessary.

Camelot

Cream of Wild Asparagus Soup*

YIELD: 6 servings

INGREDIENTS

Butter	1 tablespoon
Onion, Small, chopped	1
Celery, chopped	1/2 stalk
Beef Stock	2 cups
Tiny Asparagus	1 pound
Salt	to taste
Pepper	to taste
Heavy Cream	3/4 cup

Heat butter in saucepan. Add onion and celery; cook until soft but not brown, stirring frequently. Add stock and bring to a boil. Trim asparagus, cutting as little as possible from the bottom. Place in stock; simmer for 5 minutes. Add salt and pepper. Pour stock and asparagus into blender and liquefy. Strain; add cream. Reheat and serve.

*The original Four Seasons recipe for this soup calls for wild asparagus. Tiny asparagus, such as is sometimes cut at the very beginning of the season when it is thin, delicate in flavor, and more readily available, has been substituted.

The Four Seasons

Soup of the season—at the Four Seasons, a spring offering, or, soup of a special cuisine, at Tony's, the foods of Italy-each has its own devotees.

Caponata alla Siciliana

YIELD: 8 servings

INGREDIENTS

Eggplant, Medium-sized	2
Olive Oil	1/2 cup
Onions, sliced	2
Tomatoes, strained	1 No. 2 can
Diced Celery	1 cup
Capers, washed	2 ounces
Sugar	2 tablespoons
Wine Vinegar	4 tablespoons
Salt	to taste
Pepper	to taste

Wash eggplant; dry with absorbent paper. Peel and dice into 1-inch cubes. Fry in very hot oil about 10 minutes, or until soft and slightly browned. Remove eggplant and put in large saucepan. Fry onions in same oil about 3 minutes; add more oil if necessary. When onions are golden brown, stir in tomatoes and celery; simmer about 15 minutes or until celery is tender. Add capers. Add this mixture to eggplant. Dissolve sugar in vinegar; season with salt and pepper to taste; heat slightly. Add to eggplant; cover and simmer about 20 minutes over very low heat. Stir occasionally to distribute flavor evenly. When done, place in bowl. Cool.

Tony's

Kidney Bean Chowder

YIELD: 25 gallons

INGREDIENTS

Dried Kidney Beans	25 pounds
Diced Onion	25 pounds
Celery, diced	8 stalks
Carrots, diced	12
Green Peppers, diced	10
Chopped Garlic	1 cup
Beef Base	1 pint
Condensed Tomato Soup	5 No. 5 cans
Bacon, diced	3 pounds
Ground Beef	10 pounds
Salt	to taste
Pepper	to taste

Place kidney beans in steam pot. Cover with water; soak 1/2 hour. Add onion and next 6 ingredients; simmer until beans are tender, about 2 hours. As beans cook, add water until total volume reaches 25 gallons of finished soup. At the last minute, saute bacon until crisp; add with drippings to soup. Saute ground beef; drain off excess fat; add meat to soup. Add salt and pepper to taste.

The Vineyards

Avocado a la Horcher's [Cocktail Sauce]

YIELD: Approximately 1 cup of sauce

INGREDIENTS

Wine Vinegar	2 tablespoons
Dry Mustard	1 tablespoon
Egg Yolks	2
Finely Chopped Celery	1 tablespoon
Horseradish	1 tablespoon
Chopped Chives and Parsley, mixed	1 tablespoon
Chopped Shallots	1 tablespoon
Salt	to taste
Pepper	to taste
Olive Oil	4 ounces
Brandy	2 ounces
Chili Sauce	2 ounces
Lemon, juice of	1/2
Avocados, sliced	2 to 3

Avocados at home are no competition for buttery ripe slices sauced with Ernie's full-bodied cocktail blend.

Mix first 7 ingredients together. Add salt and pepper to taste and beat well. Add olive oil and mix thoroughly. Stir in brandy, chili sauce, and lemon juice; mix thoroughly. Serve over buttery ripe avocado slices.

Ernie's

Jimmy's Famous Fish Chowder

YIELD: Approximately 2 quarts

"I prefer to be with our customers or to prepare something special for them in the kitchen," says Jimmy Doulos. *It could be the chowder for which the Harborside has long been famous.*

INGREDIENTS

Whole Haddock, 4 to 5 pounds	1
Water	1-1/2 quarts
Salt	1 tablespoon
Diced Potatoes	1-1/2 pounds
Salt Pork *or* Bacon, chopped	2 slices
Onion, Small, chopped	1
Flour	1 tablespoon
Light Cream, warmed	1 cup
Milk, warmed	1 cup

Clean haddock thoroughly. Cut into 3 pieces. Place in water. Add salt. Bring to boil, then simmer for 1 hour. Strain broth; cool. Remove bones and skin from fish. Set fish aside. Cook potatoes in fish broth until tender. Meanwhile, in shallow pan, braise salt pork for 5 minutes. Add onion; cook for 5 minutes. Strain; save fat. Add flour to fat in pan, braise slowly, stirring with wire whip. Stir in cream and milk. Combine all ingredients with fish and potatoes. Heat, but *do not boil.*

Jimmy's Harborside

Canadian Cheese Soup

YIELD: 1-1/2 gallons

INGREDIENTS

Green Peppers	3
Carrots	3
Celery Stalks	3
Onion	1
Butter	4 tablespoons
Flour	1-1/2 cups
Milk, warmed	4 quarts
Chicken Broth	1 quart
American Cheese	3 cups
Cheddar Cheese	2 cups
Dark Beer *or* Ale	6 ounces

Dice and saute vegetables; set aside. Make roux of butter and flour. Blend milk into roux. Stir in chicken broth; heat. Add cheese; stir until melted and well blended. Stir in vegetables. Finish with beer or ale.

Michigan State University

Petite Marmite of Seafood

YIELD: 6 servings

INGREDIENTS

Ingredient	Amount
Onion, Medium-sized, chopped	1/2
Oil	1 ounce
Lobster, Small, cooked in shell	1
Shrimp, cooked in shells	12
Dover Sole or Other White Fish (include bones, head, skin), diced	3/4 pound
Celery, coarsely chopped	1 stalk
Leek, green part, chopped, white part, cut julienne	1
Fresh Mushrooms (separate caps and stems)	6
Bay Leaf	1
Thyme Sprig	1
Parsley Sprigs	2
Water	2 quarts
Dry White Wine	4 ounces
Lemon Juice	few drops
Chopped Fresh Dill	4 teaspoons
Oil	1 ounce
Celery, cut julienne	1 stalk
Carrot, Medium-sized, cut julienne	1
Salt	to taste
Pepper	to taste
Tomato, peeled, diced	1
Mussels, shelled, poached	24
Oysters, shelled, poached	6

When Don Smith was at Chateau Louise in the early 70s, he taught his midwestern clientele to clamor for seafood specialties. They still do and with good reason.

Prepare a fumet: Slowly cook onion in oil until transparent. Remove shells from lobster and shrimp. Set meat aside. Add shells, fish, celery, green leek, mushroom stems, bay leaf, thyme, and parsley to onion. Stir over low heat for 1 to 2 minutes. Add water, wine, lemon juice, and 2 teaspoons chopped dill. Cook gently 45 minutes. Strain through cheesecloth into saucepan.

Note: Make sure fumet does not boil too fast. It must look like a consomme—very clear.

Slowly cook white leek, celery, and carrots in oil for one minute. Add mushroom caps. Pour fumet over all. Add salt and pepper to taste. Cook gently for 15 minutes. Add tomato, 2 teaspoons dill, lobster meat, shrimp, mussels, and oysters; simmer for 2 minutes. Serve with croutons.

Chateau Louise

Cocktail Sauce for Crabmeat

YIELD: 4 servings

INGREDIENTS

Mayonnaise	1 cup
Worcestershire Sauce	1 teaspoon
Tomato Paste	1 teaspoon
Catsup	1 teaspoon
Chopped Fresh Parsley	1 teaspoon
Cognac	1 ounce
Pepper, freshly ground	to taste
Fresh Tomato, Medium-sized, peeled, diced	1

Make a *thick* mayonnaise with peanut oil and red wine vinegar; omit sugar.   Incorporate into the mayonnaise, the worcestershire sauce and next 5 ingredients. Add the diced tomato just before serving over fresh crabmeat.

La Maisonette

Cream of Artichoke Soup with Crushed Hazelnuts

YIELD: 20 servings

INGREDIENTS

Artichokes	2 pounds
Chicken Stock	4 quarts
Hazelnuts	4 ounces
Rice Flour	8 ounces
Salt	to taste
Pepper	to taste
Heavy Cream	1 pint
Sherry	2 ounces

Remove all leaves and stems from fresh large artichokes. Clean and scoop artichokes, utilizing bottoms, or pedestals, only. Poach artichoke bottoms in water for one hour. Remove and place in chicken stock. Roast hazelnuts in oven at 250°F. until golden brown, approximately 10 minutes. Crush hazelnuts to a fine consistency. Place in chicken stock with artichoke bottoms. Simmer for 1/2 hour. Pass all ingredients through china cap. Thicken with rice flour. Simmer for 1/4 hour. Add salt and pepper to taste. Stir in heavy cream. Just before serving, stir in sherry.

Fournou's Ovens Restaurant, The Stanford Court Hotel

Appetizers and Soups listed on the Camelot luncheon menu.

APPETIZERS

Cantaloupe, Honey Dew, Cranshaw Melons . . . in season   Blue Points and Clams . . . in season

Crab Meat Cocktail   **$3.50**   Marinated Herring   **$1.75**   Shrimp Cocktail   **$3.50**

Tomato Juice   **.75**   Supreme of Fruit   **$2.00**   Fresh Orange Juice   **$1.00**

SOUPES (SOUP)

Soupes Dorroy — Soup of the King, Onion Soup Gratinee   Cup **$1.00**   Bowl **$1.25**

Potages Dyuers — Soup of the Day   Cup **.75**   Bowl **$1.00**

In season . . . Jellied Consomme, Jellied Madrilene   **$1.25**

Soup 'n Sandwich Special of the Day   **$2.95**

Quiche of Seafood with Curry

YIELD: 5 servings

INGREDIENTS

PASTRY

Flour	1-1/2 cups
Salt	pinch
Sugar	1/2 teaspoon
Firm Butter	1/2 cup
Cold Water	1-1/2 to 2 tablespoons

FILLING

Milk, warmed	1 cup
Heavy Cream, warmed	1/4 cup
Eggs, beaten	3
Salt	1/4 teaspoon
Pepper	pinch
Curry Powder	1/4 ounce
Shrimp, cooked, shelled, diced	7 ounces
Mussels, cooked	7 ounces
King Crab Meat	7 ounces
Mushrooms, Canned *or* Fresh, sliced, lightly cooked in butter	7 ounces

PASTRY

Sift flour, salt, and sugar into mixing bowl. Add butter cut in small pieces. Sprinkle with enough water to bind mixture to a firm but pliable dough. Turn dough onto floured board. With hand, press dough down and away a few times, then roll in a ball. Wrap in wet cloth. Let stand 1-1/2 hours in a cool place. Roll out dough and put into an 8-inch floured pan. Set an aluminum foil pan on it and weight down with a salad plate. Bake in oven at 400°F. for 10 minutes. Remove aluminum pan and weight.

FILLING

Stir warm milk and cream into beaten eggs. Add salt, pepper, and curry Powder. Put seafood and mushrooms into pastry shell. Strain custard over seafood. Bake in oven at 400°F. for about 40 minutes. Serve at once.

Note: This is a very tasty appetizer which can also be served as a main dish with a salad accompaniment.

Chateau Louise

Schuler's Swiss Onion Soup

YIELD: 12 servings

INGREDIENTS

Butter	1/2 cup
Thinly Sliced Onion	2 pounds
Paprika	1-1/2 teaspoons
Flour	3/4 cup
Vegetable Oil	1/2 cup
Beef Stock	1-1/2 quarts
Celery Salt	3/4 teaspoon
Salt	to taste
Pepper	to taste
Dark Beer	12 ounces
Bread (buttered, sprinkled with parmesan cheese and paprika, toasted)	12 slices
Mozzarella Cheese	12 slices

Melt butter; add onion; cook over low heat until tender. Add paprika. Make a roux by browning flour in vegetable oil. Pour beef stock into large pot; add roux, celery salt, salt, pepper, and onion mixture. Heat to boiling, stirring often. Reduce heat; simmer for 2 hours. Add beer. Pour soup into warmed ovenproof bowls. Float croutons on soup; top with mozzarella slices. Place under broiler until cheese is bubbly.

Win Schuler's Restaurant

Tony's Antipasto Salad

YIELD: 100 servings

Credit to the originator is included in the name of this dish which gets its spicy flavor from the marinated celery and cauliflower.

INGREDIENTS

Vinegar	4 ounces
Salad Oil	12 ounces
Salt	2 ounces
Garlic Powder	1/2 teaspoon
Oregano	1 teaspoon
Pepper	1/2 teaspoon
Celery, cut diagonally 4 inches long	15 pounds
Cauliflower Buds, Fresh or Frozen (thawed)	12 pounds, 8 ounces
Stuffed Olives	1 quart
American Cheese, cubed	3 pounds, 4 ounces
Egg, hard-cooked, quartered	25
Cucumber Pickle Slices, drained	1 No. 10 can
Tomato Wedges	5 pounds

Combine first 6 ingredients thoroughly. Pour over celery and cauli-flower; marinate overnight. Drain. On each lettuce-lined salad plate, place 2 pieces of celery, 2 to 3 cauliflower buds, 2 stuffed olives, 1 cube of cheese, a hard-cooked egg quarter, 2 pickle slices, and 1 tomato wedge.

Massachusetts General Hospital

Pasta Con Vongole

YIELD: 8 servings

INGREDIENTS

Littleneck Clams	3 dozen
Garlic Cloves, chopped	2
Olive Oil	1/4 cup
Chopped Parsley	1/4 cup
Pepper	dash
Pasta, cooked	1 pound

Steam the clams; put 8 to the side, keeping them warm. Save the clam broth.   Remove the remaining clams from the shells and chop. Saute garlic in olive oil but do not brown. Add parsley, pepper, and chopped clams. Mix with pasta. Add 4 cups of clam broth. Garnish with the reserved clams.

Tony's

Huitres a l'Echalote [Oysters in Shallot Butter]

YIELD: 4 servings

INGREDIENTS

Butter, softened	1/2 pound
Chopped Fresh Parsley	1 tablespoon
Fresh Shallots	3 ounces
White Wine	1/4 cup
Salt	to taste
Pepper, freshly ground	to taste
Oysters (preferably Long Island Bluepoints)	24

Combine first 4 ingredients. Season to taste. Open oysters, cut them free, and place in hollow halves of shells. Embed shells in rock salt on a tray. Place a spoonful of shallot butter on each oyster. Bake in oven at 350°F. for 5 minutes. Before serving, sprinkle oysters with bread crumbs. Glaze under salamander.

La Maisonette

Pineapple Appetizer — A Nut Tree Tradition

To prepare fresh pineapple Central American style as served at the Nut Tree, cut off top and bottom of a chilled, thoroughly ripe pineapple. Discard bottom. Now, working from bottom of fruit with a long, slender, sharp knife, cut around fruit inside shell, leaving a thin but firm wall. Push out the cylinder thus formed, and slice it. Put slices back into shell in their original order and position. If half-slices are wished, cut down through stack inside shell. Turn the filled shell upside down (so the sweeter bottom slices of fruit are at the top) and place spiky top alongside. Serve Marshmallow Sauce separately. (See recipe, p. 117.)

The Nut Tree

Cut

Cut

Cut around inside shell

Cut slices in half, in the shell

Slice cylinder of fruit

Replace in shell

Serve on tray,

with sauce

Bay Shrimp in Sour Cream with Mushrooms

YIELD: 1 serving

INGREDIENTS	
Bay Shrimp	2 ounces
Sour Cream	3 tablespoons
Horseradish	1 teaspoon
Cognac	dash
Mushrooms, cut julienne	1 to 2
Chopped Parsley	1 teaspoon

In a stainless steel mixing bowl, combine bay shrimp and sour cream.
Add horseradish, cognac, and julienne mushrooms.   Serve in fluted
white ramekin dish underlined with lettuce leaf.   Sprinkle with finely
chopped parsley.

Fournou's Ovens Restaurant, The Stanford Court Hotel

A porpoise presides over the appetizer table at Maile Terrace,
Kahala Hilton Hotel, Honolulu.

Breads

Lavosh

YIELD: 3 sheets

INGREDIENTS

Milk	1 cup
Eggs	2
Bread Flour	3 cups
Salt	1-1/2 teaspoons
Sugar	1-1/2 teaspoons
Shortening	1/4 cup
Poppy Seeds	as desired
Sesame Seeds	as desired

Work first 6 ingredients into a firm dough. Let stand for one hour. Divide dough into three equal parts. Roll out dough very thinly on floured surface. Sprinkle generously with poppy seeds and sesame seeds; roll again. Arrange on greased sheet pan. Place in oven at 425° to 450°F. Set a pan of hot water on shelf below bread for first 5 minutes of baking. Turn down heat to 300°F., remove pan of water, and bake for 15 minutes more.

The Kahala Hilton Hotel

Cheese Muffins

YIELD: 3 dozen

INGREDIENTS

Salt	2 teaspoons
Butter	3 ounces
Sugar	2-1/2 ounces
Shortening	3 ounces
Egg Yolks	1/2 cup
Yeast	2 ounces
Milk	2-1/2 cups
Bread Flour	1 pound, 11 ounces
Grated Cheddar Cheese	4 ounces

Blend first 4 ingredients together. Slowly add egg yolks, continuing to beat. Dissolve yeast in milk and add to egg mixture. Add flour and cheese; mix until a smooth dough is formed. Let rise until double in bulk. Spoon into greased muffin pans. Let rise again. Bake in oven at 400°F. for 25 to 30 minutes.

Michigan State University

Hot breads are a welcome sign of caring to students, especially at universities where the student population is so great one is apt to feel "lost in the crowd."

Pumpkin Bread

YIELD: 1 loaf

INGREDIENTS

Sugar	1-1/2 cups
Salad Oil	1/2 cup
Eggs	2
Pumpkin	1 cup
Flour	1-1/4 cups
Raisins	1/2 cup
Nutmeg	1/2 teaspoon
Cinnamon	1/2 teaspoon
Ground Cloves	1/2 teaspoon
Allspice	1/2 teaspoon
Baking Powder	1/4 teaspoon
Soda	1 teaspoon
Water	1/3 cup
Chopped Nuts	1/2 cup

Combine all ingredients. Bake for 70 minutes in deck oven at 350°F. or 45 minutes in a convection oven at 350°F.

Southern Methodist University Food Service

Schuler's Homemade Bread

YIELD: 9 small loaves

INGREDIENTS

Active Dry Yeast	2 packages
Warm Water	1/2 cup
Scalded Milk	1-3/4 cups
Sugar	1/4 cup
Salt	1 teaspoon
Salad Oil	1/4 cup
Sifted All-Purpose Flour	6 to 7 cups
Eggs, beaten	2

Soften yeast in water. In large mixing bowl, combine milk, sugar, salt, and salad oil. Add 2 cups of the flour; beat well with electric mixer. Add softened yeast and eggs; beat well. Remove from mixer; add enough remaining flour to make a moderately stiff dough. Turn out on a lightly floured surface; knead until smooth and satiny, 8 to 10 minutes. Cover; let rest 10 minutes. Divide into 9 balls; mound each like a bun; fold over sides and tuck in ends. Place each in a greased 5-1/2-inch by 3-inch by 2-inch baking pan; butter tops generously. Cover; let double, about 45 minutes. Bake in oven at 350°F. for 30 minutes, or until done.

Win Schuler's

Win Schuler's
...a dining tradition

Oatmeal Muffins

YIELD: 15 to 20 dozen

INGREDIENTS
Rolled Oats	8 cups
Bread Crumbs	8 cups
Sifted Flour	4 pounds
Baking Powder	5-1/3 tablespoons
Soda	2-2/3 tablespoons
Salt	5-1/3 tablespoons
Eggs	16
Brown Sugar	8 cups
Shortening	3 pounds
Buttermilk	1 gallon

*Down home heartiness—
a cuisine basic at Stephenson's
Apple Farm Restaurant—
is nowhere better illustrated than
in these crisp, brown muffins.*

Combine the rolled oats and bread crumbs. Sift together the flour, baking powder, soda, and salt. Blend with the oats and crumbs. Put the eggs, brown sugar, and shortening in the mixer. Blend until creamy. Using No. 2 speed of mixer, add the oats and flour mixture alternately with the buttermilk. Mix just enough to moisten dry ingredients. Fill the muffin tins 2/3 full. Bake in oven at 400°F. until brown, 10 to 12 minutes.

Stephenson's Apple Farm Restaurant

Carrot Bread

YIELD: 3 small loaves

INGREDIENTS
Sifted All-Purpose Flour	2 cups
Sugar	2 cups
Soda	1 teaspoon
Salt	1 teaspoon
Cooking Oil	1 cup + 1 tablespoon
Eggs	4
Grated Carrots	3 cups
Cinnamon	1 teaspoon
Chopped Pecans	3/4 cup

Into large bowl, sift together flour, sugar, soda, and salt. Add oil, beating constantly. Add eggs, one at a time, while continuing to beat. Stir in carrots, cinnamon, and pecans. Turn batter into 3 greased 5-inch by 2-1/2-inch by 2-1/4-inch loaf pans. Bake in oven at 350°F. for 45 minutes.

Michigan State University

M.G.H. Homemade Graham Bread

YIELD: 12 1-pound, 1-ounce loaves

INGREDIENTS

Milk	2 quarts
Compressed Yeast	4 ounces
Molasses	6 ounces
Salt	2 ounces
Granulated Sugar	6 ounces
Lard *or* Vegetable Shortening	6 ounces
Whole Wheat Flour	2-1/2 pounds
Enriched Bread Flour	3-1/2 pounds
	to 4 pounds

Place all ingredients in a mixing bowl in the order listed. Mix at low speed for 15 minutes. Allow to rise until double in volume. Knead. Divide dough into 12 pieces. Let stand for 20 minutes. Shape dough into loaves. Proof until loaves double in volume. Bake in oven at 380°F. for 45 minutes.

Massachusetts General Hospital

Special Yeast Biscuits

YIELD: Approximately 300 biscuits

INGREDIENTS

Powdered Milk	6 cups
Lukewarm Water	1 gallon
Mashed Potatoes	4 cups
Shortening	4 cups
Sugar	4 cups
Dry Yeast	8 packages
Lukewarm Water	1 cup
Flour	14 pounds
Salt	4 teaspoons
Soda	4 teaspoons
Baking Powder	8 teaspoons

Dissolve powdered milk in 1 gallon of lukewarm water. Add potatoes, shortening, and sugar and blend. Dissolve the dry yeast in 1 cup luke-warm water, then add to the milk mixture. Stir in just enough flour to make a soft sponge. Let stand in a warm place for 1 hour or until double in bulk. After one hour, punch down, then stir in salt, soda, and baking powder. Add remaining flour. Knead on mixer (No. 1 speed) until dough is very stiff. Place in a greased 12-inch by 20-inch by 6-inch pan. Grease top of dough; cover with cloth. Let stand in refrigerator at least 5 hours. Shape into rolls. Let rise until double in bulk. Bake in oven at 375°F. until golden brown, for 10 to 12 minutes.

Stephenson's Apple Farm Restaurant

Apricot-Orange Bread

YIELD: 12 loaves

INGREDIENTS

Dried Apricots	1 pound, 8 ounces
Raisins	2 pounds
Oranges	1 pound
Granulated Sugar	5 pounds, 4 ounces
Margarine	10 ounces
Salt	1-1/2 ounces
Eggs	3 cups
Milk	2 quarts, 1/2 cup
Cake Flour	7 pounds, 8 ounces
Baking Powder	4-1/2 ounces

Unusual breads are made "from scratch" at MGH and patients and cafeteria patrons alike look forward to their favorites.

Soak apricots and raisins for one hour in enough hot water to cover them. Drain well. Grind whole, unpeeled oranges in a meat grinder, using medium blade. Lightly grease 12 loaf pans (9 inch by 4-1/2 inch by 3 inch); dust lightly with flour. In mixer, beat sugar, margarine, and salt until well blended. Add eggs slowly while continuing to beat. Fold in the ground oranges and the drained apricots and raisins. Add 2/3 of the milk and mix slightly. Scrape sides of the bowl. Add flour and baking powder. Mix at low speed until flour is incorporated, then add remaining 1/3 of the milk. Mix to an even consistency. (Do not overmix.) Fill loaf pans 2/3 full of batter. Bake in oven at 350°F. until done.

Massachusetts General Hospital

Crisp, freshly baked, crescent-shaped rolls are an attractive part of the food display selected to show the highlights of the cuisine available in the Grand Ballroom at The Brown Palace.

Bishop's Bread

YIELD: 1 loaf (16 servings)

INGREDIENTS

Brown Sugar	1 pound, 7 ounces
Shortening	7 ounces
All-Purpose Flour	1 pound, 3 ounces
Cinnamon	2 teaspoons
Salt	1 teaspoon
All-Purpose Flour	6 ounces
Baking Powder	1-1/4 teaspoons
Baking Soda	1 teaspoon
Buttermilk	3-3/4 cups
Eggs	2

Cream sugar and shortening. Mix in next 3 ingredients. Reserve 1 cup of mixture for topping. Sift 6 ounces all-purpose flour with next 2 ingredients; add sugar mixture. Combine eggs and milk. Stir into flour mixture until dry ingredients are moistened. Pour mixture into 12-inch by 10-inch by 2-inch pan. Top with flour and sugar mixture. Bake in oven at 375°F. for 30 minutes or until center springs back from a light touch.

Michael Reese Hospital and Medical Center

Squares of Bishop's Bread featured in a midwestern hospital are as popular as the hot, puffy popovers being placed in the heated roll server at Anthony's Pier 4, Boston.

Salads

Caesar Salad

YIELD: 4 servings

INGREDIENTS

Anchovies	8
Garlic, finely chopped	1 clove
Dry Mustard	1/2 teaspoon
Lemon, juice of	1
Worcestershire Sauce	8 drops
Olive Oil	1/4 cup
Red Wine Vinegar	2 tablespoons
Egg, coddled	1
Salt	to taste
Pepper, freshly ground	to taste
Romaine, chilled	1 head
Bibb Lettuce, chilled	2 heads
Parmesan Cheese	1/2 cup
Croutons	1/2 cup

Blend first 5 ingredients together to paste-like consistency. Slowly blend oil into this paste, then the vinegar. Stir in egg; add salt and pepper to taste. Pour this dressing over the chilled greens; toss lightly. Sprinkle greens with cheese; toss lightly. Add croutons and toss lightly again.

Tony's

Tony's Spinach Salad

YIELD: 4 servings

INGREDIENTS

Fresh Spinach Leaves	10 ounces
Ripe Avocados	2
Salt	to taste
Pepper	to taste
Olive Oil and Wine Vinegar Dressing	1/4 cup
Roquefort Cheese, crumbled	4 ounces

This not-often-encountered combination of ingredients is a favorite with patrons of St. Louis' leading Italian dinner house.

Trim ends from spinach leaves; wash well and dry. Peel and slice avocados; mix with spinach in salad bowl. Season with salt and pepper. Add dressing, toss gently. Add cheese and toss gently again.

Tony's

Korean Spinach Salad

YIELD: 24 servings

The adventurous approach to food among college students is illustrated by these two popular salads featured at MSU. Far Eastern foods have a sizable following.

INGREDIENTS

Fresh Spinach, cleaned, drained	4 12-ounce bags
Bean Sprouts, drained	1 cup
Sliced Water Chestnuts	1 cup
Eggs, hard-cooked, grated	3
Crisp Bacon, crumbled	5 strips
Salad Oil	1 cup
Vinegar	1/4 cup
Worcestershire Sauce	1 tablespoon
Brown Sugar—*DO NOT PACK DOWN*	1/3 cup
Catsup	1/3 cup
Diced Onion	1 cup
Red Wine	1 tablespoon

Combine spinach and next 4 ingredients. Blend salad oil and remaining ingredients in blender. Pour desired amount over spinach mixture; toss. Place in salad bowl and serve.

Michigan State University

Kellogg Center Gourmet Salad

YIELD: 16 servings

At MSU's Kellogg Center which is the headquarters for many educational meetings, attended by people interested in light luncheons, this salad is a special favorite.

INGREDIENTS

Lettuce	5 heads
Fresh Spinach, washed, trimmed	1 pound
Bleu Cheese, crumbled	1 pound
Parmesan Cheese	1 pound
Croutons	2 cups
Eggs, hard-cooked, finely chopped	4
Italian Dressing	1 cup
Lettuce Cups	16
Pepper Rings	16
Stuffed Green Olives	16
Radish Roses	16
Parsley Sprigs	16
Tomato Wedges	32

Combine bite-sized chunks of lettuce, spinach, bleu cheese, parmesan cheese, croutons, and eggs. Add dressing just before service and toss. Line individual salad bowls with lettuce cups. Spoon dressed salad greens into bowls. Garnish each with one pepper ring and olive (top center), radish rose, parsley sprig (next to radish) and two tomato wedges per bowl.

Michigan State University

Chicken Salad

YIELD: 6 servings

INGREDIENTS

English Dry Mustard	1 teaspoon
Mayonnaise	1-1/2 cups
Cooked, Cubed Chicken *or* Turkey* Breast	3 cups
Diced Celery	1-1/2 cups
Halved White Grapes	1 cup
Crisp, Salted Almonds	1/2 cup
Salt	to taste
Pepper	to taste
Lettuce, chilled	as needed
Tomatoes, peeled, quartered	18 quarters
Eggs, hard-cooked, quartered	18 quarters
Parsley	to garnish

*To get the best results, place chicken breast in soup kettle on range and cover with water. Add 2 to 4 stalks each (depending upon the size of the breast) of celery and carrots, 1 medium-large onion, 1 bay leaf, and a pinch of salt. When tender, cool chicken quickly in the stock. The meat will then be nice and moist. The stock can be used for soup, consomme, etc.

Blend mustard and mayonnaise thoroughly. Mix gently with chicken, celery, grapes, and almonds. Season to taste with salt and pepper. Serve on chilled lettuce-lined salad plates, garnished with tomato and egg quarters and parsley.

Camelot

Wilted Spinach and Bacon Salad

YIELD: 4 servings

INGREDIENTS

Fresh Spinach	10 ounces
Wine Vinegar	1 ounce
Olive Oil	3 ounces
French Mustard	1 teaspoon
Salt	pinch
Pepper	pinch
Sugar	pinch
Bacon, cut 1-1/2-inch squares	6 slices

Wash and clean spinach in cold water. Dry; chill to crisp. Thoroughly combine vinegar and next 5 ingredients. Saute bacon until crisp and brown. Pour off excess fat from pan, and drain bacon. Just before serving, warm salad dressing with bacon. Pour over the chilled fresh spinach and serve immediately.

The Four Seasons

Italian Salad

YIELD: 1 serving

INGREDIENTS

Red Wine Vinegar	1 cup
Salad Oil	3 cups
Salt	4 teaspoons
Sugar	to taste
Black Pepper	to taste
Garlic Powder	to taste
Fresh Mushrooms, sliced	1-1/2 ounces
Canned Artichoke Hearts, quartered	2
Head Lettuce, chopped	3 ounces
Titi Shrimp	1-1/2 ounces
Turkey, cut julienne	1-1/4 ounces
Endive, chopped	1 ounce
Escarole, chopped	1 ounce
Romaine, chopped	1 ounce
Lettuce Cup	1
Purple Onion Rings	3
Cherry Tomatoes, halved	2
Black Olives	2

Combine first 6 ingredients. Marinate mushrooms and artichoke hearts in this oil and vinegar dressing. Toss together the head lettuce, shrimp, turkey, endive, escarole, and romaine. Line salad bowl with lettuce cup and place salad mixture in it. Top with drained marinated mushrooms and artichoke hearts. Garnish with onion rings, cherry tomatoes, and olives. Just before serving, spoon 2 ounces dressing over all.

Win Schuler's

Raw Mushrooms, Malabar Dressing

YIELD: Approximately 6 servings

INGREDIENTS

Onion, Medium-sized, finely diced	1
Diced Celery	1 cup
Diced Red Radishes	1/4 cup
Minced Parsley	1 tablespoon
Minced Truffle	1 tablespoon
Lemon Juice	2 tablespoons
Olive Oil	6 tablespoons
Cracked Malabar Pepper	1 teaspoon
Coarse Salt	2 teaspoons
Mushrooms, Medium-sized, thinly sliced	18 to 24
Boston Lettuce Leaves	as needed

Combine first 9 ingredients in a bowl. Toss well and let stand 5 minutes. Add mushrooms and toss lightly. Serve on bed of lettuce leaves. *Note:* This salad is prepared tableside at The Four Seasons.

The Four Seasons

On The Lighter Side

Country Salad Plate
Chunky chicken salad with almonds and celery, served on a bed of lettuce. Accompanied by a wedge of molded gelatin salad and frosted grapes 2.95

Gourmet Salad
*A large bowl of crisp greens combined with crabmeat, tiny shrimp and grated Swiss cheese.
A special Schuler dressing 3.10*

Schuler's Slim'n Trim
Choice ground steak cooked as you like it, served with cottage cheese and fresh fruit 2.95

Schuler's spotlights his salad selections.

Zucchini and Hearts of Palm Salad

YIELD: 6 servings

INGREDIENTS
Hearts of Palm	12
Bibb Lettuce Leaves	6
Zucchini	1

Split hearts of palm lengthwise. Arrange in row on individual salad plates; place a lettuce leaf at one end. Cut zucchini into thin slices and insert between hearts of palm halves. Serve with french dressing.
Note: Hearts of palm are a delicate vegetable which come to us in cans from Brazil or from Florida where the state tree, Sabal Palmetto, is the source. The hearts make fine salads. They are used also in many cooked dishes, particularly in **Brazil**.

The Four Seasons

Sunset Salad

YIELD: 3 to 4 servings

INGREDIENTS
Cabbage, sliced julienne	1/2 head
Lettuce, sliced julienne	1/2 head
Tongue, sliced julienne	5 thin slices
Chicken Breast, sliced julienne	1
Chicken Thighs, sliced julienne	2

Combine ingredients and serve with choice of dressing.

The 21 Club

Marshmallow Sauce*

YIELD: Approximately 3 cups

INGREDIENTS
Sugar	1 cup
Corn Syrup	2/3 cup
Hot Water	1/2 cup
Egg Whites	2
Salt	dash
Vanilla	1/4 teaspoon
Mayonnaise	1/4 cup
Grated Orange Rind	1 tablespoon

Combine sugar, corn syrup, and hot water. Heat, stirring, until sugar dissolves. Boil without stirring to firm ball stage (244°F. to 248°F. on candy thermometer; 248°F. in humid weather). Beat egg whites until stiff. Slowly add hot syrup, beating at high speed until thick and fluffy. Add salt and vanilla. Gently fold in mayonnaise and orange rind.
Note: If thicker than desired, fold in 1 or 2 tablespoons more mayonnaise or 1 or 2 teaspoons water.
*Delicious with Fresh Fruit Salads.

The Nut Tree

Polynesian Seafood Salad

YIELD: 6 servings

INGREDIENTS

Crabmeat	1 cup
Shrimp	1 cup
Finely Chopped Onion	1/4 cup
Sliced Celery	1 cup
Sliced Water Chestnuts	1/2 cup
Cubed Pineapple Slices	4
Pine Nuts	1/2 cup
Currants	2 tablespoons
Chutney	1/4 cup
Salt	to taste
DRESSING	
Mayonnaise	1 cup
Coconut Milk, Frozen, thawed	1/4 cup
Sour Cream	1/4 cup
Curry Powder	2 teaspoons

Mix first 10 ingredients thoroughly. Chill. Blend mayonnaise and next 3 ingredients. Arrange chilled seafood salad mixture on salad greens. Serve with the mayonnaise dressing.

Marie Marinkovich

Spinach Salad

YIELD: 4 servings

INGREDIENTS

Fresh Horenso Spinach	2 bunches
Olive Oil	1 cup
Fresh Lemon Juice	1/2 cup
Salt	to taste
Pepper	to taste
Bacon, crisply fried, crumbled	2 slices
Egg White, hard-cooked, chopped	1

Wash and trim spinach well. Dry thoroughly; chill. In a salad bowl mix olive oil, lemon juice, salt, and pepper. Add spinach and crumbled bacon; toss gently. Sprinkle with chopped egg white.

The Kahala Hilton Hotel

A specialty among salad listings in the Kahala Hilton's Maile Restaurant menu shown below.

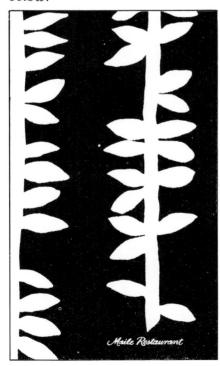

V.I.P. Salad

YIELD: 8 servings

INGREDIENTS

Lettuce	2 small heads
Romaine	10 leaves
Cauliflower, separated into small flowerets about 3/4 inch in diameter	2 cups
Avocado, peeled, diced	1
Tomatoes, Medium-sized, peeled, quartered	4
Blanched, Sliced Almonds, roasted	1 cup

Tear and mix salad greens in salad bowl rubbed with garlic. Add cauliflower and avocado. Mix. Place in individual salad bowls. Sprinkle 1 ounce almonds over top and garnish with 2 quarters of tomatoes. Serve with V.I.P. Dressing on the side.

V. I. P. Dressing

YIELD: 10 ounces

INGREDIENTS

Garlic Cloves	2
Salt	2 teaspoons
Sugar	1/2 teaspoon
Pepper	1/2 teaspoon
Celery Seed	1/4 teaspoon
Paprika	1/8 teaspoon
Dry Mustard	1-1/2 teaspoons
Lemon Juice	1/4 cup
Salad Oil	3/4 cup

Chop garlic very fine with salt. Add dry ingredients to garlic and salt mixture. Mix. Slowly add lemon juice and oil, stirring constantly. Chill and shake well before serving. Recipe can be doubled, if desired.

Michael Reese Hospital and Medical Center

Special dishes make patients and personnel feel special: VIP Salad fits the category well. Other gestures that meet specific patient needs at this hospital are the Rosh Hashanah luncheon and Yom Kippur menus. These items are offered as alternates to items on the regular menu. The Rosh Hashanah luncheon includes: APPLE SLICES dipped in a bowl of HONEY ROAST CHICKEN LIMA BEAN TZIMMES CHALLE ROLL SPONGE CAKE

Apple Farm Waldorf Slaw

YIELD: 100 to 120 servings

"Salads are truly American, that is as we know them today. Europe, Asia and the rest of the world cannot take away from America the production and perfection of the salad. So . . . we claim for America the credit of assembling, blending and bringing to perfection this health-giving item, the salad." Arnold Shircliffe, The Edgewater Beach Salad Book (out of print).

INGREDIENTS

Cabbage, finely shredded	20 pounds
Grated Carrots	2-1/2 cups
Cubed (1/2 inch) Red Apples	2-1/2 quarts
Seedless Raisins, plumped in hot water, cooled	2-1/2 cups
Pineapple Tidbits	5 cups
Diced (1/2 inch) Celery	5 cups
Chopped English Walnuts	2-1/2 cups
Salad Dressing	2-1/2 quarts
Lemon Juice	1-1/4 cups
Orange Juice	1-1/4 cups
Grated Orange Rind	1/2 cup
Sugar	2/3 cup
Salt	5 tablespoons
Pepper	2 teaspoons
Paprika	2 teaspoons
Heavy Cream	5 cups

Mix first 7 ingredients together lightly. Using No. 1 speed, blend salad dressing, juices, rind, sugar, and seasonings in mixer. Whip the heavy cream, then fold into salad dressing mixture. Blend dressing with slaw just before serving.

Stephenson's Apple Farm Restaurant

Princess Salad

YIELD: 1 salad

INGREDIENTS

Lettuce Cup, Medium	1
Tomato Slice, 1/2 inch thick	1
White Asparagus Spears, Medium to Large	2
Pimiento Strips, 1-1/2 inch by 1/4 inch	2
Green Pepper Strip, 2 inch by 1/4 inch (cut across the pepper)	1

In the lettuce cup, place the slice of tomato. Arrange the asparagus spears on the tomato. Crisscross the pimiento across the center of the spears and then arch the green pepper over the center of the pimiento cross. Serve with Vinegar and Oil Dressing.

Michael Reese Hospital and Medical Center

Perfect Pear Salad

YIELD: 12 servings

INGREDIENTS

Ripe Pears	12
Roquefort Cheese	10 ounces
Cream Cheese	5 ounces
Butter Lettuce Leaves	as needed
Tarragon Vinegar	2/3 cup
Salad Oil	2 cups
Chili Sauce	1/2 cup
Chopped Watercress	1 cup
Salt	1 teaspoon
Sugar	3 teaspoons
White Pepper	to taste

Scoop out blossom end and core of pears with corer. Peel and fill with blended roquefort and cream cheese. Arrange on lettuce-lined salad plates. Serve with dressing made by blending vinegar with next 6 ingredients.

Marie Marinkovich

Raspberry Tang Salad

YIELD: 50 to 60 servings

INGREDIENTS

Gelatin, Raspberry Flavor	1 package
Boiling Water	5 cups
Cottage Cheese	4 cups
Salad Dressing	2 cups
Crushed Pineapple	6 cups
Diced Bananas	2 cups
Shredded Coconut	2 cups
Chopped Pecan Meats	3 cups
Whipped Cream OR	
Whipped Topping	3 cups

This mold of shimmering raspberry gelatin blended with cottage cheese, fruit, and crunchy nuts may be chosen as a salad or a dessert.

Dissolve gelatin in boiling water and set aside to cool. Soften the cottage cheese with the salad dressing, mixing well so the mixture will be smooth. When the gelatin mixture begins to congeal, whip until very light. Add cheese mixture. Fold in rest of ingredients. Spoon into individual molds and chill until firm.

Purdue University

Sweetheart Molded Salad

YIELD: 48 servings

Molded salads add color and interest to salad displays and can also do double menu duty— providing either a salad or dessert course. These two colorful versions can be cut in various dimensions or can be individually molded.

INGREDIENTS

Pineapple, Crushed	1 No. 10 can
Gelatine, Unflavored	1/2 cup
Cold Water	2 cups
Hot Water	1 quart
Cold Pineapple Juice and Water to equal	1 quart
Granulated Sugar	1 pound, 8 ounces
Lemon Juice	1 cup
Salt	1/2 teaspoon
Cream Cheese	1 pound
Maraschino Cherry Juice	2 cups
Maraschino Cherries, chopped	2 cups
Whipped Topping	1 quart

Drain pineapple well, saving juice. Soak gelatine in cold water. Dissolve in hot water. Add cold pineapple juice and water, sugar, lemon juice, and salt. Stir thoroughly. Whip cream cheese, gradually adding all the cherry juice. Mix thoroughly with the gelatine mixture. Add drained pineapple and chopped cherries. Whip topping. Blend with pineapple mixture. Scale 4-1/2 quarts into each of 2 baking pans. Refrigerate until firm.

Michigan State University

Heavenly Fruit Mold

YIELD: 8 servings

INGREDIENTS

Gelatin, Lemon Flavor	6 ounces
Boiling Water	8 ounces
Crushed Ice	8 ounces
Cream Cheese	2 ounces
Mayonnaise	2 teaspoons
Chopped Maraschino Cherries	1/8 cup
Fruit Cocktail	3/4 cup

Dissolve gelatin in boiling water. Add crushed ice and stir until melted. Mix cream cheese and mayonnaise well; add cherries and fruit cocktail; stir to blend. Add this mixture to gelatin and blend. Pour into 4-ounce molds. Refrigerate and allow to congeal. To serve, arrange curly endive or lettuce cup on salad plate. Dip mold in warm water and then remove from mold by tapping bottom. Garnish each with 1/2 fresh strawberry or 1/2 maraschino cherry.

Michael Reese Hospital and Medical Center

Lime-Pear Sea Foam Salad

YIELD: 100 servings

INGREDIENTS
Pears	1-1/2 No. 10 cans
Gelatin, Lime Flavor	3 pounds, 8 ounces
Cream Cheese	2 pounds
Whipped Topping Base	1-1/4 quarts liquid

Drain the juice from canned pears. Reserve the pears. Add enough water to the juice to make 3-1/4 quarts. Heat this mixture. Dissolve the lime flavor gelatin in the warm juice and water. Cool. Puree the pears and blend with cream cheese in mixer until smooth. Add the pear-cream cheese mixture to the gelatin mixture. Beat whipped topping base without adding water to it. Fold into pear-cheese gelatin mixture. Pour into 2 pans (20 inch by 12 inch by 2-1/2 inch), or individual molds. Chill. Serve on lettuce.

Massachusetts General Hospital

Vinaigrette Dressing for Hearts of Palm Salad

YIELD: 1 pint (6 to 8 servings)

INGREDIENTS
Pickle, chopped	1 large
Green Onions, finely chopped	1/2 bunch
Pimiento, coarsely chopped	1
Paprika	3/4 teaspoon
Oil	3 ounces
White Vinegar	1 cup

Mix all ingredients together.
Note: Arrange 8 quarters of hearts of palm on lettuce-lined plates. Spoon dressing over top.

Commander's Palace

Commander's Palace also suggests these:
ENTREE SALADS
Crabmeat and Shrimp Salad, Louis Dressing . . . 4.75
Backfin lump crabmeat and shrimp on greens with devilled egg and tomato.
Avocado Filled with Shrimp Remoulade 3.50
A Commander's Specialty
Chef Salad. 3.50
Demi-julienne of ham, Swiss cheese and chicken with tomato and devilled egg on greens. Choice of dressing.
Chicken Salad Almond. 3.25
Jill Jackson Salad. 3.00
Wilted greens, crumbled Bleu cheese, bacon, hard-cooked egg and a sharp dressing.

Brown Palace Club Dressing

YIELD: 2 quarts

INGREDIENTS
Vinegar	1 pint
Chopped Garlic	1/4 teaspoon
Dry Mustard	1/4 teaspoon
Liquid Hot Pepper Seasoning	1/4 teaspoon
Worcestershire Sauce	1/4 cup
Salt	to taste
Pepper	to taste
Salad Oil	1-1/2 quarts

Combine first 7 ingredients. Add oil, a small amount at a time, beating with a wire whip until mixture thickens. Chill and serve.

The Brown Palace Hotel

Celery Seed Dressing

YIELD: 4 to 6 servings

INGREDIENTS

Vinegar	2 ounces
Celery Seed	1 teaspoon
French Mustard	1 teaspoon
Garlic Salt *or* Powder	pinch
Egg, beaten	2 tablespoons
Oil	6 ounces
Salt	to taste
Pepper	to taste
Worcestershire Sauce	to taste

Combine first 5 ingredients thoroughly. Blend in oil slowly. Season to taste with salt, pepper, and worcestershire sauce.

The Kahala Hilton Hotel

Lorenzo Dressing

"Stir the mixture (Lorenzo Dressing) in a bowl with a small lump of ice until thoroughly chilled, then serve," August C. Dietrich, maitre d'hotel, The Blackhawk, Chicago, as quoted in The Edgewater Beach Hotel Salad Book, Arnold Shircliffe, 1928 (out of print).

YIELD: 1 cup

INGREDIENTS

Chili Sauce	2 tablespoons
Chopped Watercress	1/2 cup
French Dressing	1/2 cup

Combine chili sauce and chopped watercress. Add french dressing. Blend well with spoon.

The 21 Club

Hot Bacon Dressing

YIELD: 4 servings

INGREDIENTS

Bacon Ends, diced	1/2 pound
White Onion, Large, diced	1
White Vinegar	1/2 cup
Wine Vinegar	1/2 cup
Salt	1 teaspoon
Black Pepper, coarsely ground	1/2 teaspoon
Sugar	1 to 2 teaspoons
Cornstarch	3 tablespoons
Consomme	1 cup

Saute bacon until crisp. Drain and set aside. Saute onion in bacon drippings until clear. Add vinegars, salt, pepper, and sugar. Dissolve cornstarch in consomme and add. Heat, stirring, until slightly thickened. Pour hot over well washed fresh spinach; toss. Garnish with crisp bacon and serve.

Karl Ratzsch's

Thousand Island Dressing

YIELD: Approximately 2-1/4 gallons

INGREDIENTS

Salad Mustard	1 cup
Salad Dressing	1 gallon
Chili Sauce	5 cups
Condensed Milk	5 cups
Lemon Juice	1 cup
Wine Vinegar	2 cups
Simple Syrup	1 cup
Minced Onion	1/2 cup
Minced Green Pepper	1/2 cup
Minced Celery	2 cups
Minced Green Olives	2 cups
Eggs, hard-cooked, minced	8
Seasoning Salt	2 tablespoons
Paprika	2 teaspoons
Monosodium Glutamate	2 teaspoons

Blend first 4 ingredients together in mixing bowl. Combine lemon juice, vinegar, and syrup; add to salad dressing mixture. Add minced vegetables, eggs, and seasonings. Blend thoroughly, using No. 2 speed of mixer. Serve 2 ounces dressing for each salad.

Stephenson's Apple Farm Restaurant

French Dressing

YIELD: 1 quart

INGREDIENTS

Egg Yolk	1
Worcestershire Sauce	dash
Vinegar	11 ounces
Paprika	pinch
Salt	1 teaspoon
Pepper	1 teaspoon
English Mustard	1/2 teaspoon
Olive Oil	22 ounces

Beat together egg yolk, worcestershire sauce, and 2 to 3 ounces vinegar. Continuing to beat, add paprika, salt, pepper, mustard, and an additional 2 ounces vinegar. Beating constantly, slowly add entire amount of olive oil until a uniform consistency is reached. Beat in remaining vinegar. Store in cool place.

The 21 Club

COUNTRY HARVEST BUFFET

In the summertime Stephenson's Apple Farm Restaurant patrons may fill their plates from the Country Harvest Buffet and dine under the trees of an apple orchard. Buffet foods, below are easily carried the few steps to the orchards.

APPETIZER TABLE
Brisling Sardines
Fillet of Sardine
Smoked Oysters
Cheese Tray
Cold Cuts
Cold Baked Whitefish (Haddock)
Tiny Smoked Sausages

SALAD TABLE
Tiny Whole Spiced Beets
Marinated Green Beans
Corn Relish
Sweet Sour Cucumber & Onion Slices
Ripe Sliced Tomatoes
Stuffed Celery Sticks
Green Onion & Radish Tray
Deviled Eggs
Creamed Cottage Cheese
Potato Salad
Garden Salad
Marshmallow Salad
Jellied Cinnamon Apple Salad
Jellied Waldorf Salad

RELISHES
Stuffed Olives
Sweet Cherry Peppers
Snef Gerkins (Mustard Pickles)

VEGETABLE TABLE
Wax Beans & Ham
Creamed New Potatoes & Peas
Green Rice
Country Style Corn in Cream
Baked Cinnamon Apples

MEAT STEAM TABLE
Hickory Smoked Brisket of Beef
Hickory Smoked Sliced Ham
Hickory Smoked BarBQ Ribs
Hickory Smoked BarBQ Chicken
Hickory Smoked BarBQ Gizzards
Hickory Smoked Weiners with
Creole Sauce

BREADS & MISCELLANEOUS
Hot Light Rolls
Muffins (variety of flavors, i.e. apple, banana, chocolate chip etc.)
Apple Butter

DESSERT TABLE
Fresh Fruit Bowl (center piece)
Old Fashioned Strawberry Shortcake
Fresh Apple or Cherry Cobbler
Tomato Cake
Caramel Pecan Pie
Butterscotch Whipped Cream Pie

Garnishes for Salads

Angelica
Beets, slices or julienne
Bon bons—marshmallow wrapped in coconut
Carrot curls or sticks
Celery curls, celery hearts
Cheese, American, Swiss—julienne, bar, sliced, shredded
Cheese balls—American, cottage, or cream—rolled in nuts, chopped parsley, chives, coconut or paprika
Cheese bars—rolled in nuts or chopped parsley
Coconut—plain or colored
Cucumber—slices or curls
Hard-cooked egg, sliced, deviled, riced
Fresh berries or fresh fruit
Green or red pepper, rings or strips
Jellies
Lemon slices or wedges
Melon balls, slices or wedges
Maraschino cherries, red or green
Nuts, whole or chopped
Olives, plain, stuffed, green or ripe
Orange curls or slices
Onion rings or scallions
Pineapple fans or fingers
Pickled fruit—pears, peaches, prunes, apricots, watermelon
Pickled fruit rind
Pickles, sweet, sour, dill, burr gherkins, fans, rounds
Pomegranate seeds
Radishes, plain, roses, or slices
Strawberries, whole with or without stem, sliced, or dipped in sugar
Stuffed prunes, apricots, dates, or plums
Sugared fresh grapes
Waffled fruit, vegetables, or cheese
Watercress, mint, parsley
Tomato, slices and wedges

Meat Entrees

Pampered Tenderloin of Beef

YIELD: 12 servings

INGREDIENTS

Beef Tenderloin	4 pounds
Salt	3 tablespoons
Pepper	1 teaspoon
Monosodium Glutamate	1 teaspoon
Burgundy	1-1/2 cups
Strong Beef Stock	1/2 cup
OR	
Beef Base	1 tablespoon
OR	
Bouillon Cubes	2
Hot Water	1 cup
Cornstarch	1/4 cup
Mushrooms, sliced	1 pint
Mushroom Caps, Large	12
Butter, melted	1/4 cup

Skin and trim tenderloin and season with salt, pepper, and monosodium glutamate. Place meat in roasting pan and cook in oven at 400°F. for 8 to 10 minutes. Then remove from oven and pour burgundy over meat. Cover tightly and let stand in warm place 10 to 15 minutes. Drain juice from meat into saucepan. Add beef stock or beef base or bouillon cubes and water. Mix cornstarch with 1/2 cup burgundy and add to liquid. Boil until clear and slightly thickened. Saute sliced mushrooms and add to sauce. Place large mushroom caps in baking dish and brush with melted butter. Broil 5 to 6 minutes. Carve tenderloin into 12 servings. Butterfly each serving. Serve 1 ounce sauce over each portion. Garnish with whole mushroom cap.

Michigan State University

Meat eaters enjoy celebrating the 41st Anniversary Dinners featured by Charlie's Cafe Exceptionale just as student banqueters feel they are getting extra attention when Pampered Beef Tenderloin is the entree of the evening.

1934 Charlie's 41st Anniversary Dinners 1975

Monday: **GLAZED ROAST LOIN OF PORK**   Wednesday: **LAMB SHANK JARDINÈRE**
Tuesday: **BRAISED SHORT RIBS OF BEEF**   Thursday: **FROG LEGS Provencale**
Friday: **PEPPERED TENDERLOIN TIPS** with Green Peppers, Onions and Mushrooms . . . served with Pasta

✳
each entree includes
Choice of dinner salad   Potato or Vegetable du jour   **Charlie's** bread basket — butter

$6.95

Monday through Saturday: **Charlie's** HICKORY SMOKED BARBECUED RIBS — *entree includes above . . . $7.50*

Beef Stroganoff

YIELD: 10 to 12 servings

INGREDIENTS

Fillet of Beef Tenderloin	3 to 4 pounds
Butter	1 cup
Onions, Medium-sized	2
Sliced Mushrooms	2 cups
Butter	1 cup
Flour	3 tablespoons
Beef Consomme, hot	3 cups
Dijon Mustard	2 teaspoons
Sour Cream	2 cups
Parsley, chopped	for garnish
Diced Dill Pickles	1 cup

Cut beef into narrow strips about 2 inches long and 1/2 inch thick. Melt butter in saucepan until it is bubbling. Add the beef and raw onions and saute quickly without overcooking. Add sliced mushrooms. Set aside. Melt butter and add flour. Blend well and gradually add hot consomme. Stir constantly until the sauce is smooth and thickened. Stir in mustard. The last minute before serving, add sour cream to sauce; stir over low heat until the sauce comes to a boil. Blend in the meat mixture and heat slowly for 5 minutes before serving. Sprinkle with chopped parsley and add diced pickles for garnish.

Camelot

Beef Rouladen

YIELD: 4 rouladen

INGREDIENTS

Round Steak, thinly sliced	4 pieces
Dill Pickle, Large	1
Green Peppers, Medium-sized	2
Bacon Strips	2
Onions, Large	2
Bouillon Granules	3 tablespoons
Salt	to taste
Pepper	to taste
Monosodium Glutamate	to taste
Burgundy (optional)	1 cup

Sprinkle meat lightly with salt and pepper. In center of each piece of meat, place 1/4 dill pickle, 1 strip green pepper, 1/2 strip bacon, and large piece of onion. Roll up. Place seamside down in hot fat; brown on all sides. Add bouillon granules and rest of green pepper and onion, finely chopped. Simmer until meat is tender. Remove meat from pan and thicken gravy with flour or roux. Season gravy to taste with salt, pepper, and monosodium glutamate. If desired, add wine at this point. Place rouladen back in gravy and heat thoroughly.

Karl Ratzsch's

Hickory Smoked Brisket of Beef

YIELD: 40 to 50 2-ounce slices

INGREDIENTS

Boneless Beef Brisket	6 to 8 pounds
Hot Water	as needed
Salt	2 tablespoons
Pepper	2 tablespoons
All-Purpose Seasoning	2 tablespoons
Monosodium Glutamate	1 teaspoon
Basil	2 tablespoons
Horseradish Sauce*	as needed

*See recipe, p. 182

Place meat in 12-inch by 20-inch pan. Add hot water to cover (to 3/4 full).   Add remaining ingredients. Place in smoke oven at 275°F. for 3 to 4 hours, or until very tender. Chill in liquid overnight. Remove layer of grease. Slice meat in 2-ounce slices. Put back in pan on edge. Pour meat liquid over slices. Heat in smoke oven until very hot. Serve 4 slices per serving with Horseradish Sauce.

Stephenson's Apple Farm Restaurant

Boeuf a la Bourguignonne

YIELD: 16 servings

INGREDIENTS

Round Steak, cubed	4 pounds
Salt	as needed
Pepper	as needed
Oil	1/2 cup
Flour	1/2 cup
Onion, finely chopped	1
Parsley Sprig	1
Garlic Clove, finely chopped	1
Oil	2 tablespoons
Burgundy	2 cups
Tomato Puree	2 tablespoons
Bay Leaf	1/2
Thyme	pinch
Beef Stock	1 cup
Diced Beef Marrow	2 cups

The Fairmont

Sprinkle meat lightly with salt and pepper. Brown quickly in hot oil, sprinkling flour over meat as it browns. In a separate pot, cook onion, parsley, and garlic in 2 tablespoons oil until golden. Add burgundy and boil 2 minutes. Add meat, tomato puree, bay leaf, and thyme; stir. Pour in beef stock and additional wine if needed to cover meat. Simmer for 2 hours over low heat. In meantime, poach beef marrow in boiling water for 3 to 5 minutes; drain. When beef is almost cooked, add marrow.

Fairmont Hotel

London Broil

YIELD: 100 servings

INGREDIENTS
Flank Steak, 1-1/2 to 2 Pounds each	25 pounds
Vegetable Oil	1-1/4 quarts
Fresh Lemon Juice	1 cup
Garlic, finely chopped	1 ounce
Bay Leaves, crushed	6
Salt	1/4 cup
Pepper	1 tablespoon

Have butcher trim off excess membrane, fat, and silver skin from meat. Run through tenderizer. Put steak in stainless steel pan. Make a marinade by combining oil and next 3 ingredients. Pour over steak. Cover; refrigerate for 1 to 3 days, turning occasionally. Remove steak from marinade; sprinkle with mixture of salt and pepper. Broil on rack farthest from heat until medium-rare. *Do not overcook.* Slice very thin diagonally across the grain.

Arizona State University

Today, that well known combination, meat, potatoes, and gravy has been permanently replaced on most menus. Ethnic foods have the appeal of the unfamiliar, especially when encountered on hospital menus.

Cantonese Pepper Steak

YIELD: 6 servings

INGREDIENTS
Cube Steaks, cut 3 to the pound	6
Oil	3 tablespoons
Sliced Celery, diagonal cuts	1/2 cup
Diced Onion	1/2 cup
Chopped Green and Red Peppers, mixed, *or* Chopped Pimiento	1/4 cup
Sliced Mushrooms	1/4 cup
Bean Sprouts, drained	1 cup
Beef Stock*	2 cups
Soy Sauce	1 ounce
Bead Molasses	1/2 teaspoon
Garlic Powder	pinch
Worcestershire Sauce	1/2 teaspoon
Cornstarch	1 teaspoon
*or 3 bouillon cubes in 2 cups water.	

Brown steaks in oil in skillet. Place steaks in baking pan. Mix the vegetables and sprinkle half of them over the meat. Combine beef stock with next 5 ingredients; bring to a boil. Pour hot sauce over vegetables and meat. Bake, uncovered, in oven at 325°F. for 20 minutes. Add remaining vegetables. Cover; bake 5 more minutes. Serve at once with vegetables as top garniture.

Michael Reese Hospital and Medical Center

Karl Ratzsch's Sauerbraten

YIELD: 4 to 6 servings

INGREDIENTS

Rump *or* Chuck Roast	2-1/2 pounds
Marinade	
Water	3 cups
Vinegar	1 cup
Sugar	1 tablespoon
Onion, Small, minced	1
Celery, finely chopped	1 stalk
Salt	pinch
Mixed Spices	pinch
Gingersnaps, crushed	as needed

Place meat in marinade for four days. Turn daily. Remove meat to roasting pan; save marinade. Brown meat. Add marinade and roast until meat is tender, about 1-1/2 hours. Remove meat. Add gingersnaps to marinade to make a gravy of desired consistency. Serve with sliced meat.

Karl Ratzsch's

GERMAN SAUERBRATEN — Potato Dumpling . . . . Beef Roast in Spicy, Sweet Sour Gravy — Supremely Old World

Tournedos aux Echalotes

YIELD: 4 servings

INGREDIENTS

Finely Chopped Shallots	1/2 cup
Chablis	1-1/2 cups
Bay Leaf	1
Cayenne Pepper	pinch
Heavy Cream	2 cups
Tournedos of Beef, 4 Ounces each	8
Salt	as needed
Pepper	as needed
Butter	1 tablespoon
Oil	1 tablespoon
Chablis	1/2 cup
Butter (optional)	2 tablespoons

In a heavy saucepan, combine first 4 ingredients. Cook over high heat until reduced to 1/3 original volume. Add heavy cream. Cook to reduce again to 1/3 of volume or until sauce is thick enough to coat a spoon. Set sauce aside. Sprinkle tournedos with salt and pepper. In heavy saucepan, heat butter and oil. Saute tournedos golden brown on both sides to the degree of rareness desired. Remove tournedos to serving platter. Remove excess fat from pan. Add 1/2 cup chablis; reduce to 1/2 volume. Add cream sauce; bring to boil. (For a richer sauce add 2 tablespoons butter, stirring it into sauce bit by bit. Do not boil sauce.) Adjust seasoning. Pour cream sauce over tournedos. Decorate with glace de viande if desired. Serve at once.

La Maisonette

Beef, in a French version, that is a hard-to-resist menu offering.

Skewered Beef and Mushrooms

YIELD: 6 servings

INGREDIENTS

*Squares of marinated beef
broiled on skewers accompanied
by small white onion halves,
green pepper squares and
mushrooms broiled on separate
skewers (the mushrooms
broil only briefly) show to
advantage when served on hot,
cooked rice garnished with
a cherry tomato.*

Ingredient	Amount
Top Sirloin of Beef, cut 1/4 inch thick	1-1/2 pounds
Garlic Clove, mashed	1
Minced Onion	1 tablespoon
Steak Sauce	1-1/2 tablespoons
Worcestershire Sauce	1 teaspoon
Catsup	2/3 cup
Sherry	3 tablespoons
Salt	1/4 teaspoon
Pepper	dash
White Onions, Small, halved	9
Green Pepper	18 1-1/2- to 2-inch squares
Fresh Mushroom Caps	30 to 36
Bamboo *or* Metal Skewers	18

Several hours before serving, cut beef into 30 1-1/2-inch squares. Combine next 8 ingredients. Add meat; stir; let stand for at least one hour. Remove meat from sauce; string 5 pieces on each of 6 skewers. String 3 pieces of onion alternately with 3 green pepper squares on each of 6 additional skewers. String 5 or 6 mushrooms on each of the 6 remaining skewers. Broil skewers of meat and onion-green pepper at same time. When ready to turn, put mushrooms on to broil. Serve on hot cooked rice with cherry tomato garnish.

The Nut Tree

Don Roth's Roast Prime Ribs of Beef

Cover oven-prepared prime ribs (short rib, excess fat, and backbone removed) completely with damp rock salt. Place in oven at 500°F. for one hour, then reduce heat to 350°F. Roast for an additional 1-3/4 hours, or until done.

BLACKHAWK AU JUS FOR PRIME RIBS

The secret of a good au jus is to combine the natural juices of good quality beef with the flavors obtained from fresh vegetables such as celery, carrots, and onions. Only the highest grade ground pepper and salt should be added for seasoning—no other spices are needed.

Put beef roast in roasting pan, fat side up. Rub a little salt and pepper on both sides of the meat. Add vegetables and attach meat thermometer. Occasionally add a little water and baste the meat.

When roast is done, let it "set" at room temperature for 30 to 60 minutes, depending on the size. Cool the juice and skim off excess fat. Add a few drops of caramel to get a more attractive color.

If the roast is too small to yield a sufficient amount of juice, get some beef rib bones and a few veal bones from your butcher. Have him chop them into small pieces. Put in a separate roasting pan, add some vegetables, pepper, and salt; simmer for 2 or 2-1/2 hours, or until bones are dark brown. Pour off juice, remove most of the fat, and add to the juice obtained from the roast.

The Blackhawk

*roast prime ribs of beef

the beef that made the blackhawk famous. aged properly and roasted to perfection. be sure to pour on the au jus (natural juices) — NO preservatives here.

regular or english cut   **$8.95**

*Graded U.S. Prime

*cabernet sauvignon,
louis martini. top
american claret. #25*

Roast Peppered Rib Eye of Beef

YIELD: 8 to 10 servings

INGREDIENTS

Boneless Rib Eye of Beef	5 to 6 pounds
Pepper, coarsely cracked	1/2 cup
Ground Cardamom	1/2 teaspoon
Tomato Paste	1 tablespoon
Garlic Powder	1/2 teaspoon
Paprika	1 teaspoon
Soy Sauce	1 cup
Vinegar	3/4 cup
Water	1 cup

Trim fat from beef. Combine pepper and cardamom; rub all over beef and press into meat with heel of hand. Place in shallow baking dish. Mix together tomato paste, garlic powder, and paprika. Gradually add soy sauce, then vinegar. Pour soy mixture over meat. Refrigerate overnight. Spoon marinade over meat. Remove meat from marinade. Let stand at room temperature 1 hour. Wrap in foil; place in shallow pan. Roast in oven at 300°F. for 1-1/2 hours (medium-rare). Open foil, ladle out and reserve drippings. Brown roast, uncovered, at 350°F. while making gravy. To make gravy, strain drippings. Skim off excess fat. To 1 cup meat juices, add 1 cup water; bring to boiling. If desired, add a little marinade. Serve au jus or thicken by mixing 1-1/2 tablespoons cornstarch with 1/4 cup cold water.

Charlie's Cafe Exceptionale

*The recipe above is featured
once a week as a 41st
Anniversary Dinner at Charlie's
Cafe Exceptionale. Other
beef items, to be prepared at
tableside, and promoted
as especially for two are listed
on the menu as shown below.*

ESPECIALLY FOR TWO — AT TABLESIDE

STEAK DIANE

Sirloin steak butterflied and sautéed in butter with herbs and spices . . . then cooked in spicey sauce with Robert and Diable sauces.

$14.00 per person

Choice of dinner salad

BEEF WELLINGTON

Tenderloin of Beef roasted with herbs and spices . . . spread with pâté de foie gras . . . covered with puff pastry

$16.00 per person

each entree includes
Choice of potato or vegetable du jour

STEAK CARÊME

Tournedos of beef sautéed in butter and garlic with herbs and spices . . . then cooked in cream sauce . . . flavored with Amantillado Sherry

$16.00 per person

 Charlie's® bread basket and butter

Lasagne

YIELD: 40 servings

INGREDIENTS

Onion, chopped	12 ounces
Garlic Cloves, mashed	3-1/2
Olive Oil	3/4 cup plus 1 tablespoon
Ground Beef	1 pound, 11 ounces
Tomato Paste	1-1/2 cups
Sweet Basil	1/4 teaspoon
Tomatoes (Standard)	1 No. 10 can
Chopped Parsley	1/4 cup
Parmesan Cheese	1/2 cup
Salt	2-1/2 ounces
Pepper	2-1/4 teaspoons
Lasagne Noodles, cooked	2 pounds, 9 ounces
Mozzarella Cheese	1 pound, 10-1/2 ounces
Cottage Cheese	1 pound, 10-1/2 ounces
Parmesan Cheese	as needed

Saute onion and garlic in olive oil. Add beef; brown lightly. Add tomato paste and next 6 ingredients. Simmer at least 45 minutes. Cover bottom of 4-inch steam table pan with some of the sauce. Place 1/2 of noodles in pan. Cover with half the mozzarella, then half the cottage cheese and half the remaining sauce. Repeat with another layer of lasagne, cheeses, and sauce. Sprinkle parmesan cheese over all. Bake in oven at 350°F. for 30 to 45 minutes.

Washington State University

A Guide to the University's Food Service System

Residence Hall Food Service at Washington State
1974-75

Washington State University
Pullman, Washington   99163

Boeuf a la Deutsch [Beef and Kidney Stew]

YIELD: 6 servings

INGREDIENTS

Beef Tenderloin	2 pounds
Salt	as needed
Pepper	as needed
Clarified Butter	1/4 cup
Lamb Kidneys (tubes and membranes removed)	4
Chopped Shallots	2 tablespoons
Garlic Clove, chopped, crushed	1
Green Peppers, blanched, cut in 1-inch pieces	2
Mushrooms, sliced, cooked in butter	1 pound
Sherry	1/2 cup
Tomato Puree	1/3 cup
Madeira Sauce	1/3 cup
Lemon, juice of	1
Potatoes, Small, sliced, browned in butter	6

During World War II, one ingenious foodservice manager put pastry tops on individual portions of her Beef Steak and Kidney Stew, converting it into a Pie. She then inserted a foil funnel into each pie and had a teaspoon of brandy poured into the funnel just before the pies came out of the oven. Since rationing made variety meats a recurring requirement, the service of this dish had not originally excited much interest. However, customers were intrigued by the funnel and when, on inquiring, they learned that "That's where the cook pours the brandy into the pie," the sale was made.

Cut beef in slivers.   Season with salt and pepper.   Brown quickly in heated butter in skillet.   Remove meat to a heated platter.   Wash kidneys; sliver like the beef; season with salt and pepper.   Brown quickly in the heated butter, then remove from pan.   Brown shallots and garlic. Add green peppers and saute for 3 minutes.   Stir in mushrooms and sherry; bring to a boil; add tomato puree and the Madeira Sauce.   Simmer all together for several minutes.   Adjust seasoning.   Add beef and kidneys; heat to boiling. Sprinkle with lemon juice and fold in potatoes. Serve on a hot serving platter.

The Greenbrier

Pepper Steak

YIELD: 10 servings

INGREDIENTS

Peppercorns	1/3 cup
Beef Sirloin *or* Tenderloin, 1/2 inch thick	4 pounds
Salt	to taste
Oil	1/3 cup
Brandy	1/2 cup
Heavy Cream	1 cup
Minced Parsley	1/4 cup

Crush peppercorns and coat steak heavily. Sprinkle with salt. Brown in oil in heavy skillet over high heat, 2 to 3 minutes each side. Remove to serving platter and keep warm. Discard most of oil, reserving 1 tablespoon of drippings. Add brandy to drippings, and flame. Add cream and heat. When sauce thickens, pour over steak. Garnish with parsley, serve at once.

Marie Marinkovich

Scallopine of Veal in Port Cream

YIELD: 4 servings

INGREDIENTS

Butter	2 ounces
Oil	1 ounce
Veal Scallops, 3 Ounces each	8
Salt	to taste
Pepper	to taste
Flour	3 tablespoons
Port	1/4 cup
Heavy Cream	1 cup
Bechamel Sauce*	1 teaspoon
Lemon, juice of	1/2
*See recipe, p. 183	

Heat butter and oil in large frying pan. Season the thin, round scallops of veal with salt and pepper. Dust lightly with flour. Cook for 3 minutes on each side, or until lightly browned. Remove meat to serving dish and keep warm. Pour excess fat from frying pan. Add wine and reduce to one-third. Slowly stir in cream; cook for a few minutes more, stirring constantly. Thicken with Bechamel Sauce. Add lemon juice. Season to taste. Pour sauce over veal just before serving.

The Four Seasons

Cotes de Veau aux Champignons de Paris
[Veal Chops with Mushrooms]

YIELD: 4 servings

INGREDIENTS

Fresh Mushrooms, sliced	1 pound
Oil	4 tablespoons
Butter	2 tablespoons
Salt	as needed
Pepper	as needed
Chopped Fresh Parsley	1 tablespoon
Chopped Shallots	2 tablespoons
Veal Chops	4
Flour	to coat
Heavy Cream	2 cups
Dry White Wine	1 cup
Brandy	1 ounce

Saute mushrooms in 2 tablespoons oil and 1 tablespoon butter. Season lightly with salt and pepper. Add the parsley and shallots and cook for 10 minutes. Season the chops with salt and pepper and roll them in flour. Heat 2 tablespoons oil and 1 tablespoon butter in a pan. Add chops and lightly brown on each side. Remove the chops from pan; discard the fat. Add cream, white wine, and brandy and simmer until sauce is thickened. Add sauteed mushrooms. Adjust seasoning and pour over the chops.

Ernie's

Veal, the most delicately flavored of all meats, has long been an important ingredient of haute cuisine. The sauce that accompanies it should add the desired contrast of flavor and color and must be carefully concocted. These recipes are two superior examples of the happy marrying of veal and sauce.

Ris de Veau des Gourmets
[Braised Veal Sweatbread "Gourmet"]

YIELD: 4 servings

INGREDIENTS

Fresh Veal Sweetbreads	2 (8 ounces per person)
Butter	4 ounces
Morels, soaked 1 hour in water until soft; washed, dried	2 ounces
Fresh Shallots, chopped	1/2 ounce
Carrots, cut julienne	2 ounces
Celery, cut julienne	2 ounces
Leek (white only), cut julienne	2 ounces
Cognac	1/4 cup
Madeira	1/2 cup
Veal Stock	1 cup
Truffles, sliced	1 ounce
Chopped Fresh Parsley	1 tablespoon

Parboil the sweetbreads. When cold, trim neatly. Cut in thick slices. Dust with flour. Season with salt and pepper. Saute in saucepan with butter. Brown on both sides. Remove the sweetbreads. Add the morels, shallots, and the vegetables. Saute in the butter used for the sweetbreads. Cook for 3 minutes. Deglaze with cognac and Madeira. Bring to a boil. Add the veal stock and reduce the volume to three-fourths. Pour the sauce over the sweetbreads. Cover. Cook in oven at 375°F. for 15 minutes. Before serving, add 1 ounce melted butter to the dish. Do not boil. Decorate with the sliced truffles and sprinkle with parsley.

La Maisonette

A menu that lists sweetbreads cognac-sauced and decorated with sliced truffles makes clear that the operation offering them caters to a discriminating clientele.

Another kind of Schnitzel from the Ratzsch menu.

Wiener Schnitzel

YIELD: 4 servings

INGREDIENTS

Veal Steak	3-1/2 to 4 pounds
Salt	3/4 teaspoon
Pepper	1/8 teaspoon
Monosodium Glutamate	1/8 teaspoon
Celery Salt	1/8 teaspoon
Eggs, beaten	2
Milk	1/2 cup
Salt	3/4 teaspoon
Flour	2 tablespoons
Dry Bread Crumbs, finely sifted	1 cup

Flatten veal with a metal or wooden meat tenderizer. Combine salt and next 3 ingredients. Sprinkle over meat. Blend thoroughly the beaten eggs, milk, salt, and flour. Dip veal in this mixture and then in bread crumbs. Fry in hot shortening, approximately 6 to 7 minutes on each side.

Karl Ratzsch's

Veal Piemontese

YIELD: 4 servings

INGREDIENTS

Veal Scallops, 2 ounces each	12
Sliced Artichoke Hearts	1 cup
Butter	1/4 pound
White Wine	3 ounces
Heavy Cream	1 cup
Salt	to taste
Pepper	to taste

Saute veal scallops and artichokes in butter; pour off butter, add white wine, and reduce to half. Add cream and seasonings. Remove veal from pan and arrange on platter. Reduce cream to a glaze, pour over veal.

Tony's

The Italians get considerable credit for their inventiveness with veal. Two classics in carefully combined versions make choices difficult for patrons studying the descriptions.

Osso Buco Milanaise

YIELD: 6 servings

INGREDIENTS

Veal Shanks	3
Salt	as needed
Black Pepper, freshly ground	as needed
Flour	1/3 cup
Oil	1/4 cup
Onion, Large, chopped	1
Garlic Clove, chopped, crushed	1
Carrots, diced	2
Celery Stalks, diced	2
Thyme	1/2 teaspoon
Oregano	1/2 teaspoon
Flour	1 tablespoon
Brown Stock, boiling	1/2 cup
Dry White Wine	1/2 cup
Tomato Puree	1/3 cup
Seeded, Diced, Tomatoes	1/2 cup
Bouquet Garni	1 small
Chopped Parsley	1 tablespoon
Chopped Lemon Rind	1 teaspoon
Saffron Rice	6 portions

Saw each of the veal shanks into 2 pieces about 2-1/2 inches thick. Season lightly with salt and pepper; dredge with flour. Brown on all sides in heated oil in skillet. When brown, pour half the oil from the skillet. Add onion and next 5 ingredients; cook 5 minutes. Blend in flour. Stir in stock, wine, tomato puree, and tomatoes. Bring to a boil; add bouquet garni. Cover; bake in oven at 350°F. for 1-1/2 hours. Place shanks in serving dish. Remove bouquet garni. Skim fat from sauce. Adjust seasoning. Pour sauce over meat. Top with parsley and lemon rind, mixed. Serve with Saffron Rice.

The Greenbrier

t Suite

Cordially

Invites You

to a

Different

Night Out!

If you have guests visiting
for a weekend—
are tired of cookouts—
why not join us for a fine
evening. Listen, dance to
the greatest music this side
of Buffalo—and dine on our
fine fare. We are serving—
in addition to our regular menu—
a specially selected and
prepared entree which will
change weekly. The price
for our special entree of the
week — $10.00 per couple.

Veal Normandy

YIELD: 6 servings

INGREDIENTS

Veal	1-1/2 pounds
Flour	1/2 cup
Salt	4 shakes
Pepper	4 shakes
Butter	2 ounces
Brandy	4 ounces
Mushrooms, sliced	1 pound
Heavy Cream	1 cup

Cut veal into 24 equal pieces and pound out until thin. Dredge veal with mixture of flour, salt, and pepper, then saute lightly in butter. Pour brandy into pan on top of veal, and flame. Let flame burn out; remove veal and place on dish. Saute mushrooms in same pan and then pour cream on top until it starts to thicken. Pour over veal and shake dish. Garnish with finely chopped parsley.

Plaza Suite

Veal Chops Saute

YIELD: 6 servings

INGREDIENTS

Veal Chops	6
Butter	4 tablespoons
Thick Cream	2 cups
Shallots, chopped	3
Fresh Mushrooms	1/2 pound
Dry White Wine	4 ounces
Lemon Juice	1 tablespoon
Broccoli, cooked	1-1/2 pounds
Parmesan Cheese	as needed

Season chops lightly with salt, pepper, and paprika. Saute in butter in a heavy frying pan. Remove to a large platter. Drain off part of butter from frying pan. Add shallots; saute for a few seconds (do not let them brown). Add white wine, reduce to one-half. Stir in cream; rapidly reduce to one-half. Strain. In another pan, saute mushrooms in butter; stir in lemon juice; add mushrooms to the sauce. Boil for a minute; season with salt and pepper. Pour sauce over the chops. Garnish platter with cooked broccoli which has been seasoned with parmesan cheese.

The Brown Palace Hotel

Osso Buco alla Milanese

YIELD: 6 servings

INGREDIENTS

Ossobuchi (veal shank)	6
Butter	1/4 pound
Carrot, Small, minced	1
Onion, Small, minced	1
Celery Stalks, tender, minced	3
Dry White Wine	8 ounces
Chopped Parsley	1 teaspoon
Flour	for dredging meat
Salt	to taste
Pepper	to taste
Tomatoes, Canned, Peeled	1 No. 303 can
Beef/Chicken Stock *or* Water	8 to 12 ounces

This classic Italian dish is a hearty, sauced-to-perfection combination of meat and vegetables.

Take a 4-inch high pan, large enough to accommodate all six pieces of veal shank in two rows. Butter sides and bottom of pan, using half the butter. Mix the other half of the butter with the minced vegetables and spread three-fourths of this mixture on the bottom of pan. Dredge each piece of veal in flour, shake well to remove all excess flour, and place in pan. Take remaining 1/4 of butter-vegetable mixture, divide into six parts, and top each piece of veal with a small part of mixture. Brown the veal on each side over high flame. When golden brown, pour wine over veal and cook until the wine evaporates. Add peeled tomatoes, salt and pepper to taste, lower flame and let cook until all water evaporates. At this point, add chicken or beef stock or, if neither is available, plain water; cover pan with aluminum foil, lower flame and allow to cook from 1 to 1-1/2 hours, depending on size of pieces. After completing the first steps of the cooking operation (to the point where the stock or the water is added), it is suggested that the cooking be completed in the oven. You can tell that the meat is cooked when it shrinks from the bone. Serve with boiled rice, dressed with some of the sauce from the meat.

Mamma Leone's

blackhawk
from the open hearth broiler

bill lawshee, our veteran broiler man (18 years), has that magic touch — he sears the meat on the outside and cooks it to the exact "doneness" of your choice.

cabernet sauvignon, louis martini. top american claret. #25

sirloin strip — our prize winning, man's size steak — thick, juicy, tender..... **9.50**

sirloin strip (8 oz.) — the same marvelous quality, for the smaller appetite............... **8.25**

filet mignon (9 oz.) — with fresh mushroom — everybody's favorite **8.50**

steak 'n lobster — filet mignon and succulent lobster tail..... **9.75**

beaujolais, louis jadot. rich, fruity, not too heavy. #7

chopped sirloin (12 oz.) — blackhawk style — topped with bleu cheese or cooked with diced onions....... **5.75**

* * *

thick steak of genuine calf's liver (or slices) with crisp smoked hickory bacon or golden french fried onions....... **6.95**

mateus rosé. light & lively ... from Portugal. #31

chicken breast teriyaki with pineapple — polynesia at its best **5.75**

BEEF OSKAR — a tantalizing taste treat: filet mignon, crabmeat, white asparagus, and our own bernaise sauce.   **8.75**

Escallopine of Veal Charleroi

YIELD: 5 servings

INGREDIENTS

Onions	2
Mushrooms	1 dozen
Butter	1/4 pound
Bay Leaves	2
Rosemary	pinch
Rice	2 cups
Chicken Broth	3 cups
Salt	to taste
Pepper	to taste
Egg Yolks	2
Whipped Cream, unsweetened	2 cups
Parmesan Cheese	1/2 cup
Veal Scallops (silver dollar size)	15 pieces
Sherry	1/2 cup
Brown Sauce	1 cup

Saute onions and fresh mushrooms in butter in casserole. Season with bay leaves and rosemary. Simmer for 15 minutes. Add rice and stir for one minute. Add chicken broth and season with salt and pepper. Cover. When mixture reaches the boiling point, place the covered casserole in oven at 350°F. for approximately 25 minutes, or until rice is done. When cooked, put into blender to make puree. Blend into puree the egg yolks, unsweetened whipped cream, and parmesan cheese. Place this blend into a pastry bag and set aside.

Saute veal scallops in pan in butter until brown on both sides. Remove to a serving dish. To pan from which veal was removed, add sherry; reduce. Add brown sauce and simmer.

Squeeze contents in pastry bag over veal in criss-cross fashion. Sprinkle some parmesan cheese over top. Place dish under broiler until top is golden brown. Encircle veal in dish with sherry sauce. Serve hot.

The 21 Club

This specialty of the house at "21" is presented with elegant simplicity. The veal is circled with a sherry sauce and accompanied by asparagus tips and puree of carrots on artichoke bottoms.

Sweet-Sour Pork Cubes

YIELD: 13 gallons

INGREDIENTS

Pork, cubed	80 pounds
Water	4 gallons
Soy Sauce	2 quarts
Brown Sugar	5-1/2 pounds
Cornstarch	3 pounds
Vinegar	2 quarts
Pineapple Juice	2 quarts
Pineapple Tidbits	3 No. 10 cans

Brown meat in oven. Add water and soy sauce. Simmer meat until tender. Skim off floating fat. In pan, blend sugar, cornstarch, vinegar, and pineapple juice until smooth. Slowly stir into meat. Cook until thickened and translucent, about 5 minutes. Stir in pineapple tidbits. Adjust seasoning to taste.

Washington State University

Mousse of Ham in Whole Peaches

YIELD: 6 servings

INGREDIENTS

Ham, cooked	1 pound
Mayonnaise	1/3 cup
Cayenne Pepper	to taste
Salt	to taste
Butter, softened	1/3 cup
Port	2 teaspoons
Peaches, Large, Ripe	6

Cut ham into small pieces and put through finest blade of meat grinder. Place in mixing bowl. Very slowly beat mayonnaise, pepper, salt, butter, and port into ham to make a fine mousse. Cool 1 hour.
Holding peach in one hand, remove pit by placing knife in the stem end and encircling pit. This will leave a center core of about 3/4 inch for stuffing. Stuff peaches with mousse and serve.

The Four Seasons

Summer is icumen in so the time has come for The Four Seasons to feature fresh fruits. One distinctive offering is a whole, fresh peach cored to leave a 3/4-inch opening that is stuffed with rich, port-flavored ham mousse.

Pork Tenderloin with Grapes

YIELD: 6 servings

INGREDIENTS

Pork Tenderloin, cut into 6 1/2-inch thick pieces	2-1/2 pounds
Flour	1/2 cup
Butter	3/4 cup
Salt	to taste
Pepper	to taste
Muscat Grapes	1 cup
Dry White Wine	1 cup
Currant Jelly	1 tablespoon
Heavy Cream	1-1/2 cups

Flour meat slices and brown very slowly in butter. Add salt and pepper to taste. Continue cooking until meat is well done. Transfer meat to hot platter and keep warm. Simmer grapes in the wine for 5 minutes. Lift grapes and arrange around meat slices. Reduce wine by one-third over high heat. Blend in currant jelly and add cream. Heat, but *do not boil.* Pour 1/2 of sauce over meat and serve remainder in sauceboat.

Marie Marinkovich

Pork Roast with Sweet and Sour Sauce

YIELD: 4 servings

INGREDIENTS

Center Cut Rib Pork Roasts	4 1-pound roasts
Sugar	2 cups
Cider Vinegar	1 cup
Diced Green Pepper	2 tablespoons
Salt	1 teaspoon
Water	1 cup
Cornstarch	4 teaspoons
Water	2 tablespoons
Paprika	2 teaspoons
Minced Parsley	2 tablespoons

Place roasts in pan, bone side down. Brown in oven at 450°F. for 30 minutes. Remove from oven and transfer to deeper baking pan, bone side up. Meanwhile, mix sugar, vinegar, green pepper, and salt with water. Simmer 5 minutes. Combine cornstarch with 2 tablespoons water. Stir into vinegar mixture; cook, stirring, until sauce thickens. Pour over pork. Bake in oven at 300°F. for 2-1/2 hours, or until pork is tender; baste occasionally. Place meat on platter. Strain sauce; add paprika and parsley. Ladle sauce over pork. Serve with garnish of baked apples.

The Vineyards

Saddle of Lamb "Gastronome"

YIELD: 2 servings

INGREDIENTS
Boned Saddle of Lamb, cut in 4 pieces	1
Clarified Butter	4 tablespoons
Puff Paste	4 10-inch squares
Fresh Mushrooms, minced, cooked in butter, drained, seasoned with salt and pepper	1/2 pound
Goose Liver (Foie Gras)	4 slices
Egg Yolk	1

Brown lamb quickly (one minute on each side) in sizzling clarified butter. Place one layer of puff paste on a cookie sheet; lay the large piece of lamb on it. Add half the mushrooms and place two slices of goose liver on top. Then place the smaller piece of lamb (fillet) on top. Bring the edges of dough up over the fillet. Top with another square of puff paste, sliding ends under the first piece of dough. Brush the top with lightly beaten egg yolk. Repeat operation with the remainder of the ingredients. Bake in oven at 400°F. for 10 minutes or until pastry is golden brown.

La Bourgogne

Sour Cream Lamb Stew

YIELD: 2 servings

INGREDIENTS
Onion, Small, quartered	1
Butter	1 tablespoon
Lamb, cubed	1 pound
Salt	2/3 teaspoon
Flour	as needed
Condensed Tomato Soup	1/2 cup
Water	1/2 cup
Ground Ginger	1/8 teaspoon
Sour Cream	1/3 cup
Egg Noodles, cooked	3 ounces

Cook onion in butter until soft. Sprinkle meat with salt, then coat with flour, shaking off excess. Brown the meat lightly on all sides in pan with the onion. Blend tomato soup with water and ginger. Pour over meat; mix well. Cover; simmer gently for about 2 hours, or until meat is very tender, stirring occasionally. Add a little water if the sauce begins to stick. Just before serving, blend some of the sauce with the sour cream and return to pan. Heat, *do not boil*. Serve with cooked egg noodles.

Win Schuler's

These lamb dishes, designed for discriminating palates, have new dimensions of flavor that win new converts and intrigue those who savor lamb, however it is prepared.

Gigot d'Agneau a la Cuillere [Braised Leg of Lamb]

YIELD: 10 to 15 servings

INGREDIENTS

Leg of Lamb	1
Sliced Onion	1 cup
Sliced Carrots	1 cup
Parsley Sprig	1
Bay Leaves	3 to 4
Boiling Water	2 cups
Sherry and Cornstarch	to thicken
Mint Jelly	to accompany

Trim the skin and fat from a leg of spring lamb. Debone and cut bone into about 4 parts. Put the sliced onion and carrots in a roasting pan and add parsley, bay leaves, and chopped bones. Add the leg of lamb. Place in oven at 375°F. and cook until it is well browned. Add the boiling water to prevent burning and cover the pan with foil. Reduce heat to 325°F.; cook for 4 hours, or until the meat is ready to fall apart, adding more water as needed. Remove lamb to a heated serving dish. Strain the liquid in the pan and thicken it with cornstarch dissolved in a little sherry. Strain the gravy through a fine sieve. Serve the meat with a spoon instead of carving it. Accompany with the gravy and mint jelly.

Camelot

Cervelles de Veau Saute Grenobloise [Calves' Brains]

YIELD: 15 to 20 servings

INGREDIENTS

Veal Brains	10
Red Wine Vinegar	1/2 cup
Peppercorns	2 teaspoons
Onion, Large, sliced	1
Carrot, sliced	1
Bay Leaves	2
Thyme	1 teaspoon
Butter	10 to 12 ounces
Lemons, peeled, diced	4
Capers	1 cup
Parsley	to garnish

Remove the membranes and any blood from the veal brains. Wash well in cold water. Soak in large amount of cold water with ice cubes for several hours. Rinse thoroughly and drain. Put into a saucepan with water to cover well; add wine vinegar, peppercorns, onion, carrots, bay leaves, and thyme. Bring to boil, then simmer for 25 to 30 minutes. Remove from the heat and let them cool in their own stock. Remove brains from stock and cut each side lengthwise. Dip the slices in flour and saute in butter until brown on both sides.

To serve, melt butter, add lemons and capers, and cook until golden brown color. Pour the butter over the brains. Sprinkle with parsley and serve very hot.

Camelot

Chef Touché

PRESENTE HIS SUGGESTIONS FOR TONIGHT

BACK DOOR KNOCKER SPECIAL
$4.95
State sales tax added

Entertainment Charge – $2.00

La FLANDRE SAUTÉE MEUNIÈRE
From the British Isles, another Seafood Special, a Flounder from the Cold Waters of the North Sea, sauteed to perfection in Butter. Served with Potato du Jour.

Le FILET de CABILLAUD FLORENTINE
Filet of Fresh Scrod poached in White Wine and topped with Cream Sauce and au Gratin.

La BROCHETTE d'AGNEAU a la TURQUE
Large Cubes of Tender Lamb expertly marinated with Choice Herbs and broiled on a skewer. Served with Rice a la Turque.

Les COTES de PORC SAUTEES GRAND MERE
Center cut Pork Chop sauteed with Pearl Onions, Mushrooms and Bacon. Served with Potato du Jour.

L'OSSO-BUCCO a la MILANAISE
Provemi Veal Shanks braised in genuine European fashion and prepared in a succulent Sauce that only our chef, Gaston, can master. Served with Rice Milanaise.

Camelot
RESTAURANT of DISTINCTION

Ox Tongue Rinaldi

YIELD: 2 servings

INGREDIENTS

Smoked Ox Tongue	4 2-ounce slices
Butter	2 ounces
Burgundy	1 cup
Onions, Medium-sized, finely chopped	2
Flour	1 tablespoon
Chicken Stock	2 cups
Salt	to taste
Pepper	to taste
Beef Marrow	6 slices
Parsley, chopped	1 ounce

Place tongue slices in skillet with 1 ounce butter. Cover with burgundy. Bring to a boil; simmer for 2 minutes. Saute onions in skillet with 1 ounce butter until transparent. *Do not brown.* Add flour; stir. Stir in stock; boil about 3 minutes. Season with salt and pepper.

Place one slice of tongue in center of each plate; top with half of the onions; cover with another slice of tongue. Reduce wine sauce to almost a glaze; top tongue with it. Poach marrow in boiling water for about 15 seconds. Cool in bowl of ice water; remove, and clean slices. Arrange marrow on top of tongue. Bake in oven at 350°F. for about 3 minutes. Sprinkle with parsley. Serve with sauteed potatoes and green salad.

The view from the cocktail areas adjacent to Victor's, the fine dining room at the Hotel St. Francis is matched only by the cuisine.

Hotel St. Francis

Calf's Liver Marseillaise

YIELD: 4 servings

INGREDIENTS

Oil	1 to 2 teaspoons
Calf's Liver, sliced	1 pound
Butter	4 tablespoons
Fresh Bread Crumbs	1/4 cup
Garlic Clove	1
Shallots, finely chopped	2
Demi-glace	1 tablespoon

Calf's liver cooked to order, a la Marseillaise with a hint of garlic and finely-chopped shallots, is a favorite luncheon choice among businessmen.

Place oil in heavy skillet over high heat. When hot, add liver and quickly cook to desired degree of doneness. While liver is cooking, melt butter in small pan. Add next 3 ingredients and saute until golden. Add demi-glace; cook 1 minute longer. Spread on top of liver.

Fairmont Hotel

Sweet and Sour Franks

YIELD: 100 servings

INGREDIENTS

Frankfurters	12 pounds
Apple-Currant Jelly	2 quarts
Prepared Mustard	1 quart

Unexpected flavor for a low cost item pleases patients and patrons at this hospital.

Cut frankfurters in quarters. Saute without fat for 10 minutes on very low heat. Add jelly and mustard. Mix well. Simmer until sauce is clear, about five minutes. Serve hot.

Massachusetts General Hospital

Poultry Entrees

Roast Duckling with Green Peppercorns and Kumquat Sauce

A flavor variation for roast duckling as exotic as the surroundings makes inspired use of two not-often-encountered ingredients: kumquats and green peppercorns.

YIELD: 6 servings

INGREDIENTS

Ducks, 4 to 5 Pounds each	3
Onion, Large, coarsely chopped	1
Celery Ribs, cut 1-inch slices	2
Carrots, peeled, sliced	6
Salt	as needed
Pepper	as needed
Fresh Kumquats	1 quart
Vinegar	1/4 cup
Sugar	1/2 pound
Fresh Orange Juice	1 cup
Fresh Lemon Juice	1/4 cup
Black Peppercorns, crushed	1/2 teaspoon
Bay Leaf	1
Thyme	1 small sprig
Leek, Small, finely sliced	1
Brown Sauce	2 cups
Tomato Paste	1/2 cup
Cointreau *or* Grand Marnier	2 tablespoons
Green Peppercorns	3 ounces

Wipe and dry ducks. Fill each duck cavity with 1/3 of the onion, celery, and carrots. Sprinkle with salt and pepper. Roast ducks in oven at 425°F. for 45 minutes on rack to allow fat to drain off. Peel half of the kumquats, removing all pulp from peels. Cut peels in fine julienne, cover with boiling water for 1 minute, drain, and reserve. In a saucepan over medium heat, cook vinegar and sugar until the mixture begins to caramelize. Add orange and lemon juice and the pulp from peeled kumquats. Cook until liquid reduces about one-fourth. Add the kumquat julienne, crushed peppercorns, bay leaf, thyme, and leek. Simmer, stirring occasionally, for one hour. Strain through a fine sieve. Add the liqueur and green peppercorns. Drain all juices and fat from roasted ducks, halve them, and arrange on heated platters. Garnish with remaining kumquats cut in thin slices. Reheat and serve sauce separately.

Fournou's Ovens Restaurant, The Stanford Court Hotel

Chef Connolly's Turkey Cluster

YIELD: 100 servings

INGREDIENTS

Turkey, cooked, white and dark meat	20 pounds
Bacon	5 pounds
Eggs	12
Milk	2 quarts
Dry Bread Crumbs	2 quarts

Cut turkey in 1-inch cubes. Wrap strip of bacon around 3 cubes of white meat and one cube of dark meat. Secure with a toothpick. Beat eggs. Combine with milk to make an egg wash. Dip wrapped turkey in egg wash and roll in bread crumbs. Fry in deep fat at 350°F. until brown.

Massachusetts General Hospital

Chicken Raphael Weill

YIELD: 4 servings

INGREDIENTS

Chicken Breasts, 6 to 7 Ounces each, boned	4
Salt	to taste
Pepper	to taste
Flour	to coat
Butter	2 ounces
Fresh Mushrooms, quartered	4 ounces
Fresh Artichoke Bottoms, quartered	2
Dry White Wine	1 cup
Flour	1 ounce
Heavy Cream	1 cup

Sprinkle chicken lightly with salt and pepper. Coat with flour on all sides. Heat 1 ounce of butter in shallow skillet; add chicken and brown on all sides. Add mushrooms and artichokes; saute for 2 to 3 minutes, then flash with wine. Cover; simmer until chicken is tender. Remove chicken from skillet. Mix 1 ounce flour with 1 ounce butter. Pour cream into skillet; bring to a boil. With a wire whip, slowly stir in flour and butter. Simmer until sauce is thick and creamy. Place chicken in sauce; cover and remove from heat at once. Do not open lid for 15 minutes. Serve with rice or noodles.

Note: Created by Chef Victor Hirtzler, Hotel St. Francis chef from 1916 to 1925, and named in honor of San Francisco merchant prince Raphael Weill, one of his favorite guests.

Hotel St. Francis

Chicken Curry with Mandarin Fruit

YIELD: 1 serving

INGREDIENTS

Chicken Breasts, boned	1 large *or*
	2 medium
Butter	1 tablespoon
Oil	1 tablespoon
Curry Powder	1 to 3 teaspoons
Chicken Broth, boiling, *or*	
Canned Consomme, diluted, boiling	3/4 to 1 cup
Monosodium Glutamate	dash
Salt	to taste
Pepper	to taste
Cornstarch	2 to 3 teaspoons
Cold Water	3 tablespoons

Cut boned chicken meat into large bite-sized pieces. Heat butter and oil in skillet; add curry to taste. Cook gently, stirring, 2 to 3 minutes. Add chicken, stirring to coat well. Add enough boiling broth to barely cover chicken. Add seasonings. Cover; cook gently 8 to 10 minutes. Mix cornstarch with cold water; add and cook, stirring, 1 to 2 minutes until liquid is slightly thickened and glazed looking. If too thick, thin with a little hot broth or water. Serve at once on hot steamed rice. Border with slices of fresh pineapple, orange, and banana, with touches of chutney, plumped raisins, and fresh coconut.

The Nut Tree

Breast of Capon Sans Souci

YIELD: 6 servings

INGREDIENTS

Double Breasts of Capon	6
Butter	4 ounces
Cognac	3 ounces
Flour	4 ounces
Chicken Stock	2 cups
Sauterne	12 ounces
Bay Leaves	2
Worcestershire Sauce	dash
Thyme	pinch
Salt	to taste
Pepper	to taste
Tomato Puree	3 ounces
Heavy Cream	2 cups

Brush capon breasts with butter. Roast in iron frying pan in oven at 350°F. for 35 minutes. Remove breasts; pour cognac into pan until flaming. Add flour and next 7 ingredients. Boil rapidly for 15 minutes; strain. Add tomato puree and cream. Boil again until of medium consistency.

Hotel St. Francis

𝒱 *indicates Victor's favourite fare.*

And this recipe is V-rated.

Cornish Game Hen with Oyster Dressing

YIELD: 6 servings

INGREDIENTS

Onion, Medium-sized, diced	1
Garlic Cloves, minced	2
Butter	1 tablespoon
Pork Sausage	1/2 pound
Oysters	1-1/2 dozen
Cooked Rice	3 quarts
Chopped Parsley	1/4 cup
Oregano	to taste
Sage	to taste
Salt	to taste
Pepper	to taste
Cornish Game Hens, 1 to 1-1/2 Pounds each	6

Saute onion and garlic in butter until onion is clear. Add the sausage and cook until done. Add the oysters and simmer for five minutes. Combine with rice. Season with parsley, oregano, sage, salt, and pepper. Stuff and tie the hens. Bake in oven at 350°F., basting frequently, until tender. Serve with white wine and tossed green salad.

Charlie's Cafe Exceptionale

Faisan Roti [Roast Pheasant a la Flamande]

YIELD: 2 servings

INGREDIENTS

Pheasant, 2 Pound	1
Sweet Butter	2 tablespoons
Madeira	1 tablespoon
Belgian Endives, blanched	4
Pommes Parisienne	1-1/2 dozen
Cognac	1 ounce
Madeira	1 ounce
Lemon Juice	few drops
Salt	to taste
Pepper	to taste

A touch of the sauce for the vegetables, left in it just long enough to absorb a bit, perfects this entree.

Dress the pheasant. Smear thoroughly with butter. Roast on a rack in an open pan in oven at 400°F. for 45 minutes. After 15 minutes, add 1 tablespoon Madeira to juices in the pan; baste with this mixture every 10 minutes. Ten minutes before the end of the roasting time, place the endives and potatoes in the sauce. (They will absorb some of the juice and roast at the same time.) Place the pheasant on a silver platter, surround with the endives and potatoes. To drippings in pan, add cognac, Madeira, lemon juice, salt, and pepper to taste; reduce over a hot flame for one minute. Strain into a sauceboat. Serve very hot with pheasant.

La Bourgogne

Roast Duckling Waia Lae

YIELD: 4 servings

INGREDIENTS

Ducklings, 4 Pounds each	2
Salt	sprinkle
Pepper	sprinkle
Sugar	1/4 cup
Wine Vinegar	1/2 cup
Oranges	2
Red Wine	3/4 cup
Espagnole Sauce, heated	2 cups
Water *or* Wine	1 cup
Liquid Hot Pepper Seasoning	few drops
Kitchen Bouquet (optional)	few drops
Lychee	16 pieces
Tangerines	16 pieces
Bananas	16 slices
Grand Marnier	1 ounce
Brandy	1 ounce

Rub ducklings with salt and pepper. Roast in oven at 350° to 375°F. for 1 to 1-1/2 hours, or until tender. Caramelize sugar in saucepan. Add vinegar and simmer for a few minutes. Peel oranges with a julienne scraper. In a separate pan, boil orange peel in red wine for 5 minutes. Squeeze juice from the peeled oranges into the caramel sauce. Add Espagnole Sauce; simmer for 15 minutes. When ducklings are done, remove from roasting pan; discard fat. Deglaze pan with water or wine; add to sauce and simmer a little longer. Strain sauce, then add orange peel and wine. Add hot pepper seasoning. If sauce is not dark enough, stir in a little Kitchen Bouquet. Carve each duckling into 4 pieces, place in flat skillet. Sprinkle with lychee, tangerines, and bananas. Heat over burner. Flame with Grand Marnier and brandy. Pour sauce over duckling. Serve with buttered wild rice and spiced peaches.

The Kahala Hilton Hotel

Chicken a la Crema

YIELD: 4 servings

INGREDIENTS

A chicken dish from Italy that helps assure a restaurant's reputation as a "great place to go."

Chicken Breasts, boned, split	4
Sliced Mushrooms	1 cup
Butter	1/4 pound
Burgundy	1/2 cup
Orange, juice of	1/2
Heavy Cream	1 cup
Salt	to taste
Pepper	to taste

Saute chicken and mushrooms in butter; add wine; reduce to one-half. Add orange juice and cream. Season to taste. Reduce to a glaze.

Tony's

Breast of Chicken Tiffany

YIELD: 4 servings

INGREDIENTS

Chicken Breasts, boneless	4
Rosemary	1 teaspoon
Poultry Seasoning	4 pinches
Butter	5 ounces
Chopped Shallots	4 teaspoons
Chopped Chives	4 teaspoons
Salt	1/8 teaspoon
Pepper	1/8 teaspoon
Bananas, halved	2
Bacon Strips	4
Egg, beaten	1
Oil	1 teaspoon
Flour	1 ounce
Dry Bread Crumbs	2 ounces
Dry White Wine	1/4 cup

Flatten chicken breasts with cleaver or heavy knife. Sprinkle inside of each breast with 1/4 teaspoon rosemary and a pinch of poultry seasoning. Mix 4 ounces of butter, shallots, chopped chives, salt, and pepper. Spoon 1/4 of this mixture onto center of each breast; top with a half banana. Roll in edges of chicken over mixture to form a ball. Wrap chicken roll with 1 to 2 strips of bacon. Mix egg, oil, pinch of salt, and a dash of pepper. Dip tops of chicken rolls (seam edge on bottom) in this mixture, then in flour, finally in bread crumbs. Place rolls in individual buttered casseroles or baking pans. Spoon a tablespoon of wine over each. Bake in oven at 400°F. for 45 minutes. Serve with Bearnaise Sauce (see recipe, p. 181) and wild rice.

Chateau Louise

Chicken Mascotte

YIELD: 4 servings

INGREDIENTS

Chicken, cut up	2-3/4 pounds
Butter *or* Margarine	2 to 3 tablespoons
Mushrooms, quartered	4 to 6
Artichoke Hearts, quartered	2
Shallots, chopped	2
Sherry	1/3 cup
Demi-glace	1 cup
Salt	to taste
Pepper	to taste

Saute chicken in butter in skillet until golden brown. Remove chicken. In same skillet, saute mushrooms, artichokes, and shallots until yellow but not brown. Add chicken, sherry, demi-glace, salt, and pepper; simmer until tender, about 20 to 30 minutes. Serve in casserole.

Fairmont Hotel

Chicken Regal

YIELD: 4 servings

INGREDIENTS

Chicken Breasts	4
Butter	1/2 cup
Fresh Mushrooms, sliced	1/2 pound
Chopped Onion	1/4 cup
Chopped Parsley	1/3 cup
Flour	2 tablespoons
Pepper	dash
Chicken Broth	1-3/4 cups
Half-and-Half	1/2 cup
Instant Rice	1-1/3 cups
Salt	1/2 teaspoon
Boiling Water	1-1/2 cups
Slivered, Blanched Almonds	1/4 cup
Butter	2 tablespoons

Remove skin from chicken breasts and dry with paper towel. Saute the breasts in the butter for 10 minutes over medium heat, turning once. Add the mushrooms to the breasts. Continue cooking, covered, 10 minutes longer, stirring occasionally. Remove chicken and mushrooms and set aside. Add onion to butter remaining in skillet; saute until lightly browned. Add parsley, flour, and pepper. Stir until blended. Then add broth and cream gradually, stirring constantly. Cook and stir over medium heat until mixture is thickened. Add chicken breasts and mushrooms. Cover; simmer 20 to 25 minutes or until breasts are tender. Meanwhile, add instant rice and salt to boiling water in pan; mix just to moisten all the rice. Cover; remove from heat. Let stand 13 minutes. Saute almonds in butter until golden brown, stirring constantly. Add almonds and butter to rice just before serving. Arrange rice on hot platter. Place chicken breast on rice; top with sauce and serve.

Note: To achieve a more golden color, 2 or 3 drops of yellow egg color may be added to the sauce.

Southern Methodist University Food Service

Cannelloni Capriccio

YIELD: 2 dozen

INGREDIENTS

PASTA

Sifted Flour	2 cups
Eggs	2 large
Water	1-1/2 tablespoons
Salt	3/4 teaspoon
Boiling Water	1 gallon
Salt	1 tablespoon

FILLING

Chicken Meat, cooked	2-1/2 cups
Cooked Spinach, well drained	1/2 cup
Fresh Mushrooms, chopped	1/4 pound
Butter	1 tablespoon
Egg, beaten	1
Egg Yolk, beaten	1
Grated Parmesan Cheese	1/3 cup

SAUCE

Butter	1/4 cup
Flour	1-1/2 tablespoons
Milk	1-1/2 cups
Salt	1/2 teaspoon
White Pepper	dash
Nutmeg	dash
Grated Parmesan Cheese	2 tablespoons
Egg Yolk, beaten	1

The best path to pasta for cannelloni is clearly detailed here by specialists in Italian cuisine.

PASTA

Place flour on pastry board; make a well in center and put eggs, water, and salt in it. Beat eggs with fork. Slowly mix in half of the flour. Mix in rest of flour by hand. Knead until dough is smooth, about 10 minutes. Cut dough in half; roll each piece on floured board until paper-thin. Cut dough in 3-inch squares. Cook 6 at a time in boiling salted water for 5 minutes. Remove from pan one at a time with perforated spoon and place unfolded on damp towels. Continue until all squares are cooked. Fill as directed.

FILLING

Cook a stewing chicken. Remove meat from bones and coarsely grind with cooked spinach. Saute mushrooms in butter. Add to chicken with egg, egg yolk, and parmesan cheese; mix well. Place filling on cooked pasta and roll up. Place seamside down in greased baking pan.

SAUCE

Melt butter in small saucepan. Stir in flour to a smooth paste. Add milk gradually, cooking and stirring over low heat for 10 minutes. (Sauce should be consistency of thick cream.) Stir in salt, pepper, and nutmeg. Remove from heat; quickly stir in cheese and egg yolk.

Cover filled pasta with sauce; sprinkle additional parmesan cheese over top. Bake in oven at 350°F. for 12 to 15 minutes.

Tony's

Brandied Chicken Breasts

YIELD: 4 servings

INGREDIENTS

Chicken Breasts, boned, halved, skinned	4
Brandy	2 tablespoons
Salt	to taste
Pepper	to taste
Marjoram	to taste
Butter	6 tablespoons
Dry Sherry	1/4 cup
Cream	2 cups
Egg Yolks	4
Nutmeg	to taste
Grated Swiss Cheese	as needed
Fine Buttered Crumbs	as needed

Rub chicken breasts with brandy and let stand for 10 minutes. Season with salt, pepper, and marjoram. Melt butter, add breasts; saute over medium heat 6 to 8 minutes on each side. Remove to heated platter and keep warm. Add sherry to butter in pan. Simmer over low heat until liquid is reduced to half. Stirring constantly, add cream beaten with egg yolks. Season with salt, pepper, and nutmeg. Stir and cook until slightly thickened. Pour sauce over chicken breasts. Sprinkle with grated cheese mixed with equal parts fine buttered crumbs. Glaze under broiler.

Marie Marinkovich

Shortened hospital stays will cease to be so welcome when dishes as exceptional as these appear on trays. They also make dinners for hospital personnel events to be remembered.

Rock Cornish Game Hen

YIELD: 6 servings

INGREDIENTS

Rock Cornish Hens, 10 to 12 Ounces each	6
Salt	as needed
Paprika	as needed
Carrots, cut julienne	2
Celery Stalks, cut julienne	3
Chicken Stock,* double strength	1 cup
Sauterne	1 cup
Cornstarch	3/4 teaspoon
Parsley Sprigs	to garnish
*Or 2 bouillon cubes in 1 cup water	

Wash hens; rub body cavities lightly with salt. Sprinkle skin sides lightly with paprika. Arrange hens in baking pan. Top with carrot and celery strips. Pour chicken stock and 1/2 cup of wine over hens. Bake in oven at 325°F. until tender, approximately 35 minutes. Remove hens from pan; discard carrots and celery. To residue in pan, add cornstarch. Cook 2 minutes, stirring vigorously. Add 1/2 cup wine; simmer 1 minute. Strain; pour 1 tablespoon sauce over each portion. Garnish with parsley sprigs at wing joints.

Michael Reese Hospital and Medical Center

Mallards Exceptionale

YIELD: 6 servings

INGREDIENTS

Stale Hard Water Rolls, halved	1 dozen
OR	
French Bread, sliced	1-1/2 loaves
Onion, Medium-sized, diced	1
Celery, diced	1 stalk
Pork Sausage	1/2 pound
Powdered Sage	1/8 to 1/4 teaspoon
Powdered Thyme	1/8 to 1/4 teaspoon
Salt	to taste
Pepper	to taste
Mallards	3

Soak the rolls or bread in cold water until soft. Use enough cold water to cover the bread. When the bread is soft, place in a colander and press thoroughly to remove moisture. Then tear the bread into bite-sized pieces. Saute onion and celery with the pork sausage until golden brown. Do not drain the juice from the pork sausage mixture. Add the bread to the pork sausage mixture. Season to taste with the sage, thyme, salt, and pepper. Stuff the mallards with the dressing. Wrap mallards in aluminum foil. Bake in oven at 350ºF. for approximately 1-1/2 hours. Open the aluminum foil wrapping and brown the mallards for approximately 1/2 hour.

Charlie's Cafe Exceptionale

Rolled Chicken Breasts

YIELD: 6 servings

INGREDIENTS

Chicken Breasts, boned, skinned, halved	3 large *or*
	6 small
Salt	to taste
Boiled Ham	6 thin slices
Natural Swiss Cheese, cut into 6 sticks	6 ounces
Flour	1/4 cup
Butter	2 tablespoons
Water	1/2 cup
Chicken Flavor Gravy Base	1 teaspoon
Broiled Sliced Mushrooms, drained	3-ounce can
(Fresh mushrooms may be used)	
Sauterne	1/3 cup
Flour	2 tablespoons
Cold Water	1/2 cup

Place chicken pieces, boned side up, on cutting board. Working from center out, pound chicken lightly with wooden mallet to make cutlets 1/4 inch thick. Sprinkle with salt. Place slice of ham and a cheese stick on each cutlet. Tuck in sides of each and roll up as a jelly roll, pressing to seal well. Skewer or tie securely. Coat rolls with 1/4 cup flour and brown in butter. Remove chicken to shallow pan. In same skillet, mix 1/2 cup water, gravy base, mushrooms, and wine. Heat, stirring to incorporate crusty bits from skillet. Pour this mixture over chicken. Cover; bake in oven at 350°F. for 1-1/4 hours, until tender. Transfer to warm platter. Blend 2 tablespoons flour with 1/2 cup cold water; add to gravy in baking pan. Cook, stirring, until thickened. Pour a little gravy over chicken. Garnish with toasted almonds. Pass gravy.

Marie Marinkovich

Fettucine

YIELD: 4 servings

INGREDIENTS
Noodles, freshly made	1 pound
Butter	1/2 pound
Pepper, freshly ground	dash
Heavy Cream	8 ounces
Grated Parmigiano (Parmesan) Cheese	1 cup

Cook noodles "al dente"; drain. Add butter, freshly ground pepper, cream, and cheese. Toss until all ingredients are blended together.

Tony's

Curry of Chicken Indian Fashion
[Curry de Poulet a l'Indienne]

YIELD: 8 servings

INGREDIENTS
Chickens, 3-1/2 Pounds each, cut into 8 pieces	2
Salt	as needed
Black Pepper, freshly ground	as needed
Clarified Butter	1/2 cup
Onions, chopped	3
Garlic Clove, chopped, crushed	1
Apples, peeled, cored, diced	2
Curry Powder	2 tablespoons
Flour	1/2 cup
Tomato Puree	2 tablespoons
White Wine	1/2 cup
Chicken Broth	1 cup
Bouquet Garni	1
Almonds, finely chopped	10
Chopped Indian Chutney	1/2 cup
Cream	1/2 cup
Garlic Clove, chopped, crushed	1
Shredded Coconut	1/2 cup

Guests who come to the Greenbrier to enjoy its superb cuisine are grateful for the excellent recreational facilities that are there to help them offset the calories in viands like these.

Season chicken pieces with salt and pepper. Saute in a casserole with heated butter until firm (not brown). Add onions, 1 garlic clove, and apples. Cook until onions are transparent. Blend curry powder and flour and sprinkle over chicken. Stir in tomato puree. Place casserole in oven at 325°F. for 3 minutes. Add wine and chicken broth and bring to a boil. Add bouquet garni; cover tightly; let simmer in oven at 325°F. for 35 minutes. Combine almonds with next 3 ingredients; marinate 1 hour. Rub mixture through a fine sieve; fold into curry and simmer for 15 minutes. Remove from heat; discard bouquet; skim fat and scum from surface.   Adjust seasoning.   Place in serving bowl; sprinkle shredded coconut on top of chicken.

The Greenbrier

French Pancakes with Creamed Chicken

YIELD: 24 pancakes

INGREDIENTS
PANCAKES

Flour	1 cup
Cream	3/4 cup
Eggs, separated	8
Salt	pinch
Sugar	1 tablespoon
Grated Orange Rind	2 tablespoons

CREAMED CHICKEN

Butter	1/4 cup
Flour	1/4 cup
Half-and-Half	1 cup
Diced, Cooked Chicken	2 cups
Sherry	2 tablespoons
Salt	to taste
Pepper	to taste

SAUCE

Egg Yolks	4
Water	1/4 cup
Butter, melted	1/2 pound
Heavy Cream, whipped	1/2 cup

Specialties like this are encountered at The Brown Palace because of general manager Mehlmann's interest in the food and restaurant business which he considers "a very important part of the overall daily business of a first-class property."

PANCAKES

Add flour to cream and whip thoroughly. Beat egg yolks with salt and blend into flour mixture. Beat egg whites with sugar until whites are fluffy but not stiff; fold into flour and cream mixture. Beat thoroughly until batter is smooth. It will be about the consistency of heavy cream. Add grated orange rind, mixing to blend. Cook pancakes in a hot 6-inch skillet which has been greased with butter. Use only enough batter to cover bottom of pan. Turn, cook on second side until pancake is golden brown; remove to platter or plate. Stack pancakes as they are cooked. This makes about 24 6-inch pancakes.

CREAMED CHICKEN

Melt butter over low heat. Add flour, stirring until blended. Gradually add half-and-half, stirring constantly until sauce is smooth and thickened. Add chicken. Continue cooking until mixture is thoroughly heated. Add sherry. Season to taste with salt and pepper. Spoon some of the creamed chicken onto the center of each thin pancake; roll pancake, jelly-roll fashion.

SAUCE

Combine egg yolks and water in top of double boiler over hot water. Beat until thick and lemon-colored and heated thoroughly. Meanwhile, melt butter and cool to lukewarm. Gradually add melted butter to egg yolks, beating constantly. When all the butter is beaten in and sauce is smooth, season with salt; then gently fold in whipped cream, using a spoon. Spoon sauce over rolled chicken-filled pancakes, allowing about 2 tablespoons for each serving of 3 pancakes. Place under broiler until sauce is golden brown. Serve immediately.

The Brown Palace

Eggs Florentine

YIELD: 6 servings

INGREDIENTS

Butter	1/2 cup
Flour	1/4 cup
Milk	1 quart
Salt	to taste
Pepper	to taste
Onion, Medium-sized, chopped	1
Butter	1/3 cup
Nutmeg	dash
Spinach, cooked, chopped	2 pounds
Eggs, poached	12
Grated Parmesan Cheese	1/4 cup
Finely Chopped Parsley	2 to 3 tablespoons

Brunch or light lunch treatment for eggs—out-of-the-ordinary recipes that can qualify as higher priced menu specialties.

Melt butter; stir in flour until a roux forms. Slowly stir in milk. Heat until sauce thickens, stirring constantly. Add salt and pepper. Set aside. Saute onion in butter. Add nutmeg and spinach. Turn into a heat-proof dish. Top with poached eggs. Cover with sauce. Sprinkle with parmesan cheese. Glaze under broiler. Garnish with finely chopped parsley.

Plaza Suite

Watercress and Sour Cream Omelette

YIELD: 2 servings

INGREDIENTS

Eggs	4
Milk	1 tablespoon
Salt	pinch
Pepper	pinch
Watercress, coarsely chopped	1/3 bunch
Butter	2 tablespoons
Sour Cream	1/4 cup

Beat first 4 ingredients lightly with a fork or a whisk. Over low heat, cook watercress with 1 tablespoon of butter until tender. Add sour cream. Heat the omelette pan; put in 1 tablespoon butter. When hot but not brown, pour in the eggs. When eggs are set, pour watercress mixture across center. Fold omelette out onto a platter. Serve at once.

Chateau Louise

Fish and Seafood Entrees

Turbot Poche Florentine

YIELD: 2 servings

INGREDIENTS

Butter, Unsalted	1 stick + 2 tablespoons
Chopped Shallots	2 tablespoons
Sliced Mushrooms	1 cup
Turbot, cleaned, skinless	2 6-ounce pieces
White Wine	1/2 cup + 1/8 cup
Salt	to taste
Pepper	to taste
Chopped, Cooked Spinach	1 cup
Egg Yolks	4
Lemon, juice of	1
Whipping Cream	1/3 cup
Flour	1 tablespoon

Melt 1 tablespoon butter in a hot skillet and saute slightly the shallots and mushrooms. Add the turbot, 1/2 cup white wine, salt, and pepper and bring to a boil. Place skillet in a preheated oven at 350°F. for 20 minutes. While the turbot is cooking, preheat the spinach in a small saucepan with 1 tablespoon butter, season, and keep hot in a serving dish. **Hollandaise Sauce:** In the top of a double boiler, beat 4 egg yolks vigorously together with 1/8 cup white wine and lemon juice until the mixture is light and fluffy. Very slowly add the 1 stick of melted butter, continuing to beat until all the butter is absorbed into the mixture, and it has a smooth and creamy consistency. Set aside. Remove the turbot from the oven and place the fish in a pan with the spinach. To the mushroom sauce, add the cream and cook for 5 minutes, stirring constantly. Make a paste by mixing the 1 tablespoon butter with 1 tablespoon flour and add it to the sauce to thicken. Taste for seasoning and combine with the Hollandaise Sauce, keeping it hot without letting it come to a boil. Pour the sauce over the turbot. Set oven at broil and pop the sauce-covered turbot under the broiler just long enough for the top to reach a golden color. Serve with boiled potatoes, if desired.

The Ninety-Fifth

Sole Ambassadeur

YIELD: 4 to 6 servings

INGREDIENTS

Sole Fillets	12
Minced Shallots *or* Onion	1 tablespoon
Salt	2 teaspoons
White Pepper	1/4 teaspoon
Dry White Wine	1/2 cup
Lemon, juice of	1/2
Chopped Mushrooms	1 cup
Butter	1 tablespoon
Salt	as needed
Pepper	as needed
Lemon, juice of	1/2
Light Cream	1/2 cup
Egg Yolk	1
Butter	3 tablespoons
Flour	1 tablespoon
Egg Yolks	2
Cream, Whipped	1/2 cup

Fold each fillet of sole in half. Butter baking pan or skillet. Sprinkle shallots in the bottom. Place sole on top. Sprinkle with salt and pepper. Pour wine and juice of 1/2 lemon on top. Cover with buttered paper or foil. Bring to a boil; bake in oven at 350°F. until tender. While fillets are cooking, melt 1 tablespoon butter in a pan. Add mushrooms, pinch of salt and pepper, and juice of 1/2 lemon. Cook 3 minutes or until juice is gone. Add cream, a little at a time; cook for another 3 minutes or until reduced to 1/3 of original volume. Remove from heat; add egg yolk and mix well. Spread mushrooms in a silver tray or in a casserole; keep hot. Place fillet of sole on top of mushrooms. Knead 3 tablespoons butter with 1 tablespoon flour; add to wine sauce remaining in baking pan. Cook for 3 minutes; remove from heat. Add egg yolks while whipping vigorously. *Do not boil.* Strain sauce; fold in whipped cream. Pour over sole. Glaze under broiler.

La Maisonette

The Comisar brothers of La Maisonette check table arrangements for a private dinner party.

Pompano Papillote, Drake Chef's Style

One of the two specialties with which the Cape Cod Room's name is most often associated is Pompano Papillote; the other is their snapper soup.

YIELD: 6 servings

INGREDIENTS

Red Wine	1 cup
Butter	2 ounces
Lobster, cooked, diced	2 ounces
Mushrooms, cut julienne	2 ounces
Shallots, chopped	1/4 ounce
Water	4 ounces
Pompano Fillets	6

Combine first 6 ingredients in a saucepot; heat to simmering. Add pompano and poach gently for 20 minutes. Remove fish to sheets of paper. Thicken the liquid with arrowroot to desired consistency. Cover fish with equal amounts of this sauce. Fold paper to form a bag. Clamp all edges so no air is allowed to escape. Bake in oven at 350°F. until bag begins to puff up.

Cape Cod Room, The Drake

Beau Rivage Trout

YIELD: 6 servings

INGREDIENTS

Garlic Clove	1
Trout	6
Chopped Parsley	2 tablespoons
Chopped Green Onions	2 tablespoons
Chopped Celery Leaves	1 tablespoon
Dry Red Wine	2 cups
Butter	1 tablespoon

Rub shallow baking dish with garlic; discard garlic. Lay trout in the dish and sprinkle with parsley, green onions, and celery leaves. Pour wine over trout and dot generously with butter. Bake in oven at 350°F. for 15 to 20 minutes. Remove trout to heated platter. Keep warm. Strain liquid and reduce to 1 cup. Blend 1 tablespoon butter with 1 teaspoon flour, then blend with liquid until smooth and thickened. Pour over fish. Garnish with lemon wedges and additional parsley.

Marie Marinkovich

Devil Crab

YIELD: 1 serving

INGREDIENTS

Butter	1 teaspoon
Shallot, chopped	1/2
Dry Mustard	pinch
Fresh Crabmeat	4 ounces
Cream Sauce*	3 ounces
Worcestershire Sauce	2 drops
Salt	to taste
Pepper	to taste

*See Bechamel Sauce, p. 183

Place butter in casserole. Add shallot; simmer 5 minutes. Stir in mustard, then crabmeat. Simmer 3 minutes. Blend with cream sauce and worcestershire. Add salt and pepper to taste. Pile into empty crab shell. Top with a little parmesan cheese, dot with butter. Bake in oven at 400°F. for 5 minutes.

Cape Cod Room, The Drake

Tenderloin of Trout Veronique

YIELD: 4 servings

INGREDIENTS

Trout	1-1/2 pounds
Water	2 cups
Sauterne	1 cup
Lemon, juice of	1
Hollandaise Sauce	3 cups
White Grapes	1/2 pound

One noon recently Lysle Aschaffenburg questioned some of his regular patrons about their favorite Pontchartrain dishes. The Tenderloin of Trout Veronique was a leading contender.

Cut trout to make 4 fillets. Poach in water, sauterne, and lemon juice until tender. Place trout on plate. Cover with split grapes and hollandaise. Brown under broiler. Serve hot.

Pontchartrain Hotel

Baked Stuffed Filet of Sole with Lobster Newburg Sauce

Sole never appeared to better advantage than in these lobster-filled rolls, served with a lobster newburg sauce.

YIELD: 4 servings

INGREDIENTS

Bread, trimmed, diced	2 slices
Cracker Crumbs	1 tablespoon
Butter, melted	1/2 pound
Sherry	2 ounces
Grated Parmesan Cheese	1 teaspoon
Lobster Meat, cut in small pieces	1/2 pound
Sole Fillets, 7- to 8-Ounce	4
Milk	1/2 cup
Flour	2 tablespoons
Milk, warmed	1/2 cup
Light Cream, warmed	1 cup
Butter	1 tablespoon
Paprika	dash

Mix bread with cracker crumbs, 4 tablespoons melted butter, 1 ounce sherry, parmesan cheese, and 1/4 pound lobster meat. Spread stuffing over sole fillets and roll up. Place seamside down in a pan, brush lightly with butter, and add 1/2 cup milk to keep moist. Bake in oven at 350°F. for 10 minutes. Meanwhile, place 4 tablespoons butter in saucepan. Add the flour and whip slowly. Add 1/2 cup warm milk and the cream; simmer until thickened, stirring constantly. Place 1 tablespoon butter in another pan; add 1/4 pound lobster meat, 1 ounce sherry, and paprika. Saute 1/2 minute. Stir in white sauce; simmer 5 minutes. Pour this sauce over the sole fillets. Bake 5 minutes.

Jimmy's Harborside

Shrimp de Jonghe en Casserole

YIELD: 10 servings

INGREDIENTS

Butter *or* Margarine	3/4 cup
Garlic Clove, grated	1
Salt	1 teaspoon
Bread Crumbs	1 cup
Cayenne Pepper	dash
Finely Chopped Parsley	4 tablespoons
Sherry	1/2 cup
Shrimp, Quick-Frozen, 20 to 25 Count, shelled, deveined	3 pounds
Butter	2 tablespoons

Stir butter or margarine to soft consistency. Mix garlic and salt and add to softened butter or margarine. Add bread crumbs, cayenne pepper, parsley, and sherry to mixture and blend thoroughly. Arrange 6 to 7 shrimp in each of 10 6-inch shirred egg dishes. Sprinkle 2 tablespoons butter and crumb mixture over the shrimp in each dish. Bake in oven at 350°F. for approximately 20 minutes. Serve piping hot.

Michael Reese Hospital and Medical Center

Boston Bluefish Casserole

YIELD: 100 servings

INGREDIENTS

Boston Bluefish Fillets	20 pounds
Medium Noodles	4 pounds
Shortening	1 pound
Flour	2 pounds
Salt	4 ounces
Pepper	1 ounce
Paprika	2 ounces
Milk	3 gallons
Cheese, grated	4 pounds
Worcestershire Sauce	3 ounces
Cooking Sherry	6 ounces
Lemon Juice	8 ounces
Bread Crumbs	as needed

Cook fish in salted water 15 minutes. Drain. Flake fish. Cook noodles in boiling water until tender. Drain. Melt shortening. Remove from heat. Add flour; stir until smooth. Add salt, pepper, and paprika. Return to medium heat. Add milk gradually, stirring constantly. Heat until sauce thickens. Stir in 2 pounds of the grated cheese, worcestershire sauce, sherry, and lemon juice. Add flaked fish and noodles to this mixture. Pour into 3 serving pans (12-inch by 20-inch by 2-inch) or individual casseroles. Combine the remaining 2 pounds of grated cheese with bread crumbs. Sprinkle over top of fish. Bake in oven at 350°F. for 1 hour.

Massachusetts General Hospital

From opposite ends of the country, these recipes for fish dishes indicate there is matching ingenuity among menu writers on both coasts. Fresh fish obviously engenders fresh ideas for ingredient combination.

Fletau en Brochette "Jean Lafitte"

YIELD: 2 servings

INGREDIENTS

Halibut Fillets	10 ounces
Virginia Ham	6 small slices
Onion	6 small slices
Tomato	6 small slices
Salt	to taste
Thyme	dash
Lemon Juice	few drops
Flour	2 tablespoons
French Pancake Batter	2 cups
Vegetable Oil	1/2 cup

Cut halibut fillets in 12 equal slices, 6 for each skewer. Place them piece by piece on skewers with ham, onion, and tomato slices. Season with salt, thyme, and lemon juice. Coat all sides with flour; dip into pancake batter. Heat oil in skillet until very hot. Gently place skewers in oil. Cook 5 to 6 minutes, turning skewers several times. Serve skewers on bed of curry rice with creole sauce or mango chutney and a green salad.

Hotel St. Francis

Seafood Casserole

YIELD: 4 servings

INGREDIENTS

Chopped Fresh Mushrooms	1/2 cup
Butter	4 ounces
Cooked, Diced Lobster	1/2 cup
Lump Crabmeat, cooked	1/2 cup
Cooked, Shelled Shrimp, deveined	1/2 cup
Medium Cream Sauce	1 cup
Sherry	1 tablespoon
Grated American Cheese	1/2 cup

Saute mushrooms in butter. Add seafood, cream sauce, and sherry; mix well. Pour into buttered casserole. Top with grated cheese. Bake in oven at 350°F. for 20 minutes.

Justine's

Baked Stuffed Lobster

YIELD: 1 serving

INGREDIENTS

Maine Lobster	1
Crabmeat	2 ounces
Sliced Mushrooms	2 tablespoons
Chopped Shallots *or* Onion	1 tablespoon
Chopped Celery	2 tablespoons
Bread Crumbs	1/4 cup
Grated Parmesan Cheese	1 tablespoon
Salt	to taste
Pepper	to taste
Sherry	as needed
Butter, melted	as needed
Lemon Wedges	2
Parsley	to garnish

Split body of lobster from head to tail. Mix crabmeat, mushrooms, shallots, celery, parmesan, salt, and pepper to taste. Moisten with sherry; add bread crumbs until mixture sticks together. Fill cavity of body with stuffing. Place on sizzler platter. Brush top with melted butter. Bake in oven at 450°F. for 8 minutes. Garnish with lemon wedges and fresh parsley. Serve with hot drawn butter.

Chateau Louise

Troute Saute Almondine

YIELD: 10 servings

INGREDIENTS

Fresh Trout, 10 to 12 Ounce, dressed, cleaned, boned	10
Salt	to taste
Pepper	to taste
Eggs	10
Coffee Cream	1 cup
Flour	2 pounds
Butter	1 pound
Salad Oil	1 cup
Almonds, Blanched, Slivered	1 pound
Butter	1 pound
Lemon, juice of	1/2

Place fish on table, skin side down, season well with salt and pepper. Beat eggs and coffee cream thoroughly in 2-quart bowl. Dip fish in this mixture and then in flour. Put 1 pound butter and oil in 18-inch frying pan. Heat to 260°F. Fry fish, 4 at a time, skin side up, until golden brown, about 5 minutes. Turn and finish cooking, about 7 minutes. In the meantime, in 12-inch frying pan, heat butter to 350°F.; add almonds and saute, stirring until golden brown. Remove from heat; add lemon juice. Serve fish topped with 1 tablespoon of almonds and a slice of lemon.

The Brown Palace Hotel

Crab Leg Ambassador

YIELD: 4 servings

INGREDIENTS

Mushrooms, finely chopped	1/2 pound
Shallots, Medium-sized, chopped	2
Butter	1 tablespoon
Lemon Juice	few drops
Heavy Cream	3 tablespoons
Nutmeg	to taste
Salt	to taste
Pepper	to taste
Crab Legs	40 pieces
Butter	2 to 3 tablespoons
Light Cream Sauce	1 to 1-1/2 cups

Nutmeg is the new note in this broiler-browned presentation of crab legs. Speedy sauteing of the legs is another key to the acceptance of this dish in high places.

Place mushrooms and shallots in pan with butter and lemon juice. Cover; simmer about 15 minutes, stirring occasionally. Add cream, nutmeg, salt, and pepper. Bring to a boil and put aside. Place crab legs in large pan with butter; saute lightly for 3 minutes. Spread mushroom mixture on serving platter and keep hot. Place crab legs on top. Cover all with a light cream sauce made with white wine and fish stock. Glaze under broiler until golden brown. Serve at once.

La Bourgogne

Opakapaka Caprice

YIELD: 4 servings

INGREDIENTS

Opakapaka	4 6-ounce pieces
Salt	to taste
White Pepper	to taste
Butter	4 ounces
Shallot, finely chopped	1
Fresh Mushrooms, Medium-sized, sliced	6
Lemon Juice	few drops
White Wine	1/3 cup
Butter, softened	2 ounces
Flour	2 tablespoons
Half-and-Half	1/2 cup
Whipped Cream	1/2 cup
Egg Yolk	1
Bananas, cut lengthwise, sauteed	2
Chopped Parsley	1 teaspoon

Season fish with salt and pepper. Saute in 2 ounces butter. In separate pan, saute shallot in 2 ounces butter. Add sliced mushrooms, salt, pepper, lemon juice, and wine. Cook rapidly. Mix 2 ounces butter with flour and blend with mushrooms. Add half-and-half; simmer for a few minutes. Remove from heat. Blend in whipped cream and egg yolk. Pour sauce into 4 shirred egg or similar type dishes. Place fish on sauce; top each serving with half a peeled, sauteed banana. Glaze in oven. Sprinkle with chopped parsley.

Note: Opakapaka is the Hawaiian name for red snapper. Many Hawaiian fish have double names—Hawaiians believe their fish is doubly delicious. Any fish may be substituted in this recipe.

The Kahala Hilton Hotel

Lobster a la Newburg

YIELD: 1 serving

INGREDIENTS

Butter	2 pats
Maine Lobster Meat, cooked, diced	4 ounces
Paprika	1/2 teaspoon
Flour	1/4 teaspoon
Sherry	1 teaspoon
Cream	1-1/4 cups
Egg Yolk, beaten	1

Melt butter slowly in skillet. Add lobster meat; saute lightly. Add paprika, stir until smooth. Stir in flour until blended. Add sherry and cream. Continuing to stir, let mixture come to a boil. Add beaten egg yolk slowly, stirring until well mixed and of desired thickness. *Remove from heat immediately.* (This is to prevent egg from becoming scrambled.)

Cape Cod Room, The Drake

Lake Trout Matelote

YIELD: 1 serving

INGREDIENTS

Lake Trout Fillet	8 ounces
Onion, cooked	2 ounces
Fresh Mushrooms	1 ounce
Red Wine	6 ounces
Water	4 ounces
Salt	to taste
Pepper	to taste
Worcestershire Sauce	1 teaspoon
Cornstarch	pinch

Put fish in pan. Add onion and next 6 ingredients. Cover; simmer for 15 minutes. Remove fish. Thicken sauce with cornstarch; simmer 15 minutes. Pour over fish. Serve hot.

Cape Cod Room, The Drake

Bouillabaisse

YIELD: 8 servings (2 cups broth, 6 ounces fish, 4 ounces shellfish)

INGREDIENTS

Onion, Medium-sized, diced	1
Fresh Leeks, sliced	3 to 4
Minced Garlic	2 teaspoons
Olive Oil	1/2 cup
Saffron	1 teaspoon
Bay Leaf	1
Liquid Hot Pepper Seasoning	dash
Prepared Mustard	2 teaspoons
Worcestershire Sauce	dash
Fish Stock	1 gallon
Lobster, Medium-sized,	1
OR	
Lobster Meat	1/2 pound
Clams	1 pound
Mussels	1 pound
Halibut, cut up	1 pound
Salmon, cut up	1 pound
Scallops	1/2 pound
Chicken Base	2 teaspoons
Canned Tomatoes, with juice	3 cups
Salt	to taste
Pepper	to taste
Chablis	1/4 cup

A Bouillabaisse that Bostonians find worth waiting for is served in its own special oven-proof bowl with plenty of bread for consuming every drop of broth.

Saute onion, leeks, and garlic gently in oil about 30 minutes. Stir in saffron and next 5 ingredients; simmer about 20 minutes. Add fish and simmer for 20 minutes. Add chicken base and remaining ingredients. Serve piping hot in an oven-proof bowl with crisp garlic bread.

Anthony's Pier 4

Filet of Sole Marguery

YIELD: 6 servings

INGREDIENTS

Whole Dover Sole *or* Flounder*	6
Shrimp, shelled, deveined	18
Sliced Carrots	2 cups
Chopped Onion	1/2 cup
Parsley Sprigs	10
Celery Stalks	2
Bay Leaves	2
Peppercorns	8
Water	3 quarts
Clam Juice	1 quart
White Wine (Domestic Chablis)	1 cup

Fillet each dover sole into four parts. Remove skins. Save bones and skin. Rinse fillets. Arrange in oven-proof cookware along with shrimp. Cover with plastic wrap to keep moist until ready to use. Clean fish bones, heads, and skins by rinsing thoroughly in cold water two or three times. Add cleaned skin and bones, vegetables, bay leaves, and peppercorns to water and clam juice. Simmer to make stock. Strain in cheesecloth. Cook liquid until it is reduced one-third. Cool. Preheat oven to 325° to 350°F. Over the fillets and shrimp, pour the wine and enough stock to barely cover. Salt and pepper to taste. Poach in oven approximately 20 minutes or until fish flakes easily when tested with a fork. Drain liquid and add it to stock mixture. (See recipe, p. 183.)

*Frozen fillets may be used if desired.   Camelot

Crab Meat Imperial

YIELD: 8 servings

INGREDIENTS

Green Pepper, Medium-sized, finely diced	1
Pimientos, finely diced	2
Chives *or* Green Onions	2 tablespoons
English Mustard	1 tablespoon
Salt	1 teaspoon
White Pepper	1/2 teaspoon
Eggs	2
Mayonnaise	1 cup
Lump Crabmeat	3 pounds
Paprika	as needed

Mix green pepper, pimientos, and chives or green onions; add mustard, salt, white pepper, eggs, and mayonnaise; mix well. Add crabmeat and mix carefully so the lumps are not broken. Divide mixture into 8 crab shells or casseroles, heaping it in lightly. Top with a light coating of mayonnaise. Sprinkle with a little paprika. Bake in oven at 350°F. for 15 minutes. Serve hot or cold.

                                    Commander's Palace Restaurant

COMMANDER'S PALACE SUGGESTS

Shrimp de Jonghe

YIELD: 1 serving

INGREDIENTS

Shrimp	8 ounces
Butter, melted	3 ounces
Garlic Clove, chopped	1
Chopped Shallots	1/4 ounce
Chopped Parsley	pinch
Liquid Hot Pepper Seasoning	1 drop
Worcestershire Sauce	4 drops
White Bread Crumbs	1/2 teaspoon

Cook shrimp in boiling salted water for 8 minutes; shell. Place in shallow casserole. Combine melted butter with remaining ingredients. Spread over shrimp. Bake in oven at 350°F. for 8 minutes.

Cape Cod Room, The Drake

Nautical artifacts that were put in place when the Cape Cod Room opened remain by popular demand.

Stuffed Flounder

YIELD: Stuffing for 8 to 10 flounders (one flounder per serving)

INGREDIENTS

Minced Onion	1 cup
Minced Shallots	1/2 cup
Minced Celery	1/2 cup
Garlic Cloves, minced	3
Margarine	1/2 pound
Flour	2 tablespoons
Salt	to taste
Pepper	to taste
Milk	1 cup
Dry White Wine	1 cup
Fish Stock	1 cup
Boiled, Chopped Shrimp	1/2 cup
Lump Crabmeat	1/2 cup
Bread Crumbs	2-1/2 cups
Flounders, Small	8 to 10
Margarine	1/2 cup
Shrimp, boiled	24 to 30
Lemon Slices	8 to 10
Parsley Sprigs	8 to 10

Saute onion, shallots, celery, and garlic in margarine until done. Add flour, salt, and pepper and blend. Stir in milk, white wine, and fish stock; cook until thick. Add shrimp, crabmeat, and parsley. Finish thickening with bread crumbs. Remove heads from flounders. Cut down center back. Remove backbone. Heap opening with stuffing; dot with margarine. Bake in oven at 300°F. until done (15 to 20 minutes). Garnish each flounder with three whole boiled shrimp, lemon slice, and parsley.

Commander's Palace Restaurant

Butterfly Shrimp Oriental

Presented in a boat-shaped dish with tomato wedge garnishes, this is a highly acceptable answer to the universal craving for something different.

YIELD: 8 servings

INGREDIENTS

Pineapple Juice	2 cups
Soy Sauce	1/4 cup
Vinegar	3/4 cup
Sugar	4 tablespoons
Clear Gel	4 tablespoons
Rice	12 ounces
Shrimp, Large	40
Lemon Juice	2 tablespoons
Seasoned Salt	2 tablespoons
Onions, Medium-sized, sliced julienne	4
Diced Green Pepper	1 cup
Tomato Wedges	16

Make sauce by combining pineapple juice and next 3 ingredients. Bring to a boil, add Clear Gel (cornstarch may be substituted), and cook until clear. Cook rice until tender. Butterfly shrimp and season with lemon juice and salt. Place shrimp, split side up, on baking sheet. Top each with half a slice of bacon. Bake in oven at 325°F. for 8 to 10 minutes. Saute onions and green pepper until clear but still crisp. Using boat-shaped dishes, place a No. 12 scoop rice in each dish; spoon onions and green pepper over rice. Arrange 5 shrimp around edges of each dish, bacon side up. Ladle sauce over all. Garnish each with 2 tomato wedges.

Michigan State University

Lobster Newburg

YIELD: 25 servings

INGREDIENTS

Lobster Meat, boiled, cut 3/4-inch pieces	3 pounds
Butter	4 ounces
Flour	1/4 cup
Milk	2 quarts
Egg Yolks	12
Salt	3/8 teaspoon
Cayenne Pepper	dash
Paprika	1/2 teaspoon
Sherry	1 tablespoon

Saute lobster meat in butter until heated through. Remove lobster. To hot melted butter, add flour to make a roux. Over a low flame, slowly add milk and allow to simmer for 1 to 2 minutes. Slowly add beaten egg yolks, salt, cayenne pepper, and paprika to cream sauce and allow to heat for 2 minutes. Add lobster meat and heat another minute. Add 1 tablespoon sherry just before serving. Serve over toast points or in patty shell. Newburg may be held for serving in double boiler over low heat. High heat will curdle mixture.

Michael Reese Hospital and Medical Center

Mousse of Sole

YIELD: 15 servings

INGREDIENTS

Scallops, chilled	1/2 pound
Sole Fillets, chilled	1/2 pound
Butter, softened	1/2 pound
Heavy Cream, chilled	2 cups
Eggs, chilled	6
Salt	to taste
Pepper	to taste
Liquid Hot Pepper Seasoning	2 to 3 drops
Lobster Sauce	1 quart

Grind scallops and sole twice through fine blade of meat grinder. Put into Buffalo chopper; add butter slowly. Add cream very slowly, then eggs, one at a time. Add seasonings. Be sure all ingredients are well blended. Allow mousse batter to rest in refrigerator for 24 hours before poaching.

To Poach Mousse: Bring lightly salted water to a simmer in shallow pan. With two tablespoons, shape mousse to an egg shape. Stir water with spoon and insert mousse in the swirling water. Poach 15 to 20 minutes. In another shallow pan, have boiling lobster sauce ready. Remove mousse from water; drain and put into lobster sauce. Cover; let stand until mousse starts to puff. Serve at once.

Hotel St. Francis

Coquille St. Jacques Bretonne
[Fresh Baby Scallops Brittany Style]

YIELD: 4 servings

INGREDIENTS

Butter	2 ounces
Fresh Baby Bay *or* Sea Scallops	2 pounds
Salt	to taste
Pepper, freshly ground	to taste
Dry White Wine *or* Sherry	1/2 cup
Mushroom Caps	8
Whipping Cream	1/2 cup
Chopped Fresh Parsley	1 tablespoon
Sliced Truffles	1 ounce

Melt 1 ounce of butter in a saucepan. Saute the scallops lightly (do not brown). Season to taste with salt and pepper. Add wine and raw mushroom caps. Cook for 3 minutes. Remove scallops and mushrooms; keep warm. Reduce the cooking liquor to 1/2 of its volume. Stir in cream. Reduce until the sauce begins to thicken; add the parsley. Correct seasoning if necessary. Finish the sauce with the remaining butter, added in small amounts. Shake the saucepan constantly until the sauce has absorbed all the butter. *Do not allow to boil.* Pour over the scallops. Decorate with the mushroom caps and truffles.

La Maisonette

Trout Amandine*

YIELD: 3 or 4 servings

INGREDIENTS

Trout Fillets	2 pounds
Egg, beaten	1
Milk	1 cup
Flour	as needed
Butter	1/2 cup
Slivered Almonds	1/3 cup
Lemons, juice of	2
Worcestershire Sauce	2 tablespoons
Chopped Parsley	1 tablespoon

Salt and pepper trout. Dip in batter of 1 beaten egg and 1 cup milk.
Drain.   Dredge in flour. In 9-inch skillet, melt butter and saute trout
about 5 to 8 minutes, or until golden brown. Remove trout to warm
platter.   Add almonds to skillet and brown lightly. Add lemon juice,
worcestershire sauce, and parsley. Heat through and then pour over fish.

*Brennan's New Orleans Cookbook   **Commander's Palace Restaurant**

Scampi Marie Jose

*Ernie's leadership among
San Francisco's dining spots is
easily understood from the
Gotti's imaginative approach in
this combination of shrimp
and crabmeat.*

YIELD: 4 servings

INGREDIENTS

Scampi, Medium-sized	20
Finely Chopped Crabmeat	2 ounces
Mustard	1 teaspoon
Bread Crumbs	2 teaspoons
Butter	2 ounces
Chopped Shallots	2 teaspoons
Salt	to taste
Pepper	to taste
Tomato Concasse	1-1/2 ounces
White Wine	2 ounces
Fish Stock	2 ounces
Cornstarch	1/2 teaspoon
Chopped Parsley	1 teaspoon

Shell scampi by cutting off the shell on the back. Leave tail part on the
meat. Mix crabmeat with mustard and bread crumbs. Butter the bottom of a shallow baking pan and sprinkle with shallots. Put the scampi
close together in the pan. Add seasonings. Spread the crab mixture on
top.   Sprinkle concasse of tomato over all; add white wine, and fish
stock. Cover with foil and cook in oven at 375°F. for about 15 minutes. Put the scampi on a plate. Bring the sauce to a boil, thicken with
cornstarch, and correct the seasoning. Pour sauce over scampi and
sprinkle with parsley.

Ernie's

Crepes "H.K.H."

YIELD: 2 servings

INGREDIENTS

Eggs, hard-cooked	2
Smoked Salmon	1/2 pound
Unsalted Butter	1 tablespoon
Hollandaise Sauce	1-1/2 cups
Lemon Juice	1 to 2 drops
Fresh Green Dill, minced	2 ounces
French Pancakes, medium-sized	6
Unsalted Butter	1-1/2 ounces

Cut eggs and salmon into very small cubes. Heat slightly in 1 tablespoon butter; put aside to cool. Blend hollandaise, lemon juice, and dill with fish-egg mixture. Place 1-1/2 tablespoons of this mixture in center of each pancake (crepe). Roll or fold crepe over filling. Place 3 crepes on each plate. Heat in oven at 350°F. about 5 minutes. Brown the 1-1/2 ounces butter in skillet. Remove plates from oven; top with the brown butter; glaze about 1/2 minute under a hot broiler. Serve immediately.

Hotel St. Francis

Baked Kumu

YIELD: 4 servings

INGREDIENTS

Kumu, Red Snapper, or Sea Bass	1 2-pound (whole)
Salt	to taste
Pepper	to taste
Lemons	2-1/2
Fennel Leaves, Dried	1 bunch
Butter, melted	4 ounces
Onion, Medium-sized, thinly sliced	1
Potatoes, Medium-sized, peeled, thinly sliced	4
Tomatoes, quartered	2
White Wine	1/2 cup
Anise-flavored Liqueur	3 tablespoons
Chopped Parsley	1 to 2 tablespoons

Operations not so fortunate as to be in Hawaii can still offer this unusual dish by substituting red snapper or sea bass for the kumu.

Season fish inside and out with salt, pepper, and juice of half a lemon. Place fennel leaves inside fish. In large skillet, brown fish in melted butter, then bake in oven at 375°F. for 10 minutes. Place onion around fish and bake for 10 more minutes. Add potatoes, sprinkle with salt; bake another 20 minutes. Add tomato quarters. Pour wine over fish; sprinkle with liqueur. Bake for 8 minutes. Place fish on large platter. Arrange tomatoes, potatoes, and onion around fish. Pour juices from baking dish over the fish, then sprinkle with chopped parsley. Garnish with 4 lemon halves.

The Kahala Hilton Hotel

Scallops Harborside Style

An entree with an impressive record as a patron first choice, scallops prepared Harborside style are equally popular when served as an hors d'oeuvre.

YIELD: 4 servings

INGREDIENTS

Cape Cod *or* Bay Scallops*	2 pounds
Butter	as needed
Bread Crumbs	1 tablespoon
Garlic Salt	pinch
Paprika	pinch
Sherry	few drops
Lemon, cut in wedges	1

*If desired, Deep Sea Scallops may be substituted for Cape Scallops. To make them more tender and reduce cooking time, slice them horizontally through the center.

Place scallops in oven platter containing a little butter. Sprinkle with topping made of bread crumbs, garlic salt, and paprika. Spread a little butter over the scallops. Preheat broiler 5 minutes. Broil scallops 5 to 7 minutes until they are brown. Turn off broiler, close door, and let scallops heat through for 3 more minutes. Add a few drops of sherry. Serve very hot with lemon.
Note: Delicious, too, served as hors d'oeuvre.

Jimmy's Harborside

Shrimp a la Grecque with Rice Pilaf

YIELD: 4 servings

INGREDIENTS

Rice, Raw	1 cup
Chicken *or* Lobster Broth	2 cups
Salt	to taste
Pepper	to taste
Shrimp, shelled, washed, dried	1-1/2 pounds
Butter	4 ounces
Sherry	2 ounces
Lemon Juice	few drops
Garlic Salt	pinch
Oregano	pinch
Paprika	pinch

Wash rice. Bring broth to a boil. Add salt, pepper, and rice; stir for 2 minutes. Cover. Bake in oven at 350°F. for 25 minutes. Meanwhile, saute shrimp in butter in skillet with sherry and next 4 ingredients for 10 minutes. Serve rice with shrimp and butter sauce.

Jimmy's Harborside

Sauces

Sauce Bearnaise

YIELD: 4 servings (approximately 1 cup)

INGREDIENTS

Egg Yolks	2
Water	2 tablespoons
Clarified Butter, warmed	6 ounces
Tarragon Leaves	1-1/2 teaspoons
Shallots, chopped	1/3 ounce
Tarragon Vinegar	2 tablespoons
Peppercorns, crushed	1 or 2
Dry White Wine	2 tablespoons
Salt	to taste
Pepper	to taste
Chopped Parsley *or*	1 teaspoon
Chopped Tarragon Leaves	1 teaspoon

Whip egg yolks and water in stainless steel bowl. Place over a pot of boiling water, making sure the bottom of bowl does not touch the hot water. Whip yolks lightly until cooked to a soft peak. Remove from heat and slowly add the warm clarified butter. Mix tarragon leaves, shallots, tarragon vinegar, crushed peppercorns, and wine. Reduce slightly. Drain and squeeze through a cheesecloth over the egg-butter sauce. Stir. Add salt and pepper to taste. Add chopped fresh parsley or tarragon leaves.

Chateau Louise

Spaghetti Meat Sauce

YIELD: 22 4-ounce servings per gallon

INGREDIENTS	40 GALLONS	50 GALLONS
Lawry's Spaghetti Sauce Mix without Mushrooms	12 (20 ounce) packages	15 (20 ounce) packages
Tomato Sauce	12 No. 10 cans	15 No. 10 cans
Water	18 gallons	22 gallons, 2 quarts
Sugar	2 pounds	2 pounds, 8 ounces
Oregano	1/3 cup	1/2 cup
Garlic Powder	3 tablespoons	4 tablespoons
Salt	1 pound	1 pound, 4 ounces
Ground Beef	150 pounds	188 pounds

Mix first 7 ingredients. Simmer 1 hour. Brown meat and drain well. Add to sauce. Simmer an additional hour.

Washington State University

Mushroom Sauce

YIELD: approximately 1 quart

INGREDIENTS

Fresh Mushrooms	1/2 pound
Butter	2 tablespoons
Burgundy	1/2 cup
Brown Gravy	2 cups
Salt	to taste
Pepper	to taste
Monosodium Glutamate	to taste

Thinly slice mushrooms. Saute in butter until soft. Add wine and gravy; simmer 10 minutes. Stir in seasonings.

Karl Ratzsch's

Horseradish Sauce

YIELD: 1 quart, 1 ounce per serving

INGREDIENTS

Heavy Cream	2 cups
Mayonnaise	1 cup
Salad Mustard	8 tablespoons
Horseradish	4 tablespoons
Lemon Juice	2 teaspoons
Seasoned Salt	1 teaspoon
Salt	1/2 teaspoon
Pepper	1/2 teaspoon

Whip cream until stiff. Fold in remaining ingredients. Chill.

Stephenson's Apple Farm Restaurant

Meat Sauce for Onion Shortcake

YIELD: 24 servings

INGREDIENTS

Chopped Celery	2 cups
Chopped Onion	1 cup
Oil	1/3 cup
Ground Beef	4 pounds
Salt	2 teaspoons
Pepper	1 teaspoon
Tomato Paste	1 cup
Tomato Juice	2 quarts
Water	1 quart

Saute celery and onion in oil. Add ground beef seasoned with salt and pepper. Cook until beef is browned. Add tomato paste, tomato juice, and water. Simmer about 1 hour. Serve on Onion Shortcake (see recipe, p. 186).

Michigan State University

Bechamel Sauce

YIELD: 1-1/2 to 2 cups

INGREDIENTS

Butter	3 tablespoons
Sifted All-Purpose Flour	1/3 cup
Milk	1-1/2 to 2 cups
Salt	to taste
White Pepper	to taste

Heat butter in saucepan. Stir in flour and cook until light and foamy. Slowly add the milk, beating constantly with whisk, while simmering for 3 to 4 minutes. Season with salt and pepper.

The Four Seasons

Sauce for Filet of Sole Marguery

INGREDIENTS

Fish Stock*	6 cups
Whipping Cream	1/2 cup
Egg Yolks	8
*If frozen fillets have been used, use clam juice as a substitute for the fish stock.	

Heat fish stock and thicken with roux. Bring to just below boiling point and stir carefully to creamy consistency. Place in double boiler. Slowly add beaten egg yolks. Add cream (unwhipped) and fold into sauce. Pour sauce over shrimp and fillets; reheat in oven. Just before serving, place under broiler to brown. Watch carefully. May be served with any vegetable. (See recipe, p. 174.)

A special offering on Karl Ratzsch's menu features Chateaubriand with Mushroom Sauce (see recipe, facing page).

Gracious Dining
For Two

CRAB LOUIE
APPETIZER

CAESAR SALAD MIXED
AT YOUR TABLE

CHATEAUBRIAND

MUSHROOM SAUCE	GOLDEN ONION RINGS

BAKED IDAHO POTATO

CHOICE OF
BEVERAGE

$22.00

Vegetables

As the level of nutrition consciousness rises, interest in vegetable selection increases. But they have to be vegetables that are not simply drab portions of what's good for you; today's vegetables have to be presented with imaginative flavor touches. The recipes in this section are clearly the result of an innovative approach to vegetable preparation.

Tiny Whole Beets in Orange Sauce

YIELD: 6 to 8 servings

INGREDIENTS

Tiny Whole Beets	1 No. 2-1/2 can
Beet Juice	1 ounce
Orange Juice	4 ounces
Butter *or* Margarine	1 ounce
Sugar	1 ounce
Salt	pinch
Cornstarch	1/4 teaspoon

Drain beets; set aside. Combine beet juice and remaining ingredients. Cook, stirring, over low heat until sauce has smooth, glossy appearance, approximately 5 minutes. Add beets to sauce; heat thoroughly.

Michael Reese Hospital and Medical Center

Fresh Green Beans, Hungarian Style

YIELD: 6 servings

INGREDIENTS

Fresh Green Beans	1-1/2 pounds
Boiling Water	3 quarts
Butter, melted	6 tablespoons
Finely Chopped Onion	1 cup
Garlic Clove, diced	1
Flour	2-1/2 tablespoons
Sweet Hungarian Paprika	1-1/2 tablespoons
Sour Cream	1-1/4 cups
Salt	1 teaspoon
Pepper	1/4 teaspoon
Diced Fresh Parsley	1 teaspoon

Prepare green beans for cooking. Place in boiling, salted water; cook until tender-crisp (do not overcook). Drain and hold beans. Melt butter, add chopped onion and diced garlic; add enough flour to make a light roux. Add paprika, sour cream, salt, pepper, and diced parsley. Pour the above sauce over cooked green beans, heat gently, and serve.

Charlie's Cafe Exceptionale

Broccoli-Stuffed Tomato

YIELD: 10 servings

INGREDIENTS

Fresh Tomatoes, Medium-sized	10
Frozen Broccoli	10 ounces
Heavy White Sauce	
Butter	1/4 pound
Flour	10 tablespoons
Salt	1/4 teaspoon
Pepper	dash
Half-and-Half	5 cups
Sherry	1/3 cup
Nutmeg	1/4 teaspoon

Remove tops from tomatoes; scoop out the inside of each. Place tomatoes, cut side down, on paper towel and let drain. Cook broccoli 6 minutes in boiling salted water. Cut in 1-inch pieces and set aside. Melt butter in double boiler and stir in flour, salt, and pepper; cook 10 minutes. Slowly add half-and-half, beating with french whip. Stir in sherry and nutmeg. Add cooked broccoli to white sauce and mix gently. Fill the tomatoes with mixture. Place filled tomatoes in buttered baking dish; bake about 25 minutes in oven at 325°F.

Michigan State University

Ratatouille Provencal

YIELD: 10 servings

INGREDIENTS

Olive Oil	as needed
Eggplant, peeled, seeded, diced	2 pounds
Zucchini, diced	1 pound
Onions, diced	3
Garlic Clove, chopped	1
Bouquet Garni	
Laurel, Thyme, Parsley,	1 sprig each
Tarragon	1 teaspoon
Green Pepper, diced	1 pound
Mushrooms, diced	12
Tomatoes, peeled, sliced	1-1/2 pounds
Tomato Paste	1 tablespoon
Salt	to taste
Pepper	to taste

As a demonstration of their belief that preparation and presentation of foods should be simple, "21" offers a low calorie, delicately flavored vegetable recipe, equally satisfying whether served hot or cold.

Put a light cover of olive oil in pan and saute eggplant and zucchini for 5 to 10 minutes. Remove vegetables and set aside. Discard oil. Put a light cover of fresh olive oil in pan and saute onions, garlic, and bouquet garni for a few minutes. Add green pepper and mushrooms; saute 5 to 10 minutes. Stir in peeled tomato and tomato paste. Bring to a boil and simmer 10 minutes. Add salt and pepper to taste. Add zucchini and eggplant. Cover and simmer 1/2 hour. Serve hot or cold.

The 21 Club

Stuffed Tomatoes

Listed on Win Schuler's menu as Kitchen Supplements are Mushrooms Saute, delicately flavored with Burgundy wine; Mushrooms dipped in batter and french fried, and Onion Rings, french fried and golden brown.

YIELD: 6 servings

INGREDIENTS

Tomatoes, Large, Ripe	6
Fresh Mushrooms, chopped	1/2 pound
Onion, Medium-sized, finely chopped	1/2
Salt	1/2 teaspoon
Chopped Parsley	1 teaspoon
Tomato Paste	3 tablespoons
Seasoned Croutons	1/2 cup
Parmesan Cheese	2 tablespoons
Butter, melted	1/4 cup
Mozzarella Cheese Slices, halved	3

Remove tops of the tomatoes and carefully scoop out pulp, seeds, and juice. Season cases with salt and pepper. Combine mushrooms, onion, and butter; cook gently until the onion is tender and has picked up some color, about 5 to 7 minutes. Add salt and next 4 ingredients; mix well. Stuff the tomatoes with the mixture. Top each tomato with half a slice of the cheese. Place under low broiler heat until tomato is tender, approximately 10 minutes.

Win Schuler's

Onion Shortcake

YIELD: 24 servings

INGREDIENTS

Flour	1 quart
Baking Powder	1-1/2 tablespoons
Salt	1-1/2 teaspoons
Shortening	3/4 cup
Eggs	2
Milk	2 cups
Sliced Onion, tiny rings	2 quarts
Salt	1 tablespoon
Shortening	1/4 cup
Egg	1
Sour Cream	1 cup

Combine flour, baking powder, and salt; cut in 3/4 cup shortening until mixture resembles coarse meal. Beat 2 eggs slightly and combine with milk. Add to flour mixture; blend only until moistened. Spread evenly in a 12-inch by 18-inch sheet pan. Sprinkle onion with 1 tablespoon salt and saute in the 1/4 cup shortening until tender but not brown. Cover shortcake, which has been spread in greased baking pan, with the sauteed onion. Beat the egg slightly and mix with sour cream. Pour over onion. Bake shortcake in oven at 425°F. for 45 minutes or until done. Serve with Meat Sauce (see recipe, p. 182).

Michigan State University

Potato Dumplings

YIELD: 5 to 6 dumplings

INGREDIENTS

Potato, pared, ground	1 large
Onion, Small, ground	1/2
Bacon Strips, diced, fried	4
Croutons	1/2 cup
Eggs	2
Minced Parsley	pinch
Flour	1 cup
Salt	pinch
Pepper	pinch
Nutmeg	pinch

Mix all ingredients thoroughly. Form into balls about the size of an egg and cook in boiling salted water for 30 minutes. Remove dumplings from water; put melted butter on top and serve immediately.

Karl Ratzsch's

Tortellini Palermitana

YIELD: 8 servings

INGREDIENTS

Butter	5 tablespoons
Garlic Clove, minced	1
Onions, Medium-sized, chopped	2
Tomatoes, Ripe, peeled, chopped	4
Tomato Paste	1 tablespoon
Flour	1 tablespoon
Beef Stock	1 cup
Thyme	1/4 teaspoon
Bay leaf	1/2
Salt	1 teaspoon
Pepper	1/2 teaspoon
Mushrooms, chopped	2
Frozen Tortellini	8 dozen
Parmesan Cheese, freshly grated	4 tablespoons

Heat 2 tablespoons butter in saucepan. Add garlic and onions; cook for about 5 minutes. Add tomatoes, tomato paste, flour, stock, and seasonings. Stir while bringing to a boil. Simmer 15 minutes. Add mushrooms; cook an additional 5 minutes. Set aside. Preheat oven to 450°F. Prepare tortellini. Cook the frozen tortellini in boiling salted water for 10 minutes. Drain. Heat 2 tablespoons butter in shallow baking dish. Add the drained tortellini and cook over moderate heat until coated with butter. Pour tomato sauce over the tortellini. Add 2 tablespoons parmesan cheese; stir gently. Top with 1 tablespoon butter, diced. Sprinkle with 2 tablespoons grated parmesan cheese and bake in oven at 450°F. for 10 minutes.

Ernie's

Happily, not everyone is a calorie counter so heartier vegetable dishes—Onion Shortcake (facing page), Potato Dumplings, and Tortellini Palermitana have their own sizable following.

Broccoli Casserole

YIELD: 6 servings

INGREDIENTS

Frozen Chopped Broccoli, thawed, drained	2 10-ounce packages
Mushrooms, drained	1 8-ounce can
Pimiento, chopped	1 2-ounce jar
Sour Cream	3/4 cup
Diced Celery	1 cup
Salt	1 teaspoon
Pepper	1/2 teaspoon
Grated Sharp Cheese	1/2 cup

Gently mix all ingredients except cheese. Turn into greased casserole dish. Top with cheese. Bake in oven at 350°F. for 25 minutes.

Marie Marinkovich

Curried Tomatoes

YIELD: 60 servings

INGREDIENTS

Tomato Halves	60
Onions, Jumbo, sliced	11
Butter	1-1/2 pounds
Curry Powder	3 tablespoons

A painterly approach to food presentation is easily possible if menu planners keep in mind the color accents that vegetable accompaniments can offer. Green, red and pale yellow possibilities offer a first step to combinations with a high color quotient.

Slice tomatoes in half. Scoop out the insides of each tomato half. Saute the sliced onions in the butter and curry powder. Fill each tomato half with this mixture; heat and serve.
Note: Top with crumbs and bake, if you prefer the crumb-top look.

Southern Methodist University Food Service

Potato Gratin

YIELD: 6 servings

INGREDIENTS

Potatoes	2 pounds
Salt	to taste
White Pepper	to taste
Grated Swiss Cheese	1/2 cup
Heavy Cream	2 cups
Eggs, beaten	4
Nutmeg	pinch

Peel and mince the potatoes. Season lightly with salt and pepper. Butter a baking dish; make layers of potatoes. Sprinkle with grated cheese. Combine the heavy cream, eggs, and nutmeg; add to the potatoes, covering them. Salt and pepper to taste. Cook in oven at 325°F. for 70 minutes.

Ernie's

Turmeric Rice

YIELD: 60 servings

INGREDIENTS

Rice, Uncooked	7-1/2 pounds
Butter	1-1/2 pounds
Onions, thinly sliced	5
Finely Chopped Chicken Livers	2-1/2 cups
or Canned Chopped Chicken Liver	4 ounces
Turmeric	2 tablespoons
Chicken Broth	1-1/2 gallons
Parmesan Cheese	to taste
Butter	as needed

Vegetables in preparations rarely encountered add new dimensions to menus, often attracting attention to an entree that is on the low cost list, and would otherwise get only a "so what's new" response from patrons.

Brown rice in the 1-1/2 pounds butter. Add onions and saute about 1 minute. Combine with chicken livers, turmeric, and chicken broth. Bake, covered, in deck oven at 350°F. or 45 minutes in a convection oven at 350°F. until rice is tender. Season to taste with parmesan cheese and additional butter. Serve with chicken.

Southern Methodist University Food Service

Pasta Verde

YIELD: 4 servings

INGREDIENTS

Flour	4 cups
Eggs	4
Olive Oil	1 tablespoon
Cooked, Chopped, Fresh Spinach	1 cup

Sift the flour into a bowl; make a well in the center and put into it the eggs and oil. Work in the flour and the spinach. (If the mixture is too dry, add a little water.) Pick up the dough and slap it down hard on rolling board a few times, then knead until very smooth. Form into a ball. Cover with a bowl. Let stand 30 minutes. Roll out thin and cut to the width desired.

Tony's

Zucchini with Walnuts

YIELD: 6 servings

INGREDIENTS

Walnut Halves	1 cup
Zucchini, Medium	6
Butter	2 tablespoons
Salt	to taste
Pepper, freshly ground	to taste

Reserve 6 walnut halves for garnish. Chop the rest. Cut unpeeled zucchini in 1/8-inch slices. Place in skillet with melted butter. Add chopped walnuts, salt, and pepper. Cook, stirring, until zucchini is tender. Garnish with reserved walnut halves.

The Four Seasons

Zucchini

Peel fresh zucchini. Steam until tender, but firm. Dot with butter. Season with salt and pepper. Sprinkle with grated parmesan cheese and white bread crumbs. Bake in oven at 350°F. for ten minutes.

Tony's

Tomato-Vegetable Medley

YIELD: 60 servings per pan

INGREDIENTS

Cut Celery, 2-inch strips	3 gallons
Cut Carrots, 2-inch strips	2-1/4 gallons
Sliced Onion	2-1/4 gallons
Cut Green Beans	4 No. 10 cans
Green Pepper Strips	1-1/2 gallons
Tomatoes	4 No. 10 cans
Salt	6 tablespoons
Quick Cooking Tapioca	1 quart
Butter	3 pounds
Pepper	1 tablespoon
Sugar	1-1/2 cups

Steam celery and carrots for 15 minutes. Mix all ingredients. Scale 2-1/4 gallons into each of 4 buttered 12-inch by 20-inch by 4-inch pans. Cover with foil and cook in steamer for 30 minutes.

Purdue University

Au Gratin Dauphinoise

Quick cooking is essential for the crisp vegetables that are preferred by many patrons today. However, the custard-like potato dish (Au Gratin Dauphinoise) offers a pleasant contrast to crisp cooked entrees.

YIELD: 6 to 8 servings

INGREDIENTS

Potatoes, Large, pared	5
Butter	4 ounces
Garlic Clove	1
Eggs	5
Heavy Cream	1 cup
Milk	1 cup
Salt	to taste
Pepper	to taste
Nutmeg	dash

Slice potatoes paper-thin. Keep covered with water so they do not turn brown. Use 2 ounces of the butter to generously butter a 2-inch deep square or oblong baking pan. Rub with garlic clove. Spread drained, sliced potatoes evenly in the pan. In blender or with an egg beater, combine eggs and next 5 ingredients. Pour over potatoes so they are just covered. Dot with 2 ounces of butter. Bake in oven at 350°F. for 10 minutes, or until brown on top. Reduce heat to 250°F. and bake for another hour, or until almost like a custard.

Hotel St. Francis

Creme Spinach

YIELD: 4 servings

INGREDIENTS
Chopped, Cooked Fresh Spinach	2 cups
Medium Cream Sauce	2 heaping tablespoons
Worcestershire Sauce	dash
Liquid Hot Pepper Seasoning	dash
Salt	to taste
Pepper	to taste
Hollandaise Sauce	1/4 cup

Mix together spinach, cream sauce, and seasonings; heat. Divide into 4 individual casseroles or 1 large casserole. Top each portion with hollandaise sauce. Lightly brown in oven at 450ºF.

Justine's

Creamed Spinach

YIELD: 8 4-ounce servings

INGREDIENTS
Salt Pork, finely ground	2-1/2 ounces
Onion, chopped	1-1/2 ounces
Frozen Spinach, thawed, finely ground	1-1/2 pounds
Salt	to taste
Pepper	to taste
Cream Sauce (Bechamel)	1 cup

Saute ground salt pork until brown. Add chopped onion and saute 2 to 3 minutes, or until golden brown. Add spinach, salt, and pepper. Bring to a boil, stirring occasionally. Add cream sauce. Cook gently about 35 minutes, stirring frequently.

The Blackhawk

Concombres a la Creme [Cucumbers in Cream]

YIELD: 15 to 20 servings

INGREDIENTS
Cucumbers	10
Butter	10 ounces
Salt	to taste
Pepper	to taste
Heavy Cream	1-1/2 cups
Parsley	for garnish

Peel cucumbers, quarter lengthwise, remove seeds, cut each in 3 pieces. Simmer the cucumber pieces in lightly salted water for 4 minutes. Drain thoroughly. Melt butter in a casserole; add the cucumbers; cook slowly for 15 to 20 minutes. Sprinkle with salt and pepper to taste. Pour cream over top; cook for 5 minutes longer. Before serving, sprinkle with chopped parsley.

Camelot

LEGUMES

Asperges au gratin
Asperges fraîches au beurre
Broccoli sauce hollandaise
Creme d' Epinards
Pomme de terre au gratin
Petits pois a la francaise
Haricots verts à la Lyonnaise
Celéris Braisés
Courgettes (en saison)

Justine's

Red Cabbage

YIELD: 6 servings

Red cabbage is featured on Ratzsch's menu with Roast Duckling and Wild Rice, and billed as a combination "once reserved for nobility."

INGREDIENTS

Bacon Strips, minced	4
Red Cabbage, finely cut	1 small head
Apple, Medium-sized, finely chopped	1
Onion, Small, finely chopped	1
Salt	1 tablespoon
Sugar	1/4 cup
Vinegar	3/4 cup
Water	2 cups
Mixed Spices (clove, mustard seed, bay leaf, dill seed, cinnamon, red pepper, coriander)	1 teaspoon

Saute bacon in kettle. Add remaining ingredients and cook until tender.

Karl Ratzsch's

Stuffed Zucchini

YIELD: 30 servings

INGREDIENTS

Zucchini Squash	15
Finely Chopped Bread Crumbs	1 cup
Mushrooms, finely chopped	2 cans
Finely Chopped Celery, sauteed	1/4 cup
Finely Chopped Onion, sauteed	1/4 cup
Crumbled Oregano	1/2 teaspoon
Salt	to taste
Pepper	to taste
Buttered Bread Crumbs	1-1/2 cups

Split zucchini or cut into portions. Steam for five minutes. Scoop out centers of zucchini; drain and save to mix with other ingredients. Mix zucchini, bread crumbs, mushrooms, celery, onion, oregano, salt, and pepper. Stuff mixture back into zucchini shell. Top with buttered bread crumbs and bake in oven at 350°F. for 20 to 25 minutes.

Michigan State University

Mushrooms a la Daum

YIELD: 2 servings

INGREDIENTS

Sliced Mushrooms	1 cup
Minced Onion	1/2 cup
Julienne Sliced Ham	1/2 cup
Salt	to taste
Pepper	to taste
Minced Parsley	to taste
Butter	4 tablespoons
Brown Gravy	1/2 cup

Mix mushrooms, onion, ham, and seasonings. Saute in butter in skillet. Before serving, stir in brown gravy. Serve over toasted white bread.

The 21 Club

Parmesan Eggplant Martinez

YIELD: 100 servings

INGREDIENTS

Eggplant, Medium-sized	21 pounds
Flour	2 pounds
Egg Wash	
Beaten Eggs	2 cups
Water	2 cups
Dry Bread Crumbs	1-1/2 pounds
Tomato Sauce	6 quarts
Parmesan Cheese	1 pound

As a hot entree or a cold appetizer, this eggplant variation is equally in demand. To serve as a cold appetizer, prepare half a recipe, chill, and cut into 1-inch squares.

Peel eggplant. Slice 1/4 inch thick. Dip eggplant slices in flour, egg wash, and bread crumbs. Fry two to three minutes at 375°F. to brown the eggplant. Alternate layers of tomato sauce, eggplant, and cheese three times in 2 baking pans (12-1/2-inch by 17-inch by 2-1/2-inch.) Bake in oven at 350°F. for 30 minutes. Cut into 3-inch squares. Serve hot as an entree.

Massachusetts General Hospital

Broccoli Polonaise

YIELD: 10 servings, 4 ounces each

INGREDIENTS
Broccoli	2-1/2 pounds
Boiling Water	to cover
Salt	1 tablespoon
Butter	1/2 pound
Fresh White Bread Crumbs	3 cups
Eggs, hard-cooked, finely chopped	5
Chopped Parsley	3 tablespoons

Place broccoli in a saucepan; cover with boiling water; add salt. Heat again to boiling, then simmer until tender. Remove from water, drain, and place on oven-proof platter. Heat butter in 10-inch frying pan until golden brown. Add bread crumbs; stir until browned. Remove from heat; add chopped eggs and parsley. Sprinkle over top of broccoli. Place in oven at 400°F. for 10 minutes.

The Brown Palace Hotel

As their promotion brochure illustrates "for more than three-quarters of a century (The Brown Palace Hotel) has been serving discriminating guests in the grand manner."

Sandwiches

Grilled Crabmeat & Monterey Jack Cheese Sandwich

YIELD: 1 sandwich

INGREDIENTS

Sourdough Bread	2 medium slices
Monterey Jack Cheese	2 1-ounce slices
Alaska Crabmeat, cooked	2-1/2 ounces
Butter, melted	1 ounce
Lettuce Leaf	1
Kosher Pickle Spear	1
Potato *or* Corn Chips	1/2 ounce

On one slice of bread, put one slice of cheese. Spread crabmeat evenly over cheese and bread. Cover this with the other slice of cheese. Top with second bread slice and apply a little pressure on sandwich. Brush both sides of sandwich well with melted butter. Preheat grill to 325°F. and grill both sides until golden brown and cheese is melted. Transfer to plate and garnish with pickle and potato chips.

Cedars-Sinai Medical Center

Wisconsin Club Sandwich

YIELD: 6 servings

INGREDIENTS

Milk	3 cups
Butter	1/4 cup
Flour	1/4 cup
Salt	to taste
Pepper	to taste
Paprika	1 tablespoon
Prepared Mustard	1 tablespoon
Liquid Hot Pepper Seasoning	2 shakes
Worcestershire Sauce	1 tablespoon
Cheddar Cheese	1 pound
Toast (white bread)	6 slices
Turkey, cooked	12 1-1/2-ounce slices
Ham	6 1-ounce slices
Tomato Slices	12

Heat milk. Melt butter; stir in flour to make a roux. Blend in milk. Fold in next 7 ingredients. Stir until mixture is smooth. Arrange a slice of toast on each of 6 heat-proof plates. Top each with 2 slices of turkey, 1 slice of ham, and 2 slices of tomato. Pour sauce over and around sandwich. Bake in oven at 375°F. until sauce bubbles around edge of plate. Garnish with paprika and parsley.

Plaza Suite

Sandwich suggestions from Win Schuler's menu:

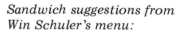

For our Daily Special
Be Sure to Check the blackboard . . . or ask your server.

In Great Haste
A department for those people who want the fastest service possible.

Broiled Sliced Beef Steak
Thinly cut juicy flank steak . . . served with crisp tossed green salad 2.95

Prime Rib Sandwich
Juicy and tender and roasted to perfection. Served open faced. Crisp green salad. 4.95

Sandwiches Combined

International
Kosher corned beef, raw sauerkraut and Swiss cheese topped with tangy dressing and grilled on dark rye. Served with a dill pickle. 2.85

Stacked Ham
Shaved ham piled high on a toasted bun. Topped with Swiss cheese and served hot or cold. 2.65

Schuler Vagabond
A plate full of sliced ham, turkey, Swiss cheese and potato salad and a loaf of bread — Do it yourself! 2.95

Schuler's Hearty Steak Burger
A very large portion of ground steak on homemade toasted bun with your favorite topping.
2.45
1. Bleu or Swiss Cheese
2. Bacon, Tomato, and Onion
3. Sliced Tomato and Onion

Grilled Crabmeat-Cheese Sandwich

YIELD: 1 sandwich

INGREDIENTS
Sourdough Bread	2 medium slices
Monterey Jack Cheese	2 1-ounce slices
Alaska King Crabmeat, cooked	2-1/2 ounces
Butter, melted	1 ounce
Kosher Dill Pickle Spear	1
Lettuce Leaf	1
Potato or Corn Chips	1/2 ounce

On one slice of bread put one slice of the cheese. Spread crabmeat evenly over cheese. Cover with other slice of cheese. Top with remaining bread slice; press down slightly. Brush melted butter on both sides of sandwich. Preheat grill to 325°F. Grill sandwich on both sides until golden brown and cheese is melted. Serve on plate with pickle, lettuce leaf, and potato chips.

The Ninety-Fifth

Cheese is the basic ingredient in sandwiches that range from a connoisseur's version served high atop Chicago's John Hancock Building to the three other hot and hearties for which recipes are also presented on these pages.

Tuna Cheeseburgers

YIELD: 40 servings

INGREDIENTS
Chopped Onion	1-3/4 cups
Tuna, drained, flaked	3 pounds, 10 ounces
Cabbage, coarsely chopped	14 ounces
Dill Relish	3/4 cup
Salad Dressing	2-1/2 cups
Pepper	1/4 teaspoon
Sandwich Buns, split	40
Tomato Slices	40
American Cheese	40 1-ounce slices

Combine first 6 ingredients. Arrange bottoms of buns on baking sheets. Spread a No. 16 scoop of tuna mixture on each bun. Top each with a tomato slice and a slice of cheese. Bake in oven at 400°F. for 10 to 15 minutes until cheese is melted. Serve open-faced with buttered bun top.

Washington State University

Cheese Barbecue Sandwich

YIELD: 6 sandwiches

INGREDIENTS

Shredded Cheddar Cheese	1-1/2 cups
Eggs, hard-cooked, shredded	2
Catsup	3/4 cup
Finely Chopped Onion	1/4 cup
Chopped Green Pepper	3 tablespoons
Chopped Stuffed Olives	3 tablespoons
Butter	1 tablespoon
Worcestershire Sauce	1/2 teaspoon
Hamburger Buns, split	6

Combine first 8 ingredients. Spread on bottom half of each bun. Broil until cheese melts. Place top halves of buns under broiler during last few seconds, or until lightly toasted. Serve immediately.

Michigan State University

Cheese Dreams

YIELD: 100 servings

INGREDIENTS

Butter *or* Margarine	1 pound
Chicken Broth	1 quart
Paprika	3 ounces
Dry Mustard	2 ounces
Worcestershire Sauce	1/2 cup
American Cheese, shredded	10 pounds
Hamburger Rolls, split	100

Melt butter. Add broth; stir in paprika, mustard, worcestershire sauce, and the shredded cheese. Mix well. Use a No. 20 scoop to portion cheese mixture onto split hamburger rolls. Spread cheese mixture with a knife to cover roll completely. Broil until lightly brown. Serve 2 halves per serving.

Massachusetts General Hospital

Denver Brunch Sandwich

YIELD: 60 servings, 12 per pan

A new lift for brunch menus is this student special—a brunch sandwich. It is a satisfying solution for breakfast skippers of every age.

INGREDIENTS

Eggs	10 dozen
Milk	6-2/3 cups
Salad Dressing	2-1/2 quarts
Bacon, cooked until crisp, crumbled	2 pounds (6 pounds raw)
Chopped Pimiento	2-1/2 cups
Salt	1 teaspoon
Pepper	1/4 teaspoon
Toast	60 slices
Green Pepper Rings	120
Tomato Slices	120
Lettuce Leaves	as needed

Beat eggs and milk together. Stir in salad dressing, cooked bacon, pimiento, salt, and pepper. Scale 2 quarts into each of 5 pans (12-inch by 20-inch by 2-1/2-inch). Set pans in pans of hot water and bake in oven at 350°F. for 30 to 40 minutes. Cut into squares and serve on toast. Garnish with green pepper rings, sliced tomatoes, and lettuce.

Purdue University

Poor Boy Sandwich

YIELD: 8 sandwiches

INGREDIENTS

Butter, melted	1/4 pound
Prepared Mustard	1 teaspoon
Mayonnaise	1 teaspoon
Chopped Onion	1 teaspoon
Poppy Seeds	sprinkle
Poor Boy Buns, split	8
Ham, baked or boiled, sliced	1 pound
Turkey, cooked, sliced	1 pound
Swiss Cheese	8 1-ounce slices
Tomato Slices	16
Lettuce Leaves	8

Blend first 5 ingredients together. Split buns. Spread the butter sauce on inside of top half of each bun. Stack 2 ounces each of ham and turkey and a slice of cheese on each bottom half. Heat under broiler until cheese melts. Top each with 2 tomato slices, a lettuce leaf, and top half of the bun.

Win Schuler's

Shrimp and Cheese Delight

YIELD: 4 servings

INGREDIENTS

English Muffins	4
Shrimp, cooked, chopped	1/2 pound
Cheddar Cheese, shredded	1/2 pound
Curry Powder	1 tablespoon
Lemon Juice	2 tablespoons
Worcestershire Sauce	2 tablespoons
Salt	to taste
Pepper	to taste

Cut muffins in half. Mix all ingredients and spread on muffin halves.
Broil until golden brown. Serve 2 muffin halves on each luncheon plate
or oval platter. Garnish with peach half and ripe olive on endive.

Plaza Suite

NEW SMORBROD
SCANDINAVIAN OPEN SANDWICHES

Alaskan Crab Salad......................$2.25

Shrimp Salad............................$1.75

Tuna Fish Salad.........................$1.45

Chicken Salad...........................$1.45

Swedish Anchovies with Scrambled Eggs...$2.25

Norwegian Sardines......................$2.50

Ham.....................................$1.45

Roast Beef with Onions..................$1.75

Corned Beef.............................$1.75

Turkey..................................$1.45

Smoked Salmon with Scrambled Eggs.......$3.25

Focus is on the filling in the open-face sandwiches listed here. Calorie counters feel freer, too, as they order the one-slice specialties.

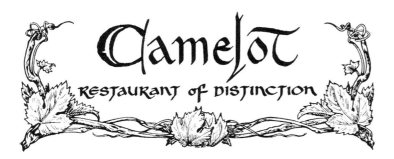

Desserts

Apple Dumplings

YIELD: 12 servings

INGREDIENTS

Apples	12
Pastry	enough for 2-crust pie
Sugar	4 cups
Water	1 quart
Butter *or* Margarine	6 tablespoons
Cinnamon	1/2 teaspoon
Nutmeg	1 teaspoon
Butter *or* Margarine	1/4 cup
Sugar)	3/4 cup
Cinnamon) mix	1 tablespoon
Nutmeg)	1 tablespoon
Milk	1/4 cup
Sugar	1 tablespoon

Peel and core apples. Roll out pastry slightly less than 1/8 inch thick; cut into 7-inch squares. Combine 4 cups sugar with next 4 ingredients; boil for 3 minutes. Place one apple in center of each pastry square. In core cavity of each apple, place 1 teaspoon of butter and 1 tablespoon of sugar-spice mixture. Bring points of pastry up over apple, and overlap. Moisten with mixture of milk and sugar. Place dumplings in baking pan. Do not let them touch. Pour hot syrup around dumplings to moisten bottom of pan. Bake in oven at 425°F. for 40 to 45 minutes.

Stephenson's Apple Farm Restaurant

Baked Cherry Pudding

YIELD: 48 4-ounce servings

INGREDIENTS

Shortening	1-1/4 pounds
Sugar	2-1/2 pounds
Eggs	15
Flour	3-3/4 pounds
Baking Powder	5 tablespoons
Salt	1/2 teaspoon
Milk	3-3/4 cups
Cherries, drained	1 No. 10 can

Cream shortening and sugar; beat in eggs. Sift dry ingredients and add to mixture alternately with milk. Fold in cherries. Bake in greased sheet pan in oven at 350°F. for 40 minutes. Serve in Champagne Sauce. Garnish with whipped cream.

Plaza Suite

Crunchy Raisin-Nut Cookies

YIELD: 5 to 6 dozen

INGREDIENTS

Seedless Raisins	1 cup
Walnuts, chopped	1 cup
Butter, softened	1/2 cup
Sugar	1 cup
Eggs	2
Vanilla	2 teaspoons
Sifted All-Purpose Flour	1-3/4 cups
Baking Powder	1 teaspoon
Baking Soda	1/2 teaspoon
Salt	1 teaspoon
Cinnamon	1 teaspoon
Nutmeg	1 teaspoon
Cloves	1/4 teaspoon

Plump raisins in boiling water; drain well. Mix with nuts and set aside. Beat butter and sugar together until creamy. Beat in eggs, one at a time. Stir in vanilla. Sift dry ingredients together. Stir into batter. Add raisins and nuts. With teaspoon, drop batter onto greased baking sheets. Bake in oven at 400°F. for about 10 minutes or until brown. Remove at once to rack to cool. Store tightly covered.

The Nut Tree

Nut Tree Chess Pie

YIELD: 1 9-inch pie

INGREDIENTS

Granulated Sugar	1 cup
Brown Sugar, firmly packed	1/3 cup
Flour	4 teaspoons
Salt	1/2 teaspoon
Chopped Walnuts *or* Other Nuts (*or* mixed)	1 cup
Seedless Raisins, plumped in boiling water, drained	1/2 cup
Eggs	3
Milk	2/3 cup
Butter, melted	4 teaspoons
Pie Shell, 9-inch, unbaked	1

Combine dry ingredients, nuts, and raisins in mixing bowl. In a smaller bowl, beat eggs with fork; add milk and melted butter. Stir into dry ingredients, mixing well. Pour into unbaked pie shell. Bake in oven at 275°F. for 2 hours. During this long, slow baking, the nuts rise and turn golden brown on top of the rich, firmly jelled filling. Serve cold. Keeps well in cool place. (Pie cuts best after is has stood for 24 hours.)

The Nut Tree

Grasshopper Pie

YIELD: 8 pies

INGREDIENTS

Marshmallows	3 pounds
Milk	1-1/2 cups
Creme de Menthe Syrup	3/4 cup
Water	2 cups
Creme de Menthe Liqueur	1-1/2 cups
Whipped Topping Concentrate	8 cups
Green Coloring	as needed
Graham Cracker Crust Pie Shells	8
Whipped Topping	to garnish
Chocolate Curls	to garnish

Melt marshmallows in the milk and syrup. Cool. Add water and liqueur to whipped topping concentrate, and whip. Fold into chilled marshmallow mixture. Add coloring. Pour into graham cracker crust. Let set until firm. Garnish with whipped topping and chocolate curls.

Purdue University

The STANFORD COURT
Hôtel on San Francisco's Nob Hill

Praline Ice Cream Pie

YIELD: 1 9-inch pie

INGREDIENTS

Brown Sugar	4 ounces
Heavy Cream	1/2 cup
Butter	1 ounce
Pecans	4 ounces
Vanilla Extract	1/2 teaspoon
Vanilla Ice Cream	1-1/2 quarts
Pie Shell, 9-inch, baked	1
Pie Meringue, using 3 egg whites	
RUM SAUCE	
Egg Yolks	2
Sugar	3 tablespoons
Butter, melted	3 ounces
Lemon Rind, grated	1 tablespoon
Lemons, juice of	2
Rum	to taste

Prepare praline mixture. Heat brown sugar until it reaches the point where it begins to turn color. Mix with heavy cream and melted butter. Add crushed pecans and flavor with vanilla extract. Whip vanilla ice cream. Fold in praline mixture. Place praline ice cream mixture in pie shell and top with meringue. Serve with Rum Sauce.
RUM SAUCE
Beat egg yolks until thick. Gradually add sugar while beating. Beat in butter, lemon rind, and lemon juice. Stir in rum to the desired flavor.

Fournou's Ovens Restaurant, The Stanford Court Hotel

Frosted Macadamia Nut Souffle

YIELD: 4 servings

INGREDIENTS

Macadamia Nut Ice Cream, softened	1 quart
Dark Rum	1 ounce
Whipped Cream	to garnish
Macadamia Nuts, chopped	to garnish

A dessert to dally over, yet one that can be prepared ahead with only the garnishing to be done at serving time.

Line edge of souffle cups with a 1/4-inch paper collar. Mix ice cream with rum. Fill souffle cups to 1/4 inch above paper collar. Freeze until solid. Before serving, remove paper collar. Garnish ice cream with whipped cream and a sprinkle of chopped macadamia nuts.

The Kahala Hilton Hotel

Fudge-Macaroon Cupcakes a la Stevens

YIELD: 120 cupcakes

INGREDIENTS
MACAROON FILLING

Granulated Sugar	1 pound, 8 ounces
Macaroon Coconut	1 pound, 2 ounces
Salt	1/4 ounce
Bread Flour	6 ounces
White Corn Syrup	8 ounces
Hot Water	6 ounces
Egg Whites	11 ounces
FUDGE CUPCAKES	
Granulated Sugar	2 pounds, 3 ounces
Shortening	1 pound, 2 ounces
Salt	2/3 ounce
Eggs, Whole	1 pound, 10 ounces
Cocoa	7 ounces
Baking Soda	1/2 ounce
Milk	1 quart
Vanilla	1/2 ounce
Cake Flour	2 pounds, 4 ounces
Baking Powder	1-1/2 ounces

Blend sugar, coconut, salt, and flour together well. Add syrup and hot water and mix well. Stir in egg whites. Place mixture in double boiler or steam kettle and heat until mixture is hot to the touch. Remove and cool to room temperature. Set aside. Beat sugar, shortening, and salt together until creamy. Add eggs slowly while continuing to beat. Sift together cocoa and soda. Add to creamed mixture. Mix well. Add 2 cups milk and the vanilla. Mix at low speed until incorporated. Add flour and baking powder. Mix at low speed until blended. *Do not over-mix.* Add the remaining milk; mix until smooth. Fill muffin tins half full with cake batter. Using a pastry bag, drop 1 heaping teaspoon Macaroon Filling into the center of cupcake batter. Bake in oven at 360°F. Serve with dusting of confectioners' sugar if desired.

Massachusetts General Hospital

Macaroons

YIELD: 6 to 8 dozen

INGREDIENTS
Almond Paste	2-1/8 cups
Sugar	2 cups
Almond Flour	1 cup
Confectioners' Sugar	1-1/8 cup
Lemon Rind	1 tablespoon
Egg Whites	1/2 cup

Mix almond paste with next 4 ingredients. Slowly add the egg whites. The mix should be medium stiff so cookies will retain their shape when bagged out. Hold back some whites to be sure mix is stiff enough. If too stiff, add whites a little at a time until the desired consistency is reached. Line baking pans with parchment paper, or grease lightly and dust with flour. Bag mixture out on pans with a No. 4 plain pastry tube. If the macaroons have a slight peak, moisten a cloth in cool water, wring out well, and place over tops. Run palms of hands lightly over top of cloth to eliminate peaks. Sprinkle macaroons lightly with granulated sugar. Bake in oven at 350°F. until golden brown.

The Greenbrier

Elegant desserts from establishments with unshakable reputations as practitioners of haute cuisine are a stimulating challenge to chefs and cooks. When such preparations are mastered, they can be featured on occasions where such specialties can earn praise for place and preparer.

Floating Island

YIELD: 4 to 6 servings

INGREDIENTS
Eggs, separated	6
Sugar	1-1/2 cups
Milk	3 cups
Vanilla Bean, split	1
Water	1/4 cup
Lemon Juice	dash

Beat egg whites until foamy. Add 1/2 cup sugar gradually, beating until stiff, shiny peaks form. Meanwhile, heat milk until just simmering. *Do not boil.* Place rounded tablespoons of meringue into heated milk. Cook 1 minute on each side. Remove with a skimmer. Drain on a clean towel or napkin. Strain milk used for cooking meringues. Add more milk to make 3 cups. Combine egg yolks with 1/2 cup sugar and vanilla bean. Bring milk to a boil; pour on top of egg yolk mixture while stirring. Return milk mixture to saucepan; cook and stir just to first boil. Remove bean. Immediately put custard into individual serving bowls. Add dash of cold heavy cream to cool more quickly. Be sure custard cools completely. Make a mound of the meringue islands on top of each portion of cold custard. Mix 1/2 cup sugar with 1/4 cup water and lemon juice. Cook until brown and syrupy. Cool slightly. As the mixture thickens, take 2 forks and work sugar right and left over wooden rod until it becomes fine like angel hair. Garnish each serving with spun sugar caramel.

La Grenouille

Apple Walnut Cake

YIELD: 1 8-inch square cake

INGREDIENTS

Sugar	2 cups
Shortening	1 cup
Eggs, beaten	2
Sifted Flour	2 cups
Soda	1 teaspoon
Nutmeg	1 teaspoon
Cinnamon	2 teaspoons
Salt	1 teaspoon
Finely Chopped Apples	5 cups
Walnuts, finely chopped	1 cup
ICING	
Cream Cheese	6 ounces
Butter	4 ounces
Powdered Sugar	2 cups
Chopped Nuts	1/2 cup
Vanilla	2 teaspoons

Cream sugar and shortening. Add eggs to creamed shortening and stir slightly. Blend together the sifted flour, soda, nutmeg, cinnamon, and salt. Add the apples and nuts; stir just enough to mix. Pour this thick batter into greased 8-inch by 8-inch pan. Bake in oven at 350°F. for 1 hour.

ICING

Blend all ingredients together well. Spread over cooled cake. Decorate with whole walnuts and apple slices.

Stephenson's Apple Farm Restaurant

Fresh Apple Pie

YIELD: 1 9-inch pie

INGREDIENTS

Sliced Apples	1 quart
Pie Shell and Top Crust, 9-inch, unbaked	1
Orange, juice of	1
Grated Lemon Rind	1 teaspoon
Flour	2 tablespoons
Sugar	1 cup
Nutmeg	1 teaspoon
Cinnamon	1 teaspoon
Butter	2 tablespoons

Place apples in unbaked pie shell. Add orange juice and lemon rind. Combine flour, sugar, and spices; sprinkle over apples. Dot butter in center of pie. Cover with top crust. Bake in oven at 450°F. for 20 minutes; reduce heat to 400°F. and bake for 15 minutes, then lower heat to 350°F. and bake 10 minutes longer. Brush top crust with mixture of 1 tablespoon sugar and 1/4 cup milk.

Stephenson's Apple Farm Restaurant

Mile High Ice Cream Pie

*It is a custom among
some Pontchartrain Hotel guests
to order Mile High Ice Cream
Pie ahead of time for
out-of-town guests. When this
large and luscious offering is
placed before them, outcries of
amazement are the common
reaction.*

YIELD: 1 10-inch pie

INGREDIENTS

Pie Shell, 10-inch, baked	1
Ice Cream*, slightly softened	1 quart
Egg Whites	1-1/2 cups
Vanilla	1 tablespoon
Sugar	1 cup
Chocolate Sauce	as needed
*Use 2 or 3 flavors	

Fill baked pie shell with alternate layers of ice cream. Beat egg whites and vanilla until frothy. Gradually add sugar, beating until the mixture forms shiny stiff peaks of meringue. Top ice cream with meringue. Brown quickly under broiler. Serve at once with Chocolate Sauce, p. 220.

Pontchartrain Hotel

Apple Brandy Cream Pie Mousse

YIELD: 1 pie

INGREDIENTS

PIE CRUST

Sifted Cake Flour	8 ounces
Butter	6 ounces
Salt	pinch
Macaroons, crushed	6
PIE FILLING	
Egg Yolks, beaten	6
Sugar	3/4 cup
Grated Lemon Rind	1 tablespoon
Gelatine, Unflavored	1/2 ounce
Cold Water	as needed
Boiling Water	2 ounces
Apple Brandy	5 ounces
Applesauce	1/2 cup
Egg Whites	2
Whipped Cream	3 cups

Sift flour into butter; blend well. Add salt. Stir in enough cold water to moisten flour. Knead until consistency is the same throughout. Chill until firm. Roll out dough, then lightly roll crushed macaroons into dough. Fit dough into pie plate. Bake in oven at 350°F. for 15 minutes. Cool. Beat egg yolks; add 1/2 cup sugar gradually while continuing to beat. Stir in lemon rind. Soften gelatine in cold water, then dissolve in 2 ounces of boiling water. Add to yolks. Stir in brandy and applesauce. Set aside. Slowly add 1/4 cup sugar to egg whites, continuing to beat until soft peaks are formed. Gently fold into yolk mixture. Fold in whipped cream. Pour into pie crust. Chill until firm. Garnish with whipped cream.

The Four Seasons

Mousse au Cafe [Coffee Mousse]

YIELD: 3 to 4 servings

INGREDIENTS

Whipping Cream	1 cup
Powdered Sugar	6 tablespoons
Egg Whites	2
Coffee Liqueur	1 ounce
Coffee Extract	1/2 teaspoon
Chocolate Candy Coffee Beans	12

This melt-in-your-mouth mousse clearly merits the champagne glass service recommended for it.

Whip the cream with 4 tablespoons of the sugar. Whip the egg whites with 2 tablespoons of sugar until very stiff. Keep separate. Mix the coffee liqueur with the coffee extract; add to the whipped cream. Fold in the egg whites. Spoon into a glass bowl or champagne glasses. Decorate with candy coffee beans. Serve well chilled.

La Maisonette

Chocolate Mousse and Sauce Sabayon

YIELD: approximately 10 servings

INGREDIENTS

Egg Yolks	1 cup
Sugar	1 cup
Half-and-Half, scalded	1-1/2 cups
Semi-sweet Chocolate, melted	5 ounces
Rum Flavoring	1 teaspoon
Vanilla	1 teaspoon
Gelatine, Unflavored	2 tablespoons
Heavy Cream, whipped	2 cups
SAUCE SABAYON	
Sugar	2 pounds, 12 ounces
Eggs	1 dozen
Instant Starch	1/2 cup
Rum Flavoring	3 ounces
Vanilla	dash
Salt	pinch
Whipped Cream	3 cups

Beat egg yolks and sugar in top of double boiler. Add half-and-half, melted chocolate, and flavorings. Soften gelatine in 1/4 cup cold water. Stir into custard mixture. Heat over hot, but not boiling, water, stirring constantly, until custard becomes thick and creamy, about 30 minutes. Cool custard over cracked ice. *IMPORTANT:* Custard must be cooled to just the right temperature—about 95°F. When this temperature has been reached, fold in the whipped cream until well blended. Pour into custard cups and cool.

SAUCE SABAYON

Beat all ingredients except whipped cream in electric mixer at low speed for at least 30 minutes. Fold in whipped cream just before serving.

Camelot

Chocolate Brownies

YIELD: 13 16-inch by 24-inch pans

INGREDIENTS

Shortening	14 pounds
Sugar	44 pounds
Cake Flour	20 pounds
Salt	8 ounces
Walnuts, chopped	8 ounces
Eggs	10 quarts
Vanilla	8 ounces
Margarine, melted	10 pounds
Bitter-Sweet Chocolate, melted	14 pounds

Mix shortening and sugar for 10 minutes using electric mixer at medium speed. Turn off mixer. Add remaining ingredients in order listed. Mix until smooth.   Scale 9 pounds 12 ounces of batter into each of 13 greased bun pans. Spread evenly. Bake in oven at 350°F. for about 25 minutes.   These are fudgy brownies—*do not overbake.* Cut each pan into 70 squares. Ice with chocolate frosting.

Michigan State University

Chocolate-lovers are legion. These two longtime leaders among favorite chocolate desserts have been refined to as nearly a perfect state as could be produced.

Chocolate Cream Pie

YIELD: 2 9-inch pies

INGREDIENTS

Pie Shells, 9-inch, baked	2
Bitter Chocolate	4 ounces
Butter *or* Margarine	1/3 cup
Sugar	1-1/4 cups
Milk	8 cups
Cornstarch	1/4 cup
Egg Yolks, beaten	3
Eggs, Whole, beaten	3
Egg Whites	3
Sugar	1/3 cup
Vanilla Extract	1/2 teaspoon
Salt	to taste
Whipped Cream	to garnish
Chocolate Shavings	to garnish

Prepare and bake pie shells. Melt chocolate and butter together. Stir in 1-1/4 cups sugar. Blend 1 cup milk with cornstarch. Add remaining milk to chocolate mixture. Bring to a boil. Blend some hot milk into beaten yolks, eggs, and cornstarch. Pour mixture into boiling milk and cook until thick. Whip egg whites, adding 1/3 cup sugar a little at a time, until soft peaks are formed. Fold meringue into cooked mixture. Add vanilla and salt. Turn into baked pie shells; cool. Top with whipped cream and chocolate shavings.

The Greenbrier

Mousse Tia Maria

YIELD: 4 servings

INGREDIENTS

Eggs, Whole	4
Vanilla Extract	3 drops
OR	
Vanilla Bean	1
Granulated Sugar	1/4 cup
Gelatine, Unflavored	1 tablespoon
Instant Coffee	1/4 cup
Salt	pinch
All-Purpose Flour	1 tablespoon
Boiling Milk	2 cups
Whipped Cream	2 cups
Tia Maria Liqueur	2 ounces

A make-ahead mousse with the unique flavor of Tia Maria is served in the fine crystal one would expect to find in the Victorian splendor of Ernie's.

In a bowl, mix together eggs, vanilla, sugar, gelatine, coffee, and salt until mixture coats heavily on a spoon. Fold in flour; mix well. Add boiling milk, stirring constantly with a soft whip. Put mixture in a pan and heat to boiling, stirring continuously. Remove from heat immediately; pour into a cold bowl. Let cool. When completely cold, fold in whipped cream and Tia Maria. Pour into glass dish of your choice. Store in the refrigerator for at least 1 hour. Serve with cookies.

Ernie's

Floating Island

YIELD: 4 servings

INGREDIENTS

Eggs, separated	8
Powdered Sugar	1/2 pound
Half-and-Half	1 pint
Homogenized Milk	1 pint
Rum	2 tablespoons
Granulated Sugar	1/2 cup
Vanilla	1 teaspoon
Nuts, chopped	to garnish

Place egg whites in a small mixing bowl and whip them to make a meringue, adding powdered sugar gradually. Beat until meringue becomes very stiff. Set aside. Combine half-and-half and next 4 ingredients; stir. Place over low heat and simmer for a few minutes. Add egg yolks and stir well into mixture. Cook over low heat, stirring frequently. (Do not allow mixture to come to a boil because eggs will cook and separate.) Remove from heat; set aside. With 2 teaspoons, mold 1 teaspoonful of meringue into ball shape. Mold 11 more of these (3 per person). Divide sauce among 4 dessert dishes, then place 3 meringue balls in each dish. Sprinkle with chopped nuts.

Commander's Palace Restaurant

Pear William

YIELD: 4 servings

INGREDIENTS

Fresh Ripe Pears	4
Rock Candy Syrup	1 quart
Sponge Cake Rounds, 2-1/2-inch by 1/2-inch	4
Vanilla Ice Cream	4 No. 20 scoops
Whipped Cream, sweetened	1 cup
Fresh Mint Leaves	to garnish
Pear William Liqueur	1/4 cup

Peel pears, cut in halves, remove cores. Poach pears in rock candy syrup until tender. Remove from heat and allow to cool in the syrup. Place a piece of sponge cake in each of 4 compote dishes. Moisten with the pear syrup. Fill pear halves with ice cream. Press 2 halves together to obtain shape of a whole pear. Place a pear on each piece of cake. Surround with whipped cream and decorate with mint leaves. In a hot shallow pan, heat the Pear William Liqueur, flame it, and pour over pears. Serve immediately.

Hotel St. Francis

Fudge Pudding

YIELD: 96 servings, 24 servings per pan

INGREDIENTS

Cake Flour	2 pounds, 4 ounces
Baking Powder	2-1/2 ounces
Sugar	3 pounds, 8 ounces
Salt	2 teaspoons
Cocoa	4 ounces
Milk	1 quart
Margarine, melted	1 pound, 2 ounces
Nuts, chopped	2 pounds
Brown Sugar	4 pounds, 8 ounces
Cocoa	8-2/3 ounces
Hot Water	1 gallon
Vanilla	1/4 cup

Mix flour, baking powder, salt, sugar, and cocoa. Blend together milk and margarine. Combine with flour mixture. Add nuts. Pour into 4 greased 10-inch by 14-inch utility pans. Scale 2 pounds per pan. Mix brown sugar and next 3 ingredients together. Pour 5 cups of this mixture over batter in each pan. Bake in oven at 350°F. for 45 minutes. Avoid overbaking.

Purdue University

Coffee Cup Souffle

YIELD: 6 servings

INGREDIENTS

Flour	4-1/2 tablespoons
Butter	4-1/2 tablespoons
Milk	1-1/2 cups
Eggs, separated	6
Instant Coffee	1 tablespoon
Sugar	3/4 cup
Coffee Ice Cream	1/4 cup

Sophisticated diners frequently select souffles after a brief study of the dessert menu. Coffee cup service is a unique variation at the Four Seasons.

Blend flour and butter thoroughly. In saucepan, heat milk to boiling. Add flour-butter mixture, stirring until thick. Cool. Add beaten egg yolks and coffee. Beat egg whites until they form soft peaks. Continue beating, gradually adding the sugar, until stiff peaks are formed. Fold into the yolk mixture. Set aside 1/4 cup of the souffle mixture. Butter insides of 6 oven-proof coffee cups and sprinkle lightly with sugar. Divide remaining mixture among prepared coffee cups. Bake in oven at 425°F. for about 11 minutes or until souffle is of desired consistency. Serve with a sauce made by mixing the reserved 1/4 cup souffle mixture with the coffee ice cream.

The Four Seasons

Souffle Grand Marnier

YIELD: 2 servings

INGREDIENTS

Milk	1/2 cup
Sugar	2 tablespoons
Salt	pinch
Sifted Flour	2 tablespoons
Cold Milk	1/4 cup
Grand Marnier	1/4 cup
Egg Yolks, beaten	3
Butter	2 teaspoons
Egg Whites, stiffly beaten	4
Powdered Sugar	as needed

Mix first three ingredients in saucepan. Bring to a boil. Blend flour with cold milk, then stir into hot milk mixture. Add the liqueur. Cook, stirring, for 2 to 3 minutes. Remove from heat. Fold in beaten egg yolks and butter. Then quickly mix in stiffly beaten egg whites. Turn mixture into a buttered and sugar-coated souffle dish. Smooth surface of souffle. Bake in oven at 350°F. for about 20 minutes, or until golden. Sprinkle with powdered sugar to glaze. Serve immediately.

La Bourgogne

Kahlua Angel Food Cake

YIELD: 1 cake, 16 servings

INGREDIENTS
Angel Food Cake	1
Kahlua	1/2 cup
Whipped Cream	2 cups
Almonds, toasted	1 cup

Cut cake, horizontally, into 3 layers. Sprinkle each layer with the Kahlua and spread with part of the whipped cream. Put layers back together and ice the cake with the remaining whipped cream. Garnish with toasted almonds; chill and serve. (For ease of cutting, chill cake and cut before adding almonds.)

Southern Methodist University Food Service

Biscuit Tortoni

YIELD: 4 to 5 servings

INGREDIENTS
Whipping Cream	1 cup
Powdered Sugar	1/4 cup
Egg White, stiffly beaten	1
Macaroon Crumbs, almond flavor	1/2 cup
Rum	2 teaspoons
Macaroon Crumbs, sieved	1/3 cup

Desserts are often the appeal that dictates the choice of the place for a party. These three would prove powerful persuaders.

Whip the cream; gradually fold in the powdered sugar. Fold in the stiffly beaten egg white. Add alternately the macaroon crumbs and rum. Pack mixture in individual paper cups. Sprinkle tops with sieved macaroon crumbs. Freeze until firm.

The Brown Palace Hotel

Macadamia Nut Pancake

YIELD: 6 servings

INGREDIENTS
Eggs	10
Sugar	6-1/2 teaspoons
Salt	1/2 teaspoon
Buttermilk	1-1/4 cups
Sifted Cake Flour	4 cups
Baking Powder	4 teaspoons
Macadamia Nuts, crushed	2 cups
Powdered Sugar	as needed

Thoroughly mix first 4 ingredients together. Add flour and baking powder; mix well. Stir 1 cup of the nuts into batter. Cook on griddle. When ready to serve, sprinkle with remaining macadamia nuts and powdered sugar.

The Kahala Hilton Hotel

Larry's Graham Cracker Pudding

YIELD: 125 servings

INGREDIENTS

Crushed Pineapple	2 No. 10 cans
Margarine	4 pounds
Granulated Sugar	10 pounds
Eggs, Whole	1 quart
Graham Crackers, finely crushed	10 pounds

Drain crushed pineapple. Strain the juice and reserve. Beat together the margarine and sugar until creamy. Add eggs one at a time, continuing to beat. Add drained pineapple; mix slowly until pineapple is completely incorporated. Cover bottoms of 2 inch deep pans with two-thirds of the crushed graham crackers. Dampen this with some of the strained pineapple juice. Spread pineapple mixture over the graham cracker crumbs. Sprinkle the remaining third of the crushed graham crackers on top. Dampen with strained pineapple juice. Refrigerate at least 6 hours. Serve garnished with whipped cream.

Massachusetts General Hospital

White Chocolate Cake

YIELD: 3 9-inch layers

INGREDIENTS

White Chocolate	1/3 pound
Water	1/2 cup
Butter *or* Margarine	1 cup
Sugar	2 cups
Eggs, separated	4
Sifted Cake Flour	2-1/2 cups
Baking Powder	1-1/2 teaspoons
Salt	1/2 teaspoon
Buttermilk	1 cup
Vanilla	1 teaspoon
Chopped Pecans *or* Almonds	1 cup
Flaked Coconut	1 can (3-1/2-ounce)

Place chocolate and water in top of double boiler; whisk until blended; cool. Beat butter and 1-1/2 cups sugar together until creamy. Add egg yolks; beat thoroughly. Sift flour with baking powder and salt; add to creamed mixture in thirds alternately with buttermilk, vanilla, and chocolate; beat until smooth after each addition. Beat egg whites until soft peaks form. Gradually add remaining 1/2 cup sugar, continuing to beat until stiff, but not dry. Fold into batter; then gently fold in pecans and coconut. Turn into three 9-inch round cake pans, which have been greased, lined with wax paper, and greased again. Bake in oven at 350°F. about 35 minutes or until done. Frost with boiled or butter icing.

Marie Marinkovich

No-Crust Coconut Pie

YIELD: 1 9-inch pie

INGREDIENTS

Eggs	2
Milk	1 cup
Sugar	3/4 cup
Flaked Coconut	1 can (3-1/2-ounce)
Flour	1/4 cup
Butter, melted	1/4 cup
Baking Powder	1/4 teaspoon
Salt	1/4 teaspoon

Even calorie-counters can often be tempted by feathery looking custard or cream pies.

With electric or rotary mixer, beat eggs until light and fluffy. Stir in remaining ingredients. Pour into a buttered and floured 9-inch pie pan. Bake in oven at 350°F. for 40 minutes. (Pie forms own crust.)

Marie Marinkovich

Bavarian Cream Pie

YIELD: 3 pies

INGREDIENTS

Sugar	1 pound
Gelatine, Unflavored	1-1/2 ounces
Milk	1 quart
Egg Yolks, beaten	4
Heavy Cream	1 quart
Dark Rum	1 ounce
Fruit (Strawberries, Blueberries, or Cherries)	3 to 4 cups
Pie Shells, baked	3

Mix sugar and gelatine. Blend into milk. Add egg yolks. Heat slowly, stirring, until gelatine is dissolved. Refrigerate until cool and starting to jell. Whip cream; add rum. Fold whipped cream into gelatine mixture. Add strawberries, blueberries, or cherries. Turn into pie shells. Chill until set.

Jimmy's Harborside

Strawberry Crepes

YIELD: 6 servings

INGREDIENTS
CREPES (12)

Sifted Cake Flour	2 ounces
Sifted Bread Flour	2 ounces
Sugar	1/2 ounce
Salt	1/8 ounce
Milk	1 cup
Eggs, slightly beaten	2
Egg Yolks, slightly beaten	2
Butter, melted	2 ounces
Vanilla	1/4 teaspoon
Grated Lemon Rind	1 tablespoon

STRAWBERRY SAUCE

Strawberries	1 quart
Sugar	5 teaspoons
Butter, melted	2 tablespoons
Triple Sec	2 ounces
Brandy	2 ounces
Vanilla Ice Cream	1 pint

Combine sifted flours, sugar, and salt in bowl. Slowly stir in milk and eggs. Add butter, vanilla, and grated lemon rind. Let batter rest 1 hour before using. Heat 6-inch cast-iron skillet; brush with butter. Pour in just enough batter to cover bottom of pan with a very thin layer. Pancakes must be very thin. Cook for 1 minute or until brown; turn over and brown other side.

STRAWBERRY SAUCE
Sprinkle strawberries with sugar. Place in pan with butter. Saute, covered, for 5 minutes to let strawberries steam. Add Triple Sec. Then set aflame with brandy. On large plates, place two crepes for each serving. Put scoop of vanilla ice cream in center of each crepe, and roll. Then spoon strawberries and sauce over crepes. Serve immediately.

Charlie's Cafe Exceptionale

FLAMING DESSERTS a la EXCEPTIONALE

BANANAS FOSTER — bananas with brown sugar, Creme de Banana, Rum and ice cream . . . . $1.75 per person

CHERRIES JUBILEE — with vanilla ice cream and a bing cherry sauce . . . flamed with brandy . . . . $1.75 per person

CREPES SUZETTES — with a sauce of butter, orange and lemon flamed with Grand Marnier, Cointreau, and Cognac . . . . $2.50 per person

SPANISH COFFEE — set ablaze with Tia Maria and Cognac . . . topped with whipped Cream . . . . $2.50 per person

(min. two orders)

Trifle Pudding*

YIELD: 12 servings

From a carefully compiled compendium of the culinary creations of certain California chefs.

INGREDIENTS

Vanilla Pudding and Pie Filling Mix	1 3-1/4-ounce package
Half-and-Half	2 cups
Puerto Rican Rum, Dark	2 tablespoons
Heavy Cream, whipped	2-1/4 cups
Sugar	3 tablespoons
Red Raspberry Preserves	2 tablespoons
Sponge Cake, layer	1 10-inch round
Brandy	1/4 cup
Dry Sherry	1/4 cup
Strawberries, whole	30 to 38

Combine pudding mix with half-and-half. Cook on temperature controlled top burner, using a low flame at 200°F. for 12 to 15 minutes, or until mixture comes to a boil and partially thickens. Stir well occasionally. Turn off flame and allow to cool slightly. Mix in rum. Chill pudding thoroughly. Whip 1-1/4 cups cream and 1 tablespoon sugar until stiff. Fold into chilled pudding mixture. Using a brush, coat a deep, 10-inch diameter bowl with raspberry preserves to within 1 inch of top.
TO ASSEMBLE:
Slice sponge cake horizontally into fourths. Place top slice, crust side up, in bottom of preserves-coated bowl, curving outer edge of layer upward. Combine brandy and sherry, and sprinkle a fourth of the mixture (approximately 2 tablespoons) over the cake slice. Next, spread one-third of the chilled pudding mixture over the surface of the cake slice. Repeat procedure two additional times. Finish by arranging 15 to 18 strawberries on the top of the third layer of pudding and cover with fourth cake layer, crust side down. Sprinkle with remaining brandy-sherry mixture. Whip remaining 1 cup cream and 2 tablespoons sugar until stiff. Place whipped cream in pastry bag fitted with a fluted tip. Make 12 mounds of whipped cream around the edge of the bowl and 3 mounds across the diameter. Top each mound with a strawberry. Refrigerate at least two hours. To serve, spoon onto chilled dessert plates.
Lawry's Five Crowns

*Where Food Is Finest, Southern Counties Gas Company

Drunken Strawberries

YIELD: 9-inch by 13-inch pan

INGREDIENTS

Strawberries	2 quarts
Confectioners' Sugar	1/4 cup
French Vanilla Ice Cream	1 quart
Whipped Cream	2 cups
Grand Marnier	1/2 cup
Cognac *or* Brandy	1/4 cup
Creme de Cacao	1/4 cup

Wash and halve strawberries. Mash a few of the softest berries to make 1/4 cup. Add confectioners' sugar to crushed berries. Place French Vanilla Ice Cream in shallow pan and let stand until semisoft. Spread evenly in bottom of pan. Gently fold whipped cream into ice cream. Add Grand Marnier, cognac or brandy, and Creme de Cacao to halved strawberries. Spread over ice cream. Spoon crushed berries on top. Cover pan with foil (tent foil in center). Chill at least 4 hours, preferably overnight.

Marie Marinkovich

Austrian Strawberry Mousse

YIELD: 8 servings

INGREDIENTS

Strawberries	1 quart
Sugar	1/2 cup
White Wine	1/2 cup
Gelatine, Unflavored	2 tablespoons
Cold Water	1/2 cup
Boiling Water	1/2 cup
Heavy Cream, whipped	2 cups

Press berries through a fine sieve, reserving a few whole strawberries for garnish. Add the sugar and wine. Stir well; chill. Soften gelatine in cold water. Add boiling water; stir until dissolved. Cool; combine with strawberry mixture. Beat until fluffy and slightly thickened. Fold in whipped cream. Turn into 2-quart oiled mold. Chill for 3 hours before serving. Unmold on chilled platter. Garnish with whole berries and mint sprigs.

Marie Marinkovich

Strawberries and cream are an age-old favorite. Contemporary treatment introduces more sophisticated ingredients that assure them haute cuisine classification.

Souffle Grand Marnier

YIELD: 8 servings

INGREDIENTS

Milk	2 cups
Orange Rind from 2 oranges	1/4 cup
Flour	1/2 cup
Butter	1/2 cup
Egg Yolks	5
Egg Whites	5
Granulated Sugar	2/3 cup
Grand Marnier	1/2 cup
Macaroons, diced	1/2 cup
Curacao	1 cup

Boil milk to which orange rind has been added. Add flour and butter to mixture and continue stirring until the mixture is stiff. Remove from heat and add egg yolks, one at a time. Beat egg whites until fluffy. Add sugar to form a stiff meringue and fold into the souffle base. Pour one-half of the mixture into a buttered and sugared dish or mold. Soak diced macaroons in orange liqueur. Place macaroons in center of mixture and add the other half of base, filling mold to one-half inch from the top. Bake in oven at 350°F. for approximately 30 to 40 minutes. To prevent burning, place souffle dish in pan of water while baking. Serve with Sabayon Sauce.

The Greenbrier

Banana Fritters

YIELD: 8 to 9 dozen

Memories of "light hands with pastry" are revived when patrons taste these feathery fritters.

INGREDIENTS

Sugar	1 cup
Butter, softened	1/2 cup
Eggs, beaten	4
Milk	1 quart
Diced Bananas	2 cups
Crushed Pineapple	1 cup
Flour	2 pounds
Baking Powder	3 tablespoons
Salt	1/2 teaspoon
Vanilla	2 teaspoons

Beat sugar and butter together until creamy. Add eggs; beat. Add milk and blend thoroughly. Fold in bananas and pineapple. Sift together the flour, baking powder, and salt. Lightly fold into banana mixture. Stir in vanilla (do not overmix). Heat fat in deep fat fryer to 325°F. Drop fritter batter from teaspoon into hot fat. Fry until golden brown.

Stephenson's Apple Farm Restaurant

Souffle Glace au Cointreau

YIELD: 6 servings

INGREDIENTS

Sugar	4 ounces
Egg Yolks	5
Cointreau	2 ounces
Heavy Cream, whipped	1-1/3 cups

Heat sugar until it melts and reaches a temperature of 245°F. Beat egg yolks and drop sugar into beaten mixture very slowly; continue beating until creamy and foamy. Add cointreau. Allow mixture to cool. Fold in whipped cream. Place mixture in souffle cups, placing a paper collar around lip of cup so as to allow mixture to rise approximately 1-1/2 inches above lip of souffle cup. Freeze for 4 to 6 hours. Sprinkle surface of souffle very lightly with powdered cocoa before serving.

Fournou's Ovens Restaurant, The Stanford Court Hotel

Praline Parfait Sauce *

YIELD: approximately 3 cups

INGREDIENTS

Dark Cane Syrup	2 cups
Sugar	1/3 cup
Boiling Water	1/3 cup
Chopped Pecans, *or* small halves	1 cup

Combine all ingredients in a saucepan and bring to boil over medium heat. As soon as mixture reaches the boiling stage, remove from heat immediately. Cool and store in a covered jar.

To make a Praline Parfait, spoon alternate layers of vanilla ice cream and Praline Parfait Sauce into a tall parfait glass, ending with a layer of sauce. Top with whipped cream. Garnish with pecan halves.

*Brennan's New Orleans Cookbook

Commander's Palace Restaurant

Other dessert selections they come back to Commander's Palace to eat, and eat again, below.

Baked Alaska (for two)

Cherries Jubilee
Made at your table

Lemon Cream Crepe Commander
Fresh lemon custard filling folded into a crepe and glazed

Strawberries Romanoff

Praline Parfait

Chocolate Mousse

Caramel Custard

Floating Island

Irish Coffee

Cafe Brulot

Chocolate Sauce

YIELD: 1 gallon

INGREDIENTS

Light Cream	3 quarts
Sugar	6 cups
German Sweet Cooking Chocolate	24 4-ounce bars

Mix cream and sugar in top of double boiler. Place over boiling water; add chocolate. Heat, stirring, until chocolate melts, about 15 minutes.

Pontchartrain Hotel

Sauces, dressings, frostings, each adds its fillip to some patron's favorite dessert.

Macadamia Rum Cream Dressing

YIELD: 1 cup

INGREDIENTS

Chopped Macadamia Nuts	1 tablespoon
Dark Rum	1/2 ounce
Lime Juice	1 tablespoon
Whipped Cream, sweetened	1 cup

Fold first 3 ingredients into whipped cream. Chill.

The Kahala Hilton Hotel

Rich Chocolate Frosting

YIELD: to frost 2-layer cake

INGREDIENTS

Powdered Sugar, sifted	1-1/2 cups
Ground Chocolate *or* Cocoa	1/3 cup
Flour	2-1/2 tablespoons
Butter, soft, *or* Margarine	3/4 cup
Egg Whites	3

Mix 3/4 cup of the sugar with ground chocolate and the flour. Blend into the butter; set aside. Beat egg whites almost stiff; gradually beat in remaining 3/4 cup sugar. Blend with chocolate mixture. Spread on cooled cake.

The Nut Tree

Index